M000206064

After racism destroys her family, a mother vows to find her sons

Love Never Leaves

A MEMOIR

DEBORAH HUSE BLANCHARD

Love Never Leaves

©2021, Deborah Huse Blanchard

Front cover, from left: Deborah Blanchard, George Fonteno, Mary Fonteno, 1982
Cover design by Don Armstrong
Author portrait (back cover) by John Blanchard

ISBN: 978-1-09838-685-6
ISBN eBook: 978-1-09838-686-3

For George and David
Dedicated to the memory of
Susan C. Darke

Special Thanks

To my husband, John, who has always encouraged and supported me, never complained that for eight long years I was living a different reality. He was right there with me, adapting to my mood swings, reading chapters before I sent them to my editor, trying to keep me balanced, and filling my nonworking hours with love and humor.

Thank you, my love.

My editor, Don Armstrong, whose patience and encouragement kept me going when my soul was bleeding and I wanted to give up. Without his expertise and his challenging me through rewrite after rewrite, *Love Never Leaves* never would have been completed.

Thanks, Don.

In Memoriam

Too much, too little.

George Armstrong Fonteno, my firstborn, succumbed to pancreatic cancer on January 5, 2021. It was very sudden and unexpected. "Just remember," he told me shortly before he died, "you only have two choices: you can drown yourself in grief or you can honor my life by moving forward and remembering all the positive memories since we reconnected."

I chose to move forward.

Author's Note

Part I of this book was more than a decade in the making. Its subject is love, but many of the events it describes were interwoven with hate. Some of those events directly involved race, and the trauma I experienced enduring them partly explains the length of time it took to complete the manuscript. Over the course of that decade, views on race evolved, picking up speed near the end. One such example is the increasingly common practice of capitalizing the first letter of words referring to race, such as *black*. I respect the reasons for that change but have chosen to stick with the form I have used throughout my nine decades of life. As described in the following pages, I have learned a lot about race over the years, yet still find it difficult to accept that there is a fundamental difference between people, including my family members, on that basis.

That gap has also caused some of the time references, particularly in Part II, which consists of essays by twenty-three other members of the adoption community, to be off by a few years. I have chosen to leave the work unchanged.

It was extremely important to me to be as exacting as possible in recounting certain events and conversations while writing my memoir. As individuals, we all remember things in our own way. These are my memories and how I remember them.

The people, places, and events in this story are all real. Some of the names have been changed to protect people's privacy.

Terms Used in Adoption

birth mother Over the years there has been different terminology to designate a woman who gives birth and then, for whatever reason, releases her child for adoption. I have chosen throughout *Love Never Leaves* to refer to myself and other like women as birth mothers.

triad In adoption, *triad* refers to the birth parents, the adoptee, and the adoptive parents.

closed adoptions This refers to a system in which no contact is allowed between birth parents and the adoptee and adoptive parents. All court records are sealed. A societal shift towards more openness began in the late 1980s or early 1990s.

open adoptions A system in which there is direct communication and full disclosure of identifying information between adoptive parents and birth parents. In this approach, arrangements on how to handle contact with the adoptee are decided by both sets of parents.

Contents

Part II
In Their Own Words

CHAPTER 1

Dark Clouds

AFTER I RETURNED to my parents' home, my marriage all but over, it took a while to settle in. Finally, I began to feel at ease and knew it was time for my two boys, George and David, to attend Sunday school and for me to rejoin the choir. This was the church I had belonged to since my early teens. As we headed out on a Sunday morning in April, the sun was shining, the forsythia was just starting to bloom, and the smells of spring were permeating the air.

Downstairs, in the Sunday school, the room was beautifully decorated for preschoolers. There were teddy bears and ducks stenciled on one wall and on another there was a picture of a pasture with sheep, black-and-white cows, and a huge yellow sun shining down on all kinds of flowers. The profusion of bright colors was everywhere.

When I returned to pick the boys up after church, I noticed children had gathered around David's playpen. George and David were the only biracial children in an otherwise all-white Sunday school class, so I thought to myself, *It's perfectly normal for them to be curious.* When they saw me coming, however, the whole class scattered like they were doing something wrong.

The teacher did not seem concerned and said she was confident things would change once the newness wore off. For the time being, I agreed with her.

There were many storms in my life that I would have to deal with, and one never knows when a cumulus cloud will turn dark and produce rain, then thunder and lightning. Perhaps a hurricane or tornado will happen, and happen it did. That morning, when the children scattered, it was a very small cumulus cloud beginning to take seed.

* * *

MY BROTHER, BOB, was the only one in the family who ever inquired about my husband, George Sr. One day when Bob dropped in, he asked if I had had any word at all from him.

"No, I have not."

"Do you know if he is working?"

"I don't know."

"Is he sending you any financial help?"

"No, he isn't."

"Do you still love him?"

"My feelings are conflicted at this point," I said. "I am not sure about anything."

It was not just uncertainty that marked the start of this dark period in my life. When I moved back home to Lowell, Massachusetts, in 1952, I was still not fully aware of what was happening in other parts of the country regarding racial discrimination and our ambivalence as a nation about interracial marriage. In 1948, 90 percent of American adults opposed interracial marriage, and 48 percent felt that a person who married someone of another race should be charged with a crime. During the 1950s, half of the states still had laws prohibiting interracial marriage. Even by 1967, when the United States Supreme Court legalized interracial marriage everywhere in the country, sixteen states still had statutes against it on the books.

Not in New Hampshire, though, where on April 22, 1950, I married George Emerson Taggart, whom I had met at the New England Conservatory of Music, in Boston, where we were both students. I was not aware at the time of the term *interracial marriage*, but that is what ours was called, because George was black and I was white. After a year and a half, we moved into a rental apartment in a predominantly black section of Boston called Roxbury. For reasons still difficult for me to comprehend seven decades later, things quickly turned sour and I found myself back home in Lowell, with one mixed-race baby boy at my side and another on the way, in a community not quite ready for their presence. I was completely unaware of what lay ahead for us. But I was about to find out.

* * *

THERE WAS JOY singing in the choir once again. It brought a light back into my soul that had been dimmed for some time. I was welcomed by some but sensed a distance from others. At home I began receiving phone calls telling me we were not wanted, but I dismissed and ignored them. There were episodes at church in which George, who was two years old, would complain about kids picking on him and David, calling them names, asking why they never washed and looked dirty all the time. One Sunday when I went downstairs to pick up the boys, George was nowhere around. I asked the teacher where he was.

"He was in the hall a few minutes ago," she said. "I saw him run out, thinking you had come to pick him up."

I went to look for him and began to get a panicky feeling in the pit of my stomach when I couldn't find him. I walked around the church and found George huddled in a corner with his nose bleeding. When I ran over to him, he was crying and nothing he was saying made any sense. I tried to calm him down and said we would pick up David and head home. He cried all the way, and it took the rest of the afternoon for things to settle down. The following week the only thing he would say was, "That big boy was bad. I don't like him."

I tried calling the teacher but was unable to reach her, so I decided to leave early the next Sunday and talk to her then. When we started to head out for church the following week, George became agitated, and as we approached the building he began to cry.

"I don't want to go to Sunday school anymore," he said.

"I need to go in and talk to the teacher about what happened last Sunday and see if we can find out who the boy was that hurt you," I told him.

"Do I have to stay?"

"No."

When I went into the classroom, George clung to my leg. I explained to the teacher what had happened and asked if she remembered seeing a bigger boy talking to George. She was unable to shed any light on what had gone on or who the bigger boy might have been. We talked for a few minutes and it became apparent she was embarrassed. I said I did not know if I could get George to come back to Sunday school.

I took the boys out into the hall and suggested to George that he could sit with Mama today upstairs in the big church.

"David too?"

"Yes, David too."

The phone calls, meanwhile, were becoming more frequent. They were always in the daytime. The language was becoming more offensive. There were threats about what would happen to me and my boys if we didn't move out of town. I learned very quickly when I picked up the phone to ask who was calling, and if they did not answer I quickly hung up.

I do not know why I did not recognize it sooner, but the boys and I were becoming isolated. Previously, I had often sung as a paid soloist for weddings in the local churches, but now no one would hire me. I would make phone calls to people I had known all of my life, and they were not returned. The boys were never invited anywhere by anyone outside the family. Bob and his family had moved up to Canada, and my sister, Priscilla, and her husband were down in Florida. When we went to the park, if other children started playing with the boys, their mothers would come over and take them away.

I fought the urge to scream out, "What is wrong with you? They are just little boys!"

The phone calls grew more threatening. I tried calling the police. They said they could do nothing. Many times I would not answer the phone, but that stopped when my mom said, "I know you are home. Why don't you answer?"

I knew I could not tell her the real reason. "I was busy changing David's diaper," I said. "Sorry about that, Mom."

From that point on I would just pick up the receiver, and once I heard the vile words spewing out of the caller's mouth I would slam it right back down again.

One afternoon the boys and I had just come back from our daily walk when the phone rang. I figured if I did not answer it, whoever was on the other end would just let it ring. The feeling of helplessness was overwhelming. What should I do? Try talking to them? That was the one thing I hadn't done. What was there to lose? I practiced what I would say but couldn't do it. A week went by. Finally I found the courage to speak out. This time when the phone rang I answered it, and the person at the other end—a male; it was always a male—went on a tirade. When he realized I was not hanging up, he asked, "Are you still there?"

"Yes, I am still here and would like to ask you and try to understand why you hate us so much."

"Well, you are right about one thing," he said. "I do hate you and do not have to explain anything to you."

He asked when I was going to move and I told him I had no intention of moving.

"I want you to listen very closely to what I am about to say," he replied, "because your life and your black n***** babies' lives depend on it. If you do not move and one of your n***** babies start school, he will disappear. You cannot be with him every minute of the day, and I promise you will never see him again."

"Are you threatening me?"

"You are damn right I am threatening you, and you better listen."

"Why would you hurt an innocent child? He is just a *child*."

"Lady, you keep referring to him as a child. He is not a child. He is a n***** baby and not a human being."

With that I vomited onto the phone and screamed, "*May you burn in hell!*" then slammed the receiver down and started walking around the house in a panic. I ran into the bathroom and vomited some more.

By now both the boys had woken up from their naps, and I ran upstairs and held them both close and vowed I would never let anything happen to them. Somehow I would keep them safe.

George asked, "Why are you crying, Mama?"

"Mama doesn't feel very well."

He looked up with those beautiful big eyes and said, "I take care of you, Mama."

"Thank you, honey."

I then suggested we get ready to take our walk and how about if we stop for ice cream today? I kept hearing my mother's words when she would tell my brother, "Sticks and stones will break your bones, but names will never hurt you."

Is that all it was? I didn't think so. The clouds were getting darker, and the thunder was not far behind.

CHAPTER 2

A Different Drummer

AT A VERY young age, I used to go into a room by myself, close the door, and sing at the top of my lungs. Singing brought joy to my heart, and when I joined the children's choir at church, I was thrilled when I noticed my singing brought joy to others as well. Music became my life.

I asked my mom if I could take singing lessons, but apparently I was too young and there wasn't a teacher who would accept me, so she signed me up for elocution lessons and promised that singing lessons would be in my future. I lived every day for that moment and finally started with a teacher near home who taught me everything she could and then recommended a vocal teacher in Boston by the name of Walter Greenwood. After two years he convinced my mother I was ready, at thirteen years old, to give my first concert.

In my teen years I began to recognize I was marching to a different drummer, because when most of my classmates were into talking, gossiping, dating, and going out with boys, I had no interest. All my energies went into my music, and by now I was singing at weddings, funerals, and other social functions and also practicing two to three hours a day for my upcoming concert. I was happy and content singing to a different drummer.

My efforts to convince my mom in the first year of high school that I wanted to pursue just music were met with disdain—not even worthy of discussion. About a month later she informed me she had located a private school close to home, called Rogers Hall, where they had a wonderful music director who put on light opera each year. She asked if I wanted her to set up an appointment. Needless to say, I was thrilled and could hardly wait to learn more. We then explored all the attributes the school had to offer. She was impressed with its academic curriculum. I was impressed with not only its music and drama courses but also the enormous pool, where swimming was taught as an elective. That was another of my favorite activities. Our conversations with the music director convinced me that if I were to pursue a music career, a well-rounded education would be not only important but necessary.

The next three years were filled with intellectual enlightenments. Not only did I have the opportunity to perform in musicals every spring, but the experience I gained with acting in my drama courses would prove to be invaluable.

We lived in a middle-class neighborhood in Lowell called the Highlands. My dad worked as an engineer for the Locks and Canals, a company that operated a complex system of canals that crisscrossed the city of Lowell, on the banks of the Merrimack River, thirty miles north of Boston. It had once been America's largest industrial center, but by the 1920s and '30s, the textile industry had begun to move south, and by the late '50s, the two biggest mills were closed and Lowell was headed towards a postindustrial era. My mom, Bertha Elzade Chapman, attended the New England Conservatory, majoring in piano. She married Earl Leslie Huse and started a family. When I came into the world, the country was in the midst of the Great Depression, and my dad was forced to take a cut in pay. My mom began to teach piano lessons and play the organ in local churches to help out.

The atmosphere I was surrounded by while growing up was one of joy, happiness, love, hope, laughter, faith, and music, with a mother who created that environment and a father who was steady and predictable. I was the youngest; my brother, Bob, was five years older, and my sister, Priscilla, was three years older. At the age of six, Bob was struck with polio, a debilitating disease caused by a virus that invades the nervous system and can result in total paralysis. In my brother's case it affected his lower limbs. In my world, he wasn't any different from anyone else. He was my big brother. As I grew older, I became aware of all the challenges he had to face outside the Huse family. Inside the family, it was instilled in each of us that there wasn't anything we could not do.

Even so, it became obvious our talents, even as young children, were as different as winter is from summer. Bob believed in free enterprise and that came out in full bloom when he was in the third grade. By then he was walking with the use of braces and crutches, but the school he was attending did not have an elevator, so my mother would get him there early and the janitor would help him up the stairs. One of his classmates asked if he could carry Bob's crutches. I am sure he just wanted to help, but my brother hated anyone to feel sorry for him, and always reacted with a stern voice, hoping it would scare people away. He probably said something like "It will cost you two cents, kid. Now get lost." Figuring that would be the end of it, Bob was surprised the next day when his classmate came to school with cash in hand. Soon other boys were waiting in line for the same privilege, and by the end of the first week, Bob had earned not only fourteen cents but a chocolate bar and some comic books. That ended quickly, however, when Priscilla informed our mom what was going on. As Bob noted later, "It was a sad day for free enterprise." There were many other efforts undertaken, some successful, some not, but eventually Bob did become financially independent.

Priscilla was a neat freak. She would play with my dolls because she didn't want to mess up her own and was always teasing me about things I should be doing or not doing. She would come home from school crying if she didn't get all As, unlike her sister, who was happy to just get by.

I remember the Christmas she found three dolls under the tree. When my mom went to clean up, she found one of them in the garbage.

"Priscilla, I found one of your dolls in the trash by mistake."

"It's not a mistake. I don't want it, because only two dolls will fit in my carriage."

"Honey, what if you have more than two children when you grow up?"

"Mom," Priscilla replied emphatically, "I am only going to have two children."

After graduating from college she became a teacher in a school a half hour east of Boston. Eventually, she married and had exactly two children.

When it came time for us to head out to college, money was scarce, but my mom managed to put all of her talents into earning extra money so we could achieve our goals and dreams. She was still playing the organ at church and teaching piano, but it was not enough, so she embarked on a whole new career, hosting a women's program, first on radio, then on television. Priscilla ended up attending Boston University on a scholarship and, three years later, I would attend the New England Conservatory of Music.

Despite the odds, Bob had already accomplished much in his life. He was married by the time he was twenty-five and working as an announcer at a local radio station, covering news events, hosting talk shows, and interviewing politicians and community leaders. After a couple of years, he decided to switch to real estate because it was much more lucrative.

It was the late '40s and early '50s. Women were just starting to make a breakthrough in jobs that had mostly been held by men. There were three television networks in the Boston area then, affiliated with NBC, CBS, and ABC. CBS and ABC already had hired women to do morning shows, and now NBC was looking to do the same. One of Mom's producers at the radio station suggested she apply. "Even if you are unsuccessful," he said, "the experience will be good for you, and you have nothing to lose and everything to gain."

She made an appointment to audition the following week.

My mother had been blessed with a photographic memory. She also had the gift of being able to converse with anyone nonstop, and the television networks were looking for people with those attributes. Teleprompters had not been introduced yet. They hired her immediately, and she came up with a morning show called *Domestic Diary*, which was a combination of interviewing celebrities, a cooking segment, and anything that might be of interest to homemakers.

Because both my sister and I were in school, we did not have an opportunity to watch those early shows, but we loved to listen to one story our aunt Nancy liked to tell. It seems on one of our mom's cooking segments she was explaining how much time you could save by preparing spaghetti in a pressure cooker and got carried away listing all the advantages. Meanwhile, the steam was building up behind her on the stove. Aunt Nancy was sitting home having her coffee and could tell by the valve jiggling on top of the pan that it was going to blow. She started yelling at the TV, like our mother could hear her. Sure enough, a few seconds later Mom ended up with spaghetti not only all over the set but also in her hair and dripping down over her glasses. Without missing a beat, she removed several strands of dangling pasta, looked right into the camera, and said, "Now, *that* is exactly what you *don't* want to have happen, and let me explain why."

Despite a few such mishaps, Mom's show was a huge success and in eight weeks went from fifteen minutes three times a week to twenty-five minutes five times a week. This was the beginning of a twelve-year career with WBZ in Boston, NBC's third-largest affiliate. So, yes, we were living our dreams.

CHAPTER 3

The Conservatory

TODAY WAS MY day. It was 1949, and I was eighteen years old. I had waited years for this day, anticipating it, working hard for it, setting goals for it, dreaming about it, and finally my day had arrived. In a few hours I would be climbing the steps of the famous New England Conservatory in Boston to register for the coming school year.

My mom came in the kitchen and asked, "What in the world are you doing up and dressed at five o'clock in the morning?"

"I just wanted to be ready when it was time to catch the train to Boston."

She smiled, knowing this was my dream playing itself out. She wanted to fix me breakfast, and even though I didn't think it would stay down, I knew that if I did not concede she would tell me what I had heard repeatedly for the last eighteen years: "You need to start the day with something in your stomach." My brother, sister, and I called her the Warrior of Worry.

The line for registration was at least a quarter of a mile long, but even that could not dampen my excitement over the fact that I was actually inside the New England Conservatory, walking the same halls as so many talented musicians had done before me. Many conversations broke out in line. The person I was talking to, whose name was George, was majoring in piano; my major, I told him, was voice. Questions flew back and forth. He informed me that his interest was classical; my focus, I said, was lieder.

"That's interesting," he said, "and what drew you to that musical form?"

"I love the pure sound and rich harmonies, along with the lyrical melodies. They're so romantic and expressive. In fact, as I'm sure you are aware, lieder is a type of German art song taken from poetry and literature of the eighteenth and nineteenth centuries."

He smiled and said, "You must be a lyric soprano."

I replied by answering in the affirmative.

As I was about to continue with more of the history, I realized I was next in line to be registered, so our conversation was cut short. George said quickly, "I would like to continue our conversation another time." I nodded my head and smiled. As the day went by, I realized there were a several different ethnic groups represented in the student body. George, for example, was black.

The first four months flew by, and I knew this was where I belonged. How nice to have other people around as interested in music as I. As the year progressed, I ran into George frequently. He would ask how my classes were going and we would stop and chat. He finally asked me to join him for coffee, and I was more than happy to accept. The conversations that followed were mostly about our love for music and how it consumed us. We talked about the different composers we liked and, after we received our grades for the semester, the conversation went in that direction. As it turned out, we had the same teacher for harmony, but George was in the advanced class and mine was Harmony 101. When he learned I was having difficulty, he offered to tutor me, but even with his patience and help, the next semester's grade was only a C. Embarrassed? I was mortified.

One of the classes we attended together was music history. It was stimulating to discuss with the others in the class the differences between the Renaissance, Baroque, Classical, Romantic, and twentieth-century composers and which era was our favorite and why. Many times George and I were the only two left talking, going deeper into the different music forms and how and why the structure of those forms changed from one era to another. Over the next few months, I discovered that many of the composers he played on the piano had also written music for singers.

George played works by Franz Schubert, Robert Schumann, Johann Sebastian Bach, and Johannes Brahms. Shubert alone wrote over 600 German lieder songs, along with operas, symphonies, sonatas, masses, and chamber and piano compositions. George was very familiar with all of these composers, whose works I had been singing all of my life.

I began preparing for a concert in the spring but did not have an accompanist. I asked George if he might be interested and he said, "I would love to accompany you."

"Would you be willing to share part of the concert with me?" I asked.

"Yes, of course," he replied.

I couldn't wait to tell my mother. After she questioned me about his qualifications, she said she was looking forward to meeting him and hearing him play.

George and I spent many hours practicing and fine-tuning in order to reach the highest level of performance we could. We were both gaining deep respect for the other's knowledge of music. We were spending more and more time together aside from practicing, and there were strange emotions stirring in me that were unfamiliar and a little unsettling.

It crossed my mind one day that we never went out to have lunch or coffee. I mentioned to George that there was this cute little café down the street from the school and suggested we go there for a change.

He got a strange look on his face and said, "We need to talk." He then asked if I had experienced any kind of prejudice where I was brought up.

"Well, I do remember my mom talking one night at dinner about this Jewish couple who she knew were being denied to live in a particular town because of their last name and how another one of her girlfriends, who was Irish, had married a man of the Jewish faith and both of their parents had disowned them."

"Do you have any black people living in town?"

"Not that I know of."

"If we are going to be friends I need to explain some things you might not be aware of. Do you have any idea what is going on down south with black Americans?"

"No."

"The prejudice down south is cruel and dangerous. We are not allowed to walk on the same side of the street as white people. We are forced to sit in the back of the bus. Restaurants are segregated. All of the public utilities, like rest rooms and drinking fountains, are marked for colored people only. Black children are relegated to attending schools that are inferior to white schools. We are not allowed to vote, because of Jim Crow laws, and marriages between the races are illegal. You can be put in jail if you break any of these rules. I could go on and on, but let me end by saying that in some southern states they are still lynching black people. There are many of us who are moving north and west because of the atrocities that are going on down south.

"Many of these laws are illegal in northern states," he continued, "and we have much more freedom. But even up north the races are silently separated in many ways, and we are dealing with prejudice every day. We live in certain sections of the city. Dating or going out with a white person is not accepted, and I have seen black men who have been killed because of it. If we go in a restaurant where white people are eating, the maître d' will inform you there are no seats available. We are excluded from any good jobs, so most of us work in menial positions like waiters, cooks, janitors, and if you are a professional person, such as a lawyer or doctor, all of your patients or clients come from the black community.

"I am telling you this because, if we are going to have any kind of a relationship, you need to know and understand that I am unable to do many of the normal things you are used to, and if I try, I put us both at risk."

As he was talking I kept thinking, *Why wasn't any of this brought up in school?* We had a current-events class every week and never once was the plight of black people addressed.

When he finished I was in shock. As my eyes began to tear up, George said, "Please don't cry. I did not tell you any of this to upset you, but I just wanted you to know the dangers we could be faced with."

I then pulled myself together and asked if he felt any of that prejudice here at the conservatory.

"No, I don't, because in the art world most people accept you for your talent, and one's ethnic background is never an issue."

When I headed home that night, the conversation we had was weighing me down and left me wondering what kind of a world were we living in, where the color of your skin could bring out such hatred. For the first time, I realized I had been brought up in not only a protective bubble but a bubble of idealism as well.

CHAPTER 4

Love Blooms

How AND WHEN love happened I am not sure. I remember rehearsing for the upcoming concert and getting the sense that George was expressing his feelings for me through his music. I also recall a time when seeing him became the highlight of my day. I was surprised one day as he was walking toward me and I had a feeling of warmth streaming through my whole body. He asked if I was ill. It looked like I was running a temperature, he said

"I think I *am* coming down with something," I said, "and I don't feel very well."

"Would you like to practice later on in the day?"

"I think I better go home."

As I was sitting on the train, listening to the thump, thump, thump of the wheels, it was duplicating the thump, thump, thump of my heart. I closed my eyes and fantasized about what it would be like to be swept away by George. I never had the desire to be physically close to anyone before in my life. It seemed like the flame of love had found its way in and was encompassing my whole body. There had been no words between us that expressed the depth of our feelings for each other, but that was about to change.

The concert date was getting closer, and we had reserved time at the Liberty Hall Theater, a part of the Lowell Memorial Auditorium, to have our final rehearsal before the concert. So our practice sessions at the conservatory became more frequent and intense, and because it was almost time for graduation, practice rooms were hard to come by. The rules at the school were that you could not book ahead. It was first come, first served, so George would get there as early in the morning as possible, but there were days when he couldn't get a room for us until six or seven o'clock at night. It was at one of those late practice sessions, as we were gathering up our things to leave, that he said, "Please stay for just one minute," then closed the door.

I was concerned that we would get into trouble, because the rules stated clearly that the doors to all practice rooms were to remain open at all times after 7:00 p.m.

"This will only take a moment," he said, then he came over and kissed me.

He immediately opened the door and, as we walked down the hall with that warm, tender kiss still on my lips, he said, "I will see you tomorrow and we will talk about what just happened."

* * *

IT WAS NEVER easy to find a place where we could go without raising looks of all kinds, especially outside of the conservatory. There was one place George found down by the Charles River, not far from the school, where trees were plentiful and, at certain times of the day, there were few people around. This is where we had our first serious conversation.

He started out by saying he had thought long and hard about this talk because it would mean changing both of our lives, as we now knew them, forever. Did I want him to continue? he asked. I said yes.

He then professed his love for me and said he was sure I felt the same way. "I do not want you to say anything," he concluded, "until you have had an opportunity to think before you consider taking our relationship any further. Will you do that for me? And we will talk again tomorrow."

The following day I professed my love as well, and over the next few months, we discussed the issues and problems we would face as a mixed couple. We practiced going out in public, riding on the subway. We could never hold hands, he said, and I was to take his lead at all times. We had a code set up, and if he sensed we were threatened in any way, he would pick up his music and act like he did not know me and either move to another seat or get off at the next stop without me. We would meet back at the conservatory. We talked about the acceptance of him by my family. I felt certain that as soon as they met him they would understand all of the reasons I had fallen in love with this wonderful, intelligent, sensitive, talented, articulate person and would not only accept him but love him as I did.

Alongside the caution, there were stolen kisses that were brief but oh so sweet and never enough. Love was piercing my being with an emotion that was beyond my comprehension.

Concert time drew near and now all the hard work and preparation was to play itself out in the form of our final rehearsal at the theater in Lowell. For a singer, there is a delicate balance between technique, interpretation, and passion. My mom would be there, and I always looked forward to going over minute details with her on how improvements could be made so my performance would be at its highest level and I could do justice to each composer's music that I had chosen.

It was a beautiful day and I was completely wrapped up in my euphoria of doing the one thing in the world I loved more than anything else, and that was to sing and impart to my audience all that the music was trying to say. To add to that euphoria, I would be performing side by side with the man I had lost my heart to.

Rehearsal time had been set for 4:00 p.m. in the theater. George would be coming in from Boston to Lowell by train, and I was to pick him up at 3:25. Luckily, the train was on time, and as we left the station by cab, George seemed very quiet. He whispered in my ear not to sit too close but took my hand, which sent a code: I love you.

My mother had not arrived yet, and as we were headed for the theater, a gentleman came up and asked if he could help us. I said we were there to rehearse for a concert that was scheduled for next Saturday. I asked if we could wait for my mother, but before I could get the rest of the sentence out I saw her, and as she walked toward us he recognized her. After a few niceties, he let us into the theater.

I introduced George to my mom and, once the pleasantries were over, I informed her we only had an hour and a half, so we had better get started right away. I just assumed there would be time to talk after the rehearsal was over. My mom had no idea her younger daughter was in love with the person she had just met.

The rehearsal went well with a couple of glitches, but nothing unusual when you have an opportunity to practice at the site where your performance will be taking place. I left with many concerns regarding lighting, the positioning of the piano, and the raising and lowering of the curtain. These were some of the things I hoped to discuss on the way home with Mom, but right then I was looking forward to spending some time over coffee, chatting and letting her get to know George. It was then that he brought to my attention how late it was and that, if he didn't leave right away, he would miss the last train back to Boston. We drove directly to the station and, after the polite conversation ended, he squeezed my hand with our special code and left.

On the way home I brought up my concerns—the lights, the piano, etc.—with Mom and she told me, "Don't worry about it. I will get there early and make sure all those issues are taken care of."

"So, Mom," I continued, "I am looking forward to your critique."

"Could it wait until tomorrow? It has been a long day and I am really tired."

"Sorry. Of course it can."

I knew she had to get up early to head into Boston for her TV show, so I dropped it, except to ask for an overall impression of how I had done.

"I think in general your stage presence and technique was good."

I asked what she thought about George's performance.

"There is no question he is brilliant, not only as an accompanist but as a performer as well, but, honey, you did not mention he was black."

Teasing her I said, "What does that have to do with the price of peas in France?"

"You didn't think that was important?"

"Never entered my head," I replied.

As we arrived home I was still trying to figure out what she had meant by her last statement, but I was too tired to pursue it. Probably it was nothing. I ran in the house and started to get ready for bed.

Mom was in the den, working on her script for the next day, when I went in to kiss her good night. I asked, "Mom, is there something we need to talk about?"

"No, I am just tired."

There was no reason for me to question her any further.

The night of the concert I got lost in the music and prayed I did justice to each composer whose composition I had chosen to sing. The audience reacted with enthusiasm and both George and I ended up performing several encores. The review the following day in the newspaper was extremely positive. However, I was never satisfied with my performance, so the following week I discussed with Mom how things like tempo and interpretation could have been improved.

"Not by much, honey, but keep up the good work and remember: the more you learn about technique the more time you can spend on interpretation.

Good advice, I thought.

The following week George headed for Atlantic City, New Jersey, where he had worked as a waiter and piano player for the past three summers. My plan was to work as a nanny for three small children in Hampton Beach, New Hampshire. We wrote to each other three or four times a week. In those letters we poured out our feelings in far greater depth than ever before.

In the last letter I received before George left New Jersey, he asked me to meet him in room 214 the first day of classes. A few days later, after registering for the following year, I was walking down the hall. I could hear him playing Schumann's Piano Concerto in A Minor, opus 54, and knew it was his dream, one day, to play it with a full orchestra. When I opened the door, he looked up at me with such tenderness I wanted to run into his arms but just stood there mesmerized, not knowing what to do with the emotions that were bubbling out of control. He said, "Let the beautiful sound of the music pour over you and imagine my arms around you, holding you close. I give you my love, I give you my heart, and I am asking you to be my wife."

It was what every girl dreams of, and I could not believe it was happening to me. The bubble burst as I ran over, took his face in my hands, looked straight into his eyes, and told him, "Yes, I would be honored to be your wife."

"No, I am the one who is honored," he said as he gently pushed me away, stood up, took my hand and sent his special code by squeezing twice, which meant I was standing too close. "Let's celebrate by buying lunch at the cafeteria and head towards our favorite spot down by the river," he said and then squeezed my hand once, which meant "I love you."

For one precious hour we were in a silent world of our own and it was magic. The love was flowing between us without any touching or physical contact. It was sad and wonderful at the same time. Sad because all I wanted at that moment was to feel his arms around me and experience the joy of his body next to mine.

George broke the silence by saying, "Deb, do you remember the conversation we had back at the conservatory about how things in our relationship were never going to be normal?"

"Of course I do."

"Well, this is one of those times. I have lived a lifetime learning when, how, and where to keep my emotions at bay, and I knew by the look in your eyes when I pushed you away today you were hurt. When we marry, there will be no honeymoon. Why? Because there is no place for us to go, and the times we can be together as husband and wife will be very few because, again, there will be no place for us to go until we have our own place. Simple things like going out to dinner, going to the movies, even driving in the same car together, is a danger. Everything we do will have to be scrutinized, even at the conservatory. From now on I am going to ask you to trust me implicitly because everything I do will be to protect us. However, right now I would like to pick you up, shower you with kisses, and yell to the world how happy I am, but I can only do that in my head, and I am asking you to do the same. Our time will come. We just have to be patient. Can you do that?"

"Yes, and I will go into this with my eyes wide open, and whatever lies ahead, we will deal with it together."

I said it and meant it and knew that, for now, the longing to be close would have to wait.

After the deliciousness of that romantic proposal, our feet hit the ground of realism. Over the next two months we ramped up our discussions on how to achieve our desire to become husband and wife without disrupting everyone else's lives.

One of my greatest fears, in light of my mother's career, was the possibility of our marriage being picked up by the media. If that happened, she could end up losing her job. I told George about a young woman who also lived in Lowell who had married a famous black entertainer, a national celebrity. She, too, was white. Her family was well-known in the community, and the story had appeared in local and national newspapers. His career was almost ruined. My mom was not known outside of New England, but I wanted to do everything I could to avoid any kind of publicity. George was in complete agreement.

Finally, we came up with a plan to elope and keep our marriage a secret. Our thinking was that the farther we could get from Massachusetts the better. The first step, by law, was to obtain blood tests and we were both able to do that in Boston. George and I then headed north by bus, sitting in separate rows, to Portsmouth, New Hampshire, and went directly to the clerk's office at city hall, where we filled out the necessary papers. I did fudge a little bit by reversing my middle and first names and changing the spelling of my last name, hoping to deflect any recognition or connection to my mother. The gentleman who performed the ceremony was gracious and wished us good luck, followed by shaking our hands. *Good omen*, I thought.

Once our vows were taken, we left the office as Mr. and Mrs. George Emerson Taggart. There was joy in our hearts because our plan had worked out, and that was enough for now.

He had to take a bus back to Boston, and I took a different one home to Lowell. On the way there my head was filled with all of the wonderful things that would have happened if we were an ordinary couple. Did it work? For now it was all that I had.

Once George was able to make arrangements, a month after we became husband and wife all of those beautiful images we'd had in our heads became reality and our bodies finally found each other and melded into a symphony of love.

He and I continued at the conservatory for another year and a half, and everything moved along as planned. Unfortunately, the times we could be together in the next few years became almost impossible because there was no place for us to go without bringing the attention to ourselves that we were trying so hard to avoid. It was easier, if we were going to keep our secret and stay focused, to physically and mentally return to the lives we were living before we married.

In many of our conversations we had talked about having children and agreed we needed to finish our education and have some financial stability before that could happen. We both took measures to prevent my getting pregnant, but it seems nature found a way to usurp our efforts and I began to notice my body was changing. *What will happen now?* I thought.

With trepidation I informed George about the pregnancy. He looked at me, smiled, and said, "Are you telling me that you are carrying my child?"

"Yes, that is what I am telling you," I replied.

"I didn't expect this so soon, but that's wonderful. I couldn't be happier."

He reached over and squeezed my hand, sending both of our special codes.

"Have you been to a doctor yet?"

"No, not yet. I wanted to tell you first."

"Well, it looks like we have some serious decisions to make, and the first one is to inform your parents about our marriage."

"But not the pregnancy," I replied. "Not yet."

* * *

I KNEW MY mom would be disappointed and hurt when she found out we had eloped, but I was confident she would understand, ultimately, that we had made those decisions to protect the family. As I look back now, I think I was too young and naïve to recognize that Mom was in a state of shock when I told her the details of what had happened over the past year and a half. I had never known her to be at a loss for words, but she stared at me for a very long time, and the first thing that came out of her mouth was "Did your brother know?"

"No, Mom, no one knew."

And then question after question came at me with that primal urgency in her voice that always made me feel frightened and infantile.

"When did you meet him, how old is he, what about children, have you met anyone else in his family, where is he from, what does he do for a living, where will you live, what were you *thinking*?"

"I met him at the conservatory," I said calmly, though I was anything but calm, my hands shaking beneath the table. "I fell in *love*. Why are you not happy for me? Mom, I know and understand how devastated you are on how I handled this, and I should have told you sooner, but I hope in time you will understand I firmly believed that keeping our marriage a secret for as long as we did was the right thing to do."

She finally calmed down and I pleaded with her to get to know George, to have a conversation with him.

"Please, Mom, let me bring him home."

"I can't do that right now. I need more time, but, yes, I will meet him along with your dad, but remember, Priscilla is consumed with wedding plans and will not be available and Bob has just taken a job in Canada."

It was a couple of months before my mom finally agreed to invite George to the house. He came the following Saturday in a cab from the train station. An hour before he arrived, my dad had to leave because he received a phone call informing him that a generator had broken down at one of the plants.

"I am sorry," he said. "I will do my best to get back."

Mom greeted him into our home with protective armor that was never penetrated. There was no handshake, no warm smile, for which she was famous, no casual conversation. Her indifference and apathy infused the atmosphere. I was so upset and tried to end the visit as quickly and quietly as possible, but George was sensitive enough to recognize what was going on and intervened in a very gentlemanly manner, reminding us that his time was limited and, because of his job, he had to return to Boston. He asked if I would please call a cab.

The meeting was quite different from what I had expected and hoped for, and after George left, I wanted to know why. With tears streaming down my face, I asked, "Why did you have George come up here and then treat him with such indifference?"

"I am your mother and it is my job to protect you."

"Protect me from what and from whom?"

"You are not going to like what I am about to tell you, but you need to hear it. Did you know the man you married had been married before and is not seven years but ten years older than you are?"

"What? Are you sure, and how do you know this?"

"I had him investigated by our lawyer."

"Why would you do that?"

"I wanted to have the marriage annulled and was informed there were no grounds for an annulment but was told an investigation might turn up further information on this man you married."

I could not believe what I was hearing but managed to keep my voice from sounding hysterical. "In the lawyer's report," I asked, "was there a mention of a divorce?"

"Yes, there was a divorce."

"So why bring it up? How could you do this? I have never done anything that would warrant you investigating the man—whose name is George, by the way—I chose to marry. You have never questioned my judgment before. Why would you do this? If you have a problem with my marriage, it is your problem, and I have to tell you, Mom, this is very disappointing and hurtful. My heart is broken because you took it upon yourself to doubt me."

"I was only trying to protect you. You're my daughter and I love you."

I grabbed my coat and ran out in tears. I was devastated, hurt, and confused, my thoughts swirling around in my head. As I walked, I kept thinking about my mother's reaction, which was out of character for her. I tried to calm down, but it all became more and more difficult to comprehend. In the years since, I have often asked myself, if my dad had made it back, would things have turned out differently? Honestly, I don't think so.

The next day I told George what had happened and asked about his previous marriage. He seemed embarrassed when he said, "I was very young and it happened a long time ago. It was over in six months. We were divorced, and to be honest, I did not think it was relevant. Are you angry?"

"No, but it would have been easier hearing it from you."

"I agree, but if you had known about the marriage, would it have made a difference in your decision to marry me?"

"Of course not," I said immediately.

"In regard to your mother, don't be too hard on her, because I am hoping she just needs time to process all of this."

CHAPTER 5

A Beautiful Baby Boy

IT WAS WELL into the summer when I finally told my mom I was five months pregnant. She had no reaction one way or another, which again left me confused and disappointed. With George in Atlantic City, I informed her we would not be getting our own place until after the baby was born. She seemed happy that I was going to be home and under the care of our family physician.

I accepted that I would not have a baby shower or many of the other things that go along with having your first child. Talking to my husband and looking forward to finally becoming a family was enough. During those conversations we both acknowledged that we needed to be strong and look forward to the joys of tomorrow. Those phone calls were my lifeline as the weeks went into months.

During the last visit I had with the doctor, he explained that the delivery of my baby was going to be a difficult one because my birth canal was exceptionally small. When he mentioned the timing of my contractions, I had no idea what he was talking about and was too embarrassed to ask.

After I returned home I got up the courage to ask my mom about contractions. What were they, and what did the doctor mean about the timing? Silence and then she said, "If they start when I'm not here, you should call a cab and get yourself to the hospital immediately."

"But, Mom, what do they feel like?"

"You will know once they begin."

OK, I thought, *she is not comfortable talking about this and that is all the information I am going to get*, so I decided to head for the library to see if I could find anything about contractions and what to expect in the delivery room. To my surprise there was very little.

George had already come back from Atlantic City and had rented a place for us to live in Roxbury. He made sure that I understood it was a middle-class, all-black neighborhood. He explained that the people he had rented from knew we were a mixed couple and would welcome us. All of this was very comforting to hear, and I could not wait to begin our life together.

It was November 13, around two o'clock in the afternoon, when I felt the contractions begin. After I notified the doctor, he told me to go to the hospital right away. I called a cab and gave the address of the private hospital where I was to give birth. I was not aware at the time that this particular hospital was where, typically, unwed mothers went to give birth to children they would never see again, and adoption was the only option they had because they had conceived a child without the sanctity of marriage. It was there that I learned, through my own experience, how these women were treated.

I was so frightened and did not have a clue what to expect. The nurse started to prep me, and I asked what she was doing.

She laughed. "Oh, this is your first, is it, sweetie? Well, maybe from this experience you will learn to keep your legs crossed."

Another nurse came in a few minutes later and asked, "Can I help?"

"No, she's being uncooperative and asking too many questions, but everything is under control."

They both left and went into an elongated room with a window, through which they watched me, incessantly urging me through a public-address system to push. Every ten minutes or so one of them would return to the delivery room to chastise me.

Although the doctor had warned me that my delivery was going to be difficult, I just knew something was not right. My legs had gone numb, my body was aching all over, and the baby was not moving. This was crazy. I had been in the delivery room for twelve hours and knew, from the nurses talking about the timing of my contractions, that the time between mine had remained the same. They had told me repeatedly they would not call the doctor until the time between contractions reached a certain point. So now, I knew, my tactics had to change in order to get one of the nurses to call him.

I yelled for a nurse to come in and please call the doctor. Again she refused.

"If you do not call him I will start screaming."

She laughed and went back into her cubbyhole. I began to scream, and when she did not respond, my screams got louder and louder, and she yelled back, through the PA system, "*Stop that right now!*" I had no intention of stopping, and when I continued screaming, she stormed back into the delivery room and, in a loud voice, said, "Dearie, it is three in the morning."

"I don't care what time it is, dearie. Call the doctor!"

"And if I do, what do you want me to say?"

"Tell him my back feels like it is on fire and whatever else you are supposed to know as a nurse about contractions."

She left the room and returned almost immediately and informed me that the doctor was on his way. She continued to swear and belittle me, but I turned a deaf ear.

The doctor arrived and, after a quick examination, sent for an ambulance to transport me to one of the bigger hospitals in the city and said he was going to have to do a cesarean section.

"Is the baby safe?" I asked. "And what is a cesarean section?"

"Yes, the baby is fine, but I have to operate as soon as possible, and the attendant in the ambulance will answer any questions you have."

As soon as I was in the ambulance I asked again, "What is a cesarean section?"

The attendant explained with a great deal of patience, "Your baby has become blocked and has stopped turning, so the doctor will make a cut in your belly, and in medical terms, that is called 'C-section.' It is done all the time, and it is perfectly safe."

As the painkiller started to take effect, I heard the doctor reprimanding the nurses, in a very loud voice, for not calling him earlier.

On November 14, 1951, at 5:56 a.m. I gave birth to a beautiful baby boy. When I came out from under anesthesia, I expected to see my husband but was told by my mom that he would not be coming to the hospital. I asked to see my son, and when they brought him in, I held him close and could not believe how precious he was. I checked him all over and noticed that he had long piano fingers like his dad and a full head of black hair. He even woke up for a few seconds, so I could see his dark brown eyes looking up at me. Even though I knew he couldn't see me, I knew he felt mother love pouring out all over him. This little fellow, my son, could not wait to be born. He had been knocking and kicking at my stomach door for weeks, and here he was, perfect and healthy in every way.

After the nurse came in to take the baby back to the nursery, I asked Mom, "Why was George not allowed to come and see his son?"

Her avoidance by telling me that I needed to get some rest was obvious. In fact, she never did answer. I asked the nurse the same question later. Her response was "You need to ask your mother."

George called the next day, and we shared our happiness. After I went over every detail of what the baby looked like, we talked about what we would name him, agreeing that he would carry the same name as his dad, George Emerson Taggart Jr. I asked him why he had not come to see us at the hospital.

"Your mom did not think it was advisable. She did call me and let me know everything went well and you and the baby were fine. I want you to promise me you will not make this an issue with her. Think about it. Maybe she was right. It is much safer for everybody this way."

"You know, George, I agree with you and my mother's decision, but the question I have is, why didn't she talk to me about this before I went into the hospital?"

"I can't answer that."

Was she still treating me like a child, or was there something else going on? Another question never answered.

CHAPTER 6

Something Is Askew

WE WERE SETTLING into our rented apartment in Roxbury. As you entered there was a foyer and, to the right, a beautiful grand piano. Down the hall, second door on the right, was where we called home. It was one room but expansive and had everything we needed to begin our life together. There was a large kitchen across the hall, which we shared with the landlord's sister, who lived in the apartment next to ours.

The neighborhood, on Munroe Street, was unwelcoming. No one came over with cookies or casseroles. The neighbors in our building simply ignored us. If mothers were sitting on the steps with their little ones when I was pushing George Jr. in the carriage, I would smile and say hello. They would immediately get up and disappear behind closed doors. By this time I had experienced prejudice from both sides of the page, black and white, so it was not unexpected.

None of that seemed to matter, because now we had our own place, and being a mother for the first time brought happiness, joy, and laughter into my life. Of course, there were the normal bumps in the road, as with any other couple just starting out. One of the first was when we had to face the realization that George would not be able to continue taking classes at the conservatory because of finances. He was holding down two jobs. One was at the historic Parker House hotel as a waiter; the other was at Massachusetts General Hospital in Boston, where he was a nurse's aid. I knew how disappointed he was and offered to go back home so he could continue with his education, but he said that was not an option.

The first few months of living together became an adventure. At George's request, I was trying to learn how to cook southern dishes, but the *Betty Crocker Cookbook*, my cooking bible, was not cutting it. There was the challenge of setting up a schedule that would allow me to tend to the baby, do the shopping, prepare dinner so it was ready when George Sr. arrived home, and go up to see my mother on occasion—all of the mundane problems I am sure every wife and mother goes through, and I loved it all.

After reading Dr. Benjamin Spock's book *Baby and Child Care*, I definitely was in tune with his commonsense approach to child-rearing. His belief was that babies do not have to be on a rigid schedule and parents should use their own instincts and try to recognize their own child's needs. It certainly was working with baby George. I don't know if it was because I was with him every minute of every day, but he never cried except to let me know when he was hungry or waking up from his nap.

It was more of a little whimper than a cry. Even the landlord's sister, Aretha, down the hall, asked how I kept the baby from crying. I told her he was more into giggling, cooing, and other baby noises.

I recognized as early as one month that George Jr. was going to be a very verbal child. I began reading to him, and he certainly responded to the sound of my voice. I knew he didn't understand a word I was saying, but just to see his smile made me happy. I was into "Pat-a-cake, pat-a-cake" with his feet, because his little hands were too small, and when I stopped, his feet would go into a rhythm, as if they were saying, "Do it again, Mama." Then we had those special moments when he just needed to be held, and I would sing him baby lullabies.

Every night when his father came home, I would go on about how George Jr. was progressing way ahead of Dr. Spock's prediction of what a baby should be doing at one, two, three, or four months old. I wanted to celebrate each and every milestone with George Sr., but the enthusiasm was one-sided. At the time, I attributed his lack of interest to being tired from a long day's work, but I may have been missing something.

The highlight of the day was taking George for a walk to the little corner store, where the proprietor and owner, Mr. Cohen, would greet us with a friendly smile and, after he got over playing and fussing with the baby, would say, "What can I do for you today, missus?"

If it were not for him and his suggestions on how to cook greens and other southern dishes, there would have been many more disasters at the dinner table. I also looked forward to the much-needed human contact, not only for myself, but for the baby as well. Mr. Cohen was our one ray of sunshine in the neighborhood.

Up to this point, Aretha had not accepted us or acknowledged me in any significant way, but I began to notice after a couple of months that baby George was beginning to melt her heart, and her attitude toward me became less hostile. She even offered to teach me how to make real southern corn bread. Once in a while when I was preparing dinner, she would come into the kitchen and interact with him. She made him laugh, and he would open his little arms when he saw her and, in her delightful southern drawl, she would say to me, "Girl, you sure produced one handsome child here. He is going to break a lot of hearts when he gets older."

* * *

AFTER ABOUT THREE months, all the exciting conversations George Sr. and I used to have about philosophy, music, and current events started to go silent. He was not utilizing the piano to practice, even though he had permission from the landlord to use it whenever he liked. When I asked him why one night, he just looked at me and smiled but didn't answer.

This pattern continued: my asking questions and George never answering. I did not want to admit to myself that something was drastically askew.

I told myself that if this was how it would be, practically no conversation at all, then I would learn to accept it. Even though it was upsetting and confusing, I was determined to make this marriage work. *Give it time*, I told myself.

There was one pattern in our marriage that had not changed, and that was when we were intimate. There was still the tenderness and words of love, always ending before he drifted off to sleep when he said, "Never doubt how much I love you." If he sensed any hesitation from me on a particular night, he never made me feel guilty by telling me a wife should acquiesce to her husband's desires.

More time passed and, still, night after night I would ask George what was wrong and night after night, if he answered me at all, he would say, "There is nothing wrong. Just leave it."

Sometimes after dinner he would engage with his son, but many times when the baby got fussy he would hand him over to me and retreat into his silent world. I kept asking myself, *Is it my fault? Where is the man I married? Where has he gone?* When I reminded him of the days when we fought so hard to be together and become a family, he replied, "Yes, we did."

"George, could we please talk about what is happening in our marriage?" I would say. "Is it me? Is it your job? Are you unhappy? Just talk to me. Why are you not practicing?"

He replied with such indifference: "What is there to talk about? Nothing is wrong."

When I told him I was pregnant with our second child, again there was very little reaction, leaving my heart heavy with hurt. He just wanted to know if I had seen a doctor yet.

"Yes, I did have an appointment with the doctor to see if everything was going along the way it should."

"And is everything all right?"

"Everything is fine, but the doctor reminded me, because he delivered George cesarean, this baby would also have to be delivered the same way. He explained, as my stomach grows, the incision will grow thinner, and his concern was it could open up. He said there was no way I should try to have a natural childbirth. The doctor suggested I have my fallopian tubes cut, because if I got pregnant again it would put us both at risk. He urged me to discuss it with you and to consider going ahead with the procedure. However, he also made it perfectly clear I would be unable to have any more children."

"I will support whatever your decision is," George replied, still essentially aloof to the reality of what was happening to our marriage.

After giving it much consideration, I decided to have my tubes cut, because getting pregnant again was a real possibility. We were not using any kind of birth control. Meanwhile, another problem arose that did not seem so serious at the outset, but was about to escalate.

George Sr. became agitated one evening when he noticed the baby sucking his middle and index fingers. I tried to tell him the baby would outgrow it, to just ignore it. His response was startlingly aggressive: "No son of mine is going to suck his fingers. I will not have it. If you had breastfed him this probably would not have happened."

He tried everything to get the baby to stop, but nothing was working. Soon it became an obsession with George Sr. One night he put vinegar on the baby's fingers and then moved on to pepper. He was walking a very thin line with me. I ran over to George Jr. and picked him up. His father looked at me and said sharply, "Don't you touch him. He is *my* son, and I will discipline him as I see fit."

I immediately headed toward the door. "It's time for his bath."

I assured myself that George Sr. was just tired. I was certain it would not happen again.

The following Saturday George Jr. and I headed up to Lowell to visit my mom. When we arrived at the house, I set up the playpen in the kitchen and put him and some of his favorite toys inside. In this way, Mom had a chance to visit with both of us. She loved her grandson and kept telling me how much he looked like me and how smart he was. There was never any mention of his father.

"Are you losing weight?" she asked. "You don't look well. Is everything all right?"

"Everything is fine, but I wanted to tell you in person that I am pregnant and, yes, I've been having morning sickness and that might clarify why I don't look so well."

She accepted my explanation, and I waited for her to congratulate me and share in my joy like she had when my sister announced her second pregnancy, but there was only silence.

Just then the doorbell rang. It was the milkman, Pete, with his usual cheery, boisterous greeting. He asked Mom if she wanted anything besides milk today. Pete was a tall man. His physique resembled George Sr.'s. He walked toward the playpen and said. "Well, who is this young man?" George Jr. started screaming and curled into a fetal position. I picked him up and immediately realized he was reacting to Pete's size. I tried to calm both him and my mother down. "It's OK, Mom," I said. "The baby was just reacting to Pete's loud voice. He'll be fine."

The baby was trembling in my arms as I took in what had just happened. I knew then that when I returned home there was no question I would have to confront George.

I managed to get through the next few hours, but inside, my anger was growing over a situation I had let get out of control. It had to be resolved.

When George arrived home I had never seen him so upset. Again, there was no conversation at dinner, but when I got up the courage to ask him what was wrong, I was met with a surprise. He looked at me and said, "You have no idea what it is like day after day after day to be invisible to people. They look right at you but don't see you."

Apparently a guest at the hotel had made a complaint about a waiter not refilling his water glass. When the manger asked which waiter, the guest shouted, "How would I know?! They all look alike."

George continued the story: "Of course, the manager knew it was my table and took me in the back room and asked me to explain what happened. When I went over to fill his glass with water," George recounted, the guest asked him to leave. "The manager then left, and when I went back in the dining room, the customer was no longer there. I never knew what had transpired."

This was the first time George had ever talked to me about his everyday experiences as a black man in a white world. Many other black men in our country went through similar things, I would imagine, but very few in the 1950s in quite the way George did. He didn't aspire to simply serve them their meals. He was trying to penetrate an almost sacred part of their world. All he had ever wanted to do was to play the great composers in concert halls around the world, which I had such deep appreciation for, his ambitions, but at the same time I was experiencing blinding confusion about how he was responding to it. I am still trying to understand the latter part seven decades later. I tried that day to reach out and comfort him, but he immediately closed up and pushed me away. I decided to put off our conversation about George Jr. until the next day. But what followed made that decision impossible.

George Jr. was exceptionally fussy that night, and George Sr. became more irritated as the evening went on. I decided to get the baby ready for bed early, hoping his bath would have a soothing effect. When I put him in his crib, he went to sleep immediately without sucking his fingers. A few hours later, however, he woke up crying. I got up and comforted him, hoping he wouldn't wake his father, but George Sr. did wake up and grabbed the baby out of my arms, shouting at him to stop sucking his fingers. The baby started crying again.

George Sr. slammed him down into the crib and tied his hands to the one of the slats on the side. I lost it and ran over and untied his hands and shouted, "George, this cannot continue!"

I tried to tell him what had happened with the milkman at my mother's house and how he could damage our son, but once again he wasn't hearing me. He started screaming at me and reiterated what he had said so many times before: "He is *my* son, and I will discipline him as I see fit."

I screamed back at him, "He is my son too, and I will not have it! I'm begging you to stop."

With the baby still crying, there was a knock on the door. It was Aretha, saying if we continued making such a row she was going to call the police. She asked if I was all right. I told her I was and apologized for the commotion.

I asked George to let me take the baby and see if I could calm him down. After George Jr. stopped crying, I put him back in his crib and he finally fell asleep. I then approached my husband and stated calmly, "George, I have reached my breaking point and if your behavior does not change toward your son, I am going to consider leaving you. Please, can't we just talk about this and come to some sort of an agreement?"

He stared at me with a look I did not recognize and started pacing back and forth. "How *dare* you question me again and again when I am disciplining my son!"

He kept pacing, then suddenly bolted toward me, picked me up, and walked to the window and said, "If you ever mention leaving me again, I will kill you." With that he began pushing me out the window.

My instincts took over and in a controlled but resolute voice I said, "Of *course* I am not going to leave you. I just said that so you would know how serious I was. I am your wife, carrying your child, and I love you. I couldn't possibly leave you."

Despite my show of composure, I was terrified. He pulled me back into the room and said over and over again, "You can't leave me. You're my wife. You can't leave me. You're my wife."

No matter what I did or said I could not get him to simmer down. I was so confused as to what to do, and as we sat on the edge of the bed I noticed his hands were shaking and he kept repeating, "I will never let you go, I will never let you go. He is *my* son, and I will discipline him as I see fit." This continued until finally, after what seemed like hours, he turned to me and said, "Let's forget everything that happened tonight." He then pulled me into bed with his arm wrapped firmly around my waist, which did not lessen until he fell asleep.

I lay awake all night deciding what I was going to do and needed to do. I could see no alternative but to leave the next morning. After George left for work I wrote him a note telling him where I would be and suggesting that it might be a good idea to spend some time apart but that, if he wanted to talk further, he knew how to reach me.

I made a phone call to my mom and made up the excuse that George was heading out to Atlantic City and asked if it would be all right with her if I came home until the baby was born.

"Of course it is, honey," she replied.

I was now six months pregnant.

On the drive home I kept going over in my head what had happened. This was my husband, whom had I pledged to love, honor, and obey. He had never shown signs of anger or rage before. I was willing to put up with almost anything but could not put up with what I now recognize as the emotional and physical abuse of our son.

I left Roxbury loving my husband and was still hoping we could find a way to work it out. As I drove I kept asking myself why I could not come up with a logical explanation for the drastic change in his behavior when we started living together as husband and wife. What was I missing? My world was changing, and this naïve, idealistic young woman who apparently knew nothing of the world would have to grow up and deal with reality no matter what that reality might be.

It was around 2:00 p.m. when I arrived home, knowing my mom would return at about 3:00. I had to wipe away the tears and put on my happy mask and pretend everything was fine.

Meanwhile, I had no idea how George Sr. was going to react to the note I had left. Would he call? I would just have to wait and have faith. At the same time, I knew I needed to deal with things the way they were.

It was three days before I heard from him. He called on a Monday night around seven thirty. I was thrilled to hear his voice and pleased when the first words out of his mouth were an apology for what happened the night he lost his temper. He promised it would never happen again. I wanted to believe him, and on some level I did. He wanted to know what I told my family.

"Nothing," I replied.

"Are you ready to come home?"

"I want more than anything to make this marriage work, but it cannot continue unless we can come to some agreement about changing the way you have been treating your son."

No answer.

"I would like to stay home until the baby is born," I said and then suggested it might be helpful to get some counseling. His response was, "Let me think about it, and I will get back to you in a couple of days."

It wasn't until the following week that he called and said he had thought over our last conversation. He agreed that if I wanted to stay home until the baby was born he would head out to Atlantic City, where he could make more money, and when he returned we could find a bigger apartment. As for our problems, he said we did not need any outside help. It was something we could work out ourselves through letters and conversations.

Hope was in the air again. My job would be to remain healthy and stay positive. Things would eventually work out, I was sure. I looked forward to receiving his letters and phone calls. However, I knew I would have to constantly remind myself to stay in the real world. Baby George's life and the new life growing inside me depended on it.

CHAPTER 7

The Clouds Melted

With me back home, Mom became the Warrior of Worry once again. I was relieved that she had a job to go to every day. However, she still managed to keep suggesting things I should be doing with the baby. By now I had learned to draw boundaries, which at times were completely ignored.

"George Jr. is almost a year old now. You should be thinking about taking him to Sunday school, and you might want to start singing in the church choir."

"Let me think about it. Maybe after the baby is born, if I am still here, I will take them both to Sunday school."

I believed that George Jr. was having repercussions from the way his father had dealt with the finger sucking episode. He had been drinking out of a cup for quite some time but now reverted to wanting his bottle. He began waking up at night crying, and it had a sound that was somewhere between a cry and a scream. It frightened me. I would get up and rock him until he settled down. My mother worried. I told her it might be the transition from one environment to another and that he would adjust soon. She said I was probably right, but suggested I take him to see the doctor if it continued.

During the day, George would not let me out of his sight. He wanted me to hold him and would lift his arms up and, with a little whimpering sound, say, "Mama, hold, Mama, hold."

I was concerned because I had not heard from George Sr. and had no way to get in touch with him to tell him I was scheduled to go into the hospital on November 3 to deliver our second child. I was beginning to feel guilty and thinking it was my fault the way George Jr. was regressing. I would tell myself I should have left his father sooner, and the next moment the love I had for my husband would envelop me.

The stress of pretending for my mom that everything was OK and the frustration and worry about what the future held for all of us was beginning to sap my energy. I kept telling myself, *You cannot get caught up in the worry trap*. I knew things would work themselves out eventually and that worrying wasn't going to change anything. I needed to stay focused.

There was one bright light, and that was the relationship developing between the baby and my dad. When we first came home, George Jr. would have nothing to do with him. My father's routine was to go in the living room after dinner and smoke his pipe and read the paper. George would peek around the corner and watch him smoke. After a few weeks he started to move around to the side of his chair and just stare, and when my dad started to blow smoke rings with his pipe, the baby went in front of the chair and continued to stare. He was fascinated but would not go any closer than a few feet from the chair.

He eventually ended up in his grandfather's lap, and every night Dad would pretend to read the paper to him, but George Jr. was enthralled with the smoke rings. His eyes would follow the rings, and he'd try to put his fingers through the middle. It brought joy to my heart to see a connection developing between the two of them.

Meanwhile, my relationship with Mom was strained. We went along like everything was normal, but the hurts we had inflicted on each other would take time to heal.

After two months, George Sr. finally called. It was good to hear his voice, and I squelched the desire to ask him what had taken so long. He did all of the talking, which was unlike him. He was living at the same boarding house, he said, and working at the same hotel he had in previous years, looking for another part-time job. As I was writing down the address, I asked him for a phone number in case of an emergency. He said he did not have one yet but as soon as it was installed he would get the number to me. He asked how I was doing. I told him when the baby was due. He said he would call me at the hospital on the fourth or fifth, then promised to write and asked me to do the same.

I tried to keep him on the phone, but he kept repeating he had to go. I wanted to make plans for after the baby was born and to know when he would be coming back. I needed to discuss issues regarding baby George.

I thought to myself, *He never asked about his son.* That should have been an omen, but I was still making excuses for him. He was busy. He had to get to work. *He will ask about George the next time he calls or writes.*

As soon as we hung up, I sat right down and wrote him a letter asking all the questions I wanted answers to, reminding him about his promise to communicate and discuss these issues by phone or in letters. I reiterated that it was imperative to resolve them before we resumed our life as a family.

After three months, I had received only one letter from George, informing me he was staying a little longer in Atlantic City because he had been hired to play in a lounge at another hotel, which would mean more money for us when he returned. Again, he never asked about George Jr. He didn't answer any of the questions I had asked in my letter. My world with the man I fell in love with was collapsing around me, and I still could not face it.

* * *

THE DOCTOR INFORMED me he wanted me in the hospital on November 3 at 8:00 a.m. I had been explaining to George Jr. that he was going to have a new baby brother or sister and that Mama needed to go into the hospital for a couple of days to make that happen. He was so excited and wanted to go with me. I told him he was a little young and that little boys were not allowed in the hospital.

My brother's family had returned from Canada and bought a home in Chelmsford, Massachusetts, just outside of Lowell. I had made arrangements for George Jr. to stay with them. This would be the first time we were separated, and he was not happy.

He would tell me, "No go, Mama, no go" and with that would pout and repeatedly stamp his feet, then stop pouting, then start again, all within a few moments.

As Dr. Spock had warned, I was seeing a little bit of a temper tantrum, and according to the doctor, that was OK. His advice was to let the child display his frustration and get it out. That made perfect sense to me.

On November 3, I called the cab company and asked to be picked up about 7:30 a.m. As we drove to the hospital, I never felt so alone. I knew when I left George three months earlier there would be times like this, when I would have to walk without my husband, but this somehow felt different. There was no shutting out thoughts of life without him, the possibility that this new life about to be born would have to grow up without a father, the possibility of a divorce in the future, the possibility that our love would not survive. I was not in a good place. However, I knew I had to focus on the life I was about to bring into the world. Whatever else was going on would have to wait.

My surgery was scheduled for midmorning, but it wasn't until three thirty that I was taken into the operating room. The medicine they had given me as they were prepping me had already kicked in, and from that point on I remember nothing.

When I came out from under the anesthesia, my mom was holding my hand, telling me everything had gone well and I had delivered a seven and three-quarter pound healthy baby boy who was twenty-one inches long. I wanted to see my son right away and asked the nurse on duty if she would bring him to me. She said it was highly irregular, but that the doctor had left word that when I requested to see my baby, the nurse on duty was to comply. As she walked out she repeated several times, "Highly irregular, highly irregular."

When she returned with the baby, I smiled and thanked her. There was no one who was going to spoil this moment for me. She put him in my arms and I was overwhelmed, unable to believe I had created another perfect human being.

I held him close and drank in the smell of my precious newborn, the love for him pouring out of me along with tears of joy. My mom broke the spell by asking me if I was all right. I told her I was thinking of how much he looked like his dad: same long fingers, just like his brother, same-shaped head, but he did have my mouth. She smiled knowingly and asked if I wanted her to call George Sr. I was whisked back to reality and explained that he was working but would be calling tomorrow. Right now there was no way to get in touch with him. Was she softening in her acceptance of George? Her hand reached over to take mine, and that is the last thing I remember.

The next day George Sr. called around 4:00 p.m. and asked if everything had gone well.

"Did he cut your tubes?"

"Yes, he did."

"Well, aren't you going to tell me what I am a new father of?"

"We have a beautiful son who looks like you."

He seemed happy and excited, which raised my hopes once again. We talked about names, and I told him I would like to name the baby David. I had always loved the name. This was my second miracle, and like the second king of Israel in the tenth century, the name David represented strength. It was biblical, which was important to me. I asked George to pick a middle name and he said he would like it to be Erwin, his mother's maiden name. So David Erwin it was.

Again he was off to work and would call again in a couple of weeks, he said. Once more confusion began clouding my mind, but when the nurse entered the room, bringing David to me, the clouds melted into bright sunlight. With the warmth of his little body next to mine, nothing else mattered.

When I returned home from the hospital with baby David, George Jr. could hardly contain himself. He would look at David in his crib for hours, touching his face so gently, patting his forehead, taking David's little hand in his own, but he could not understand why the baby did not talk.

After about three days the newness wore off and George began showing signs of regression—acting out, asking for his bottle. *What is this all about?* I asked myself. Again I turned to Dr. Spock and learned that the behavior was perfectly normal, part of the big adjustment to becoming a sibling. The book suggested spending a little more time with the older child and including him in the care of the new family member, so I started asking George to get me some diapers or bring the baby's bottle or changing pad or blanket. Soon things got a little easier, but I was learning quickly that having two babies eleven months apart was a gift but also a challenge, especially without their father on hand.

After two months I still had not heard from George Sr., either by phone or mail, and hope began to wane. I knew now I had to think seriously about life without him. My mom suspected something was wrong. I was relieved and grateful that she never asked. I prayed for guidance. My emotions were conflicted as to how I should proceed.

CHAPTER 8

"What Am I Doing Here?"

IT WAS MID-FEBRUARY. David was sleeping, and George Jr. was getting restless because a severe nor'easter had hit the area and we were unable to get out for our daily walk, so I was spending more time reading him stories, playing games, and making special lunches. I had just put George down for his nap when the phone rang. I was thrilled when I heard my husband's voice say, "How are you and the boys doing? I am so sorry it's taken me this long to get back to you, but I have been doing some heavy thinking and wanted to know if you would consider bringing David down to Atlantic City."

His question took me by surprise and I asked, "Does that mean you are willing to talk about our future as a family?"

"Yes."

"Why now?"

"Because it has been a year since we have seen each other and I would like to meet my son. I know you have many more questions, but would you please consider waiting so we can have this conversation face-to-face?"

"Where will we be staying?"

"You and the baby can stay with me."

"George, I need reassurance from you that no matter how the conversation goes—"

He interrupted me. "I know what you are going to ask, and I understand my actions were reprehensible, and when I said it would never happen again I meant it. If you are still concerned, I can arrange to have the landlord come in and be with us when we talk."

"I believe you, and thanks for the offer, but I don't think that will be necessary. Before I accept, let me see if I can make arrangements for someone to take care of George Jr. How can I reach you?"

"I now have my own phone, so you can call me directly."

That night I went into the boys' room, got down on my knees, and prayed things would work out for all of us. When I informed my mom I was making plans to go to see George Sr. in New Jersey, she said she was going to New York on business for a couple of days and it might be a good idea, since I would be traveling with the baby, to stay at the hotel with her before I headed down to Atlantic City. One of her sponsors was paying all her expenses. I found some comfort in her suggestion.

How I wished I could have talked to Mom about everything that was going on, but the fear of how she might react always stopped me.

I informed George Sr. I would be arriving in New York in fourteen days. The next couple of weeks were filled with putting all the pieces together for the trip. Along with the flurry of activity, there was the uncertainty of not knowing what would happen once I arrived in New Jersey. Having complete responsibility for the welfare of the boys had brought about an independence that had given me more confidence in making decisions on my own. However, that confidence seemed to dissipate when I heard George Sr.'s voice. I kept telling myself to have faith in him but also have faith in myself so I could see things clearly.

At some point my mother overheard me telling George Jr. I was going to be in New York for a few days with David and Gugga, which is what the boys called her, something they picked up from their cousins. She questioned why I hadn't told him about meeting up with his father. But I couldn't tell her that if I mentioned his dad, my firstborn was very likely to go into spasms, so I simply said, "Mom, he would have wanted to go with us."

Bob's wife, Connie, had once again agreed to take care of George Jr. and decided that, with my brother away on business, she would stay at my parents' house while we were gone. It was school vacation, so she and my nieces and nephews would be company for my firstborn. He was looking forward to having someone to play with while I was away.

The taxi arrived at eight thirty on a cold February morning to take us to the airport. I had never flown in a plane before and was looking forward to it.

From the moment we took off, I marveled at the ability of this large, heavy piece of equipment to lift itself into the air and cruise along like we were sitting in our favorite chair at home and the fact that we would reach New York City in less than an hour. When we landed, there was a car waiting, and it drove us to the hotel. I looked at Mom, smiling, and said, "So is this the way the other half lives?"

As we walked into the Drake Hotel, I was amazed at how beautiful the huge, wide-open lobby was, with its grand chandeliers along with comfortable-looking chairs and sofas. I pictured my husband working in a place similar to this one. After registering, we were escorted up to our room, which looked like something out of a movie.

Once we unpacked, changed, and fed David, Mom and I were both anxious to walk around the city and see some of the landmarks, like the Empire State Building and the Museum of Natural History, and possibly get a glimpse of the Metropolitan Opera House. We obtained a carriage for David from the front desk and off we went, managing to get a peek at the Empire State Building before he got fussy, and then we returned to the Drake. We ordered lunch and settled in for the remainder of the day.

I kept looking at my son, wondering what his father would say when he saw him for the first time. I became quiet and pensive and Mom wanted to know if I was all right.

"I am fine, just excited, Mom."

I knew she wanted to press for more, but when she recognized that I was retreating, she backed off. My avoidance side of the ledger was filling up quickly.

I checked in with Connie to see how things were going. She said George Jr. was not acting out as much as he had the last time, when I went into the hospital to give birth to David, but he was asking when Mama was coming home. This made me a bit anxious. I told her I would check in again day after tomorrow.

I called George Sr., who gave me directions to the bus depot near Grand Central Station, assuring me he would be waiting when my cab dropped us at his Atlantic City address.

I was up and down all night, lecturing myself to stay positive, to have an open mind. The next morning Mom had an appointment with the chief executive officer of the company she was representing. She would be busy most of the day. I wished her good luck as she headed out.

The morning quickly flew by as I fed and bathed David. Wanting to make a good impression on his father, I changed the baby's outfit two or three times. My own choices of what to wear were more limited because I only had brought one change.

There was a light snow falling as we headed out to catch the bus to Atlantic City. Holding the baby close to me, I dreamed of our being a family once again. When we arrived in south Jersey, I quickly found a taxi. It was much colder with the wind coming off the ocean. When I gave the driver the address he said, "I assume you know where you are headed is a colored area."

I shook my head up and down, hoping to avoid any more questions, but he continued: "You must be a social worker."

I just smiled and said nothing, and we rode the rest of the way in silence. When we finally arrived, it took forever to pay him because my hands were shaking. I dropped some coins on the floor of the cab and just left them, then headed up the front stairs to ring the bell. When George opened the door, he smiled and my heart started to ache.

He introduced me to his landlady, who was a lovely middle-aged woman with a warm, welcoming smile. She immediately took the baby and started fussing over him, telling me how handsome he was. George took us one floor up and the landlady followed, still holding David. It was a good-sized room with a double bed, a dresser, a full-length mirror, one chair, along with an end table and lamp. No pictures around anywhere. George was meticulous, and the room represented that part of his personality.

The landlady offered to take the baby, which struck me as strange since his father had not even held him yet. I thanked her and said, "No, I would like him to stay with me."

I was feeling a little awkward until George came over and gave me a welcoming hug. It was comforting being in his arms after such a long time. All of the feelings of when we first met came rushing back. Then David began to get fussy and I asked if there was someplace to run hot water over his bottle. George said he would take it to the bathroom down the hall. I was changing David's diaper when he returned. I asked if he would like to feed the baby. He said no, he did not want to disrupt David's pattern. Instantly, I could feel my anger beginning to stir. I should have voiced what I felt inside but instead said nothing.

I was just finishing feeding David when there was a knock on the door. George said he had paid his landlady to fix dinner for us, and as she brought the food in, he brought the end table, which he had covered with a white napkin, closer to the bed. She set the tray down on top of it. There was fried chicken with gravy, corn bread, greens, and for dessert a sweet-potato pie.

"Thank you so much for this wonderful meal," I told her. "It looks delicious."

Our conversation during dinner was mostly about David and how he was doing. George never asked about George Jr. The air was tense. Again, I should have spoken up but did not. I was still looking for the man I used to know who was always so concerned and caring.

After dinner George stacked the plates on a tray to take downstairs. He wanted to take the baby down as well and let the landlady care for him for a while. Knowing he had more on his mind than David, I said, "Let me think about it."

George still had not held our son, and when he returned and asked whether I had thought about it, I replied, "I don't think so."

"Why?"

"First we need to talk about your plans for our family."

He sensed the agitation in my voice and started to walk toward me. "It has been a long time since we have been together. I would like to make love to you first."

I pushed him away and repeated, this time with more irritation, "We need to talk about your plans for our family. Isn't that why you brought me down here?"

"Yes, but can't that wait until later?"

I wanted so much to give in and just fall into his arms, but my need for clarity was too great. "George, it is not going to happen until we talk."

He, too, was irritated now but began to acquiesce. I asked why he had not responded to the questions I brought up in my last letter.

"I don't want to go back there," he said.

"How can we proceed if we don't work out some of those problems that separated us in the first place, like the issue with George, for one?" I said, referring to the finger sucking.

"I didn't see them as problems."

"What do you mean you don't see them as problems? You don't see it as a problem the way you were treating your son? You don't see it as a problem that he was afraid of you?"

As our voices rose, David started to cry. I asked George to take him downstairs so we could finish our conversation. He just stood there and did not move.

I said sternly, "George, pick up your son and take him downstairs."

He did without even looking at David, slamming the door as he went out. My heart was beating so hard it frightened me. I sat down, put my head between my knees, and slowly breathed in and out.

When George returned he approached me and said softly as though I were still that idealistic girl he had met at the conservatory, "I love you," as though mere words could wipe away everything that had happened.

I stood up and repeated, "We need to continue our conversation so we can make plans for the future."

"I do not want to go back to the past," he said again.

"All right then, let's head toward the future. Tell me what your plans are for us as a family."

"I would like you to stay here with me in Atlantic City for a while."

I walked over to the bed and sat on the edge. "George, this room you are living in is not big enough for the boys and I. Were you planning to rent an apartment?"

No answer.

"Does your silence mean you have no plans for our future? Why did you have us come down then?"

"I wanted to see my son."

"You haven't looked at him since we've been here."

Again no response.

What am I doing here? I thought to myself.

I broke down in tears and said, "George, I don't know what you expect from me. I came all the way down to New Jersey because you promised me there was a possibility we could work things out, and you're giving me nothing. My faith in you is lessening by the minute." Frustration, anger, and lingering love were swirling in a confusing jumble in my mind, and I just wanted to get out of there. "Would you please go down and get David, because I want to go back to New York."

"You cannot leave at this hour of the night. It is ten o'clock and not safe. I don't know the schedule of the buses, and I will not allow you to go anywhere until morning."

He had always kept me safe, so I agreed to stay if he would bring the baby upstairs and sleep anywhere but in the bed with me. He agreed.

I lay awake thinking about what had just happened and why he would not try to work things out. Was it me? Was I being unreasonable? I heard George get up. He came over and sat on the side of the bed. In his most gentle tone he said, "I know things have not been easy for you, and I do understand what you have been through, but I can't promise things will ever change."

It didn't surprise me, but it wasn't what I wanted to hear. At least it was honest. "George," I told him, "I need time to think and sort things out, but if I have not heard from you within three to four months, I will be taking steps to end our marriage."

His silence was deafening.

I remember nothing after that except pulling the blanket over my head and holding my precious son close to me. George was not there in the room when I woke up the next morning.

CHAPTER 9

"Was It a Race Issue?"

FOR THE NEXT three months the only way I could head into the future was to continue to feel nothing. I developed a routine of being and doing only what was necessary. I was unaware that eventually I would have to grieve the loss of the man I once loved and tell my mom my marriage was coming to an end. However, the stark reality of what was happening was slowly beginning to surface.

But where children are concerned, there is *only* reality, and life goes on for them. My instinctive mothering took over, and the dense fog and dust began to lift. I had to make a future for my boys, without their father.

The dance between my mother and me continued. I knew she wanted to ask questions, lots of them, but to her credit she was using some restraint. I told her on the way home from New York that our plans were still indefinite but that I would have some answers for her shortly. In addition to all the stress of my broken marriage, I detested the idea that I was so financially dependent on my parents, even though I knew it was not an issue for them.

There was one little ember of hope still burning that maybe I would hear from George Sr. within three months. Those embers would have to be stone cold before I would think about ending our marriage. I learned much later in life that my method of avoiding painful issues was to become a work-aholic, and so all my efforts were focused on being the very best mother I could to George and David. I was still blaming myself for not finding a way to save my marriage and was determined to have no more failings in my life.

David was now six months old and precocious like his brother. He was sitting, eating solid food, playing, almost walking, and examining his toys and learning by observing George. They had very distinct personalities, however. From the time George was very small, he was exceptionally verbal and phys-ically active and had no trouble making his wants known. His brother, on the other hand, never made his wants known. David was an observer, and there was no question in my mind he was going to be an intellectual and a thinker.

Each morning after breakfast I would set the playpen up for David with the toys he liked. George would then do everything he could to engage him. He kept asking me to take David out of the playpen. I tried to explain that David was too young and couldn't walk yet.

"George, your toys are not appropriate for David, because some of them have sharp edges and could hurt him."

He would just look at me and smile like he understood but would continue trying to get his brother to play with him.

As I was watching them play from a distance one morning, George kept walking around the playpen talking to David in gibberish. David just looked at him with a quizzical expression on his face, and that was the only reaction his brother was going to get. So George began taking the toys out of the playpen one at a time. Still no reaction. This went on until there was one toy left. David held that toy with a tight grip, and there was no way his brother was going to take it away from him. They just sat and stared at each other, both defiant and determined not to let go. George finally tired and began to play with David's other toys until I walked in and asked, "George, why are your brother's toys out of the playpen?"

"I like to play with them."

"George, you have some stuffed animals upstairs. I think you better put David's toys back in the playpen right now and apologize to your brother."

He looked up at me with an inquisitive expression and said, "What does 'polgizise' mean, Mama?"

"It means telling someone you are sorry."

He then hung his head and very softly said, "I polgize, Dave, and I am sorry too."

Was this jealousy he was showing toward David or was he just being competitive? Time to consult with Dr. Spock.

In his second book, Dr. Spock explains that what works with one child does not necessarily work with another and you have to continually try different ways to find a method that matches your child's personality. It is up to the parents to observe and learn, he writes, and by all means trust your instincts. Up until now just a stern look had worked with George Jr.

* * *

THE TIME WAS fast approaching when I was going to have to inform my parents that there was no chance of reconciliation in my marriage. I knew Mom would want some questions answered, and I felt she had a right, since I would be living at home indefinitely.

One night, after the boys were in bed, Mom and I were out on the back porch, having a conversation about one of my childhood friends who was getting a divorce.

"Does she have any children?" Mom asked.

"Yes, she has a little boy."

"It's tough being a single parent."

"Yes it is, and it looks like I am going to be one also."

Mom did not seem surprised. "I knew something was going on," she said. "I just didn't know how serious it was."

Then the questions came: "What are your plans? Will you be getting a divorce? Is there any chance of reconciliation?"

Those I expected and was prepared for, but not the ones that followed—about what had happened.

OK, I thought, *that was a fair question*, but before I had a chance to answer, she added, "Did he become violent? Was it a race issue?"

"What do you mean by 'a race issue'?"

"You know, because he is black and you are white?"

Even now she is still asking that question? I tried not to show my frustration when I said, "Mom, please try to understand that race never played any role in our relationship, but George did have to deal with racism every single day, and I am sure that must have raised his tension level on how he dealt with everything in his life. As far as to why our marriage broke up, let me try and explain.

"Why does any marriage break up?" I said as calmly as I could manage. "There's an old saying I heard you use when you told us about our two uncles getting divorced, and I quote, 'You never really know a person until you live together as man and wife.' And that certainly was true for us. Did we try to work it out? Yes, we did, but let me repeat loud and clear, it had nothing to do with the fact that I am white and he is black. We had our differences, and the marriage became toxic, and it seems I did not live up to his expectations, and he didn't live up to mine."

My mom was one of the people whom I loved, trusted, and respected most in the world, but on that particular day, at that particular time, I did not like her nor understand where she was coming from. I managed to cut the conversation short and we never discussed it again. There were many issues we never talked about, and this was simply another one. Do I regret it? Do I wish I could have been more forthcoming about my inner thoughts and feelings and change what happened regarding conversations we never had? Yes, I do.

I know now that some choices I made with my mom were because I learned some of life's lessons too late and did not understand that by cutting off meaningful dialogue I was multiplying the pain for both of us.

CHAPTER 10

"There Has to Be Another Way"

AGONIZING MONTHS WENT by. The menacing phone calls from anonymous racists kept coming. Over and over they would say that I would never see my son once school started. I was overcome with a sense of hopelessness and lack of control. I found myself filled with anxiety that went beyond fear.

In spite of those threats I was trying hard to keep a normal routine, like going to the library, taking daily walks, reading to the boys at night, but when George Jr. asked me, "Why you sad, Mama?" I replied by saying, "I'll be fine, honey," but I wasn't fine. I feared for my son's life. My dream of becoming a family had died, communication with my mom became impossible, and all of that tension and anxiety was affecting the boys. These were my problems, and I needed to find some answers. Yet at every road I went down I found a sign saying, we cannot help you. I recognize now that depression had found its way in and was affecting my mind, body, and soul, but at the time, *depression* was not a word anyone used or understood.

My mom became aware that something was not right and became more assertive in her quest for answers. How could I possibly answer her questions when she wanted to know why I wasn't registering George for school or buying things for his first day and why I wasn't taking the boys to church anymore? Every question was like an arrow in my heart, and the only answer I could give her was, "Please, Mom, I will get to it."

I will never forget the day my brother, Bob, dropped in when I was lying on the couch in what he called a "coma." I was still in my robe, and the boys were on the floor playing with their toys beside me. The house was a mess. He said, "You look terrible. What is going on with you? Mom is worried sick and now after I see you, so am I."

My brother knew how to use words in a way that would cut right through you. He developed this talent as a defense with people who treated him differently because of his polio. He kept staring me down, saying things to intimidate me and demanding to know why I was in such a state of turmoil.

I started sobbing, unable to speak, and hid my face in the pillow. I did not want the boys to see me completely out of control, so I took them in the kitchen and made their favorite breakfast, oatmeal. When I returned, Bob apologized for coming on so strong, then said, "You know I love you, but I need to know what has happened to make you so unresponsive. Talk to me. Is it George Sr.?"

"No," I answered, then I told him everything that was going on: the phone calls and threats, how I was afraid to send George to school, how the boys had no friends and their lives were not normal in any way.

It took a lot to shock my brother, but I could tell I had done just that when he used a word I had never heard him speak: "Oh, shit, I had no idea. Why haven't you talked to anyone about this?"

"Bob, who am I going to talk to?

"Have you called the police?" he asked.

"Yes, several times, but they refuse to do anything and told me that it might be a good idea if I moved out of the neighborhood."

He immediately understood what I was dealing with and said, "OK, let's try to figure out some options and see if we can't get your lives back on track. I have an appointment this afternoon, but we will talk again tomorrow morning."

Before he left I made him promise not to tell Mom about our discussion, and he agreed but also made it clear it would only be until we sorted things out.

"Agreed?"

"Agreed."

The next morning, after we had coffee, his first question was "What is the most important thing you want for George and David?"

"I want them to be safe and have normal lives."

"Have you come up with any ideas on how to achieve that?"

"I know it sounds crazy, but I would like to move to Germany, France, or to England, where I have heard people in our circumstances are treated like everyone else."

"Any others?" he asked.

"None. It seems we are not accepted in the black community and are isolated with silence. We are not accepted in the white community, where they are more vocal and shun us like we have a deadly disease."

"Well, let's look at your option for heading to Europe, which is not a bad idea. However, if you go to Germany, you do not speak German, and if you go to France, you do not speak French, and you know absolutely no one in any of those countries, including England. What would you do for work? How would you live? And, most importantly, you have no money to carry off any of this. You know if I could afford to send you abroad I would, but I have five children to support and another one on the way, and we both know Mom and Dad do not have the resources to support that option, and even if they did, I don't think they would agree to such a move."

As my eyes filled up with tears, I looked at my brother and told him I was feeling trapped in a storm that was never going to end.

He looked at me and said, "You are right, hon. What you are dealing with is not going to change in our generation, and hopefully someday it will, but right now we have to deal with what is out there and find a way to protect the boys. Are we on the same page?"

I nodded in the affirmative.

There was sadness but resolve in his voice when he said finally, "Yesterday I did some research and, like you, have found your options are limited. I did talk to a woman who deals with children who have all kinds of problems and tries to find solutions. She mentioned that one you might want to consider is adoption, where you could request a black couple who can provide the boys with the love and normalcy you want for them, along with the tools to live in the society as it exists today."

As the word *adoption* started to register with me I thought, *Is he crazy?* I just stared at him for a moment, then responded hysterically: "Why would you even make such a suggestion? Are you really asking me to give up my children?"

"I am not suggesting it," he said calmly. "I'm just saying it is an option and you might want to talk to her and get some objective input. I am putting it out there for you to think about, because whatever road you choose to travel is your road and no one else's, and that includes me, your sister, Mom, and Dad. You and you alone need to take full responsibility for whatever decision you make."

The truth of his statement stung like a snakebite, making me feel even more isolated and trapped.

"I'm sorry, I have to go," he said, handing me a piece of paper with information about the woman. I crumpled it up and put it in my pocket.

As he left, my thoughts were screaming at me over and over again: *Flesh of my flesh, blood of my blood. I have to find another way. Adoption is not an option. There has to be another way.*

CHAPTER 11

The Toughest Call

THERE WAS NOT a moment during the day, every day, that I wasn't trying to figure out some way to protect my boys. I was tired, my brain cells were tired. I spent many hours praying and asking God to help me find a solution that I could live with.

One thing that kept reverberating through my head was a question my brother had asked me: "What is it you want for George and David?"

My mother continued to press me for answers. I needed some time away from her constant questions and asked if she would look after the boys for a couple of hours. She wanted to know where I was going. My reply was intentionally nebulous: "I just have a few errands to run, and it would be easier if the boys were not with me."

In truth, I wanted refuge, so I headed to the nearest Catholic church, where the doors were always open, because during the week the Methodist church, where I was a member, was closed. As I climbed the church stairs, I noticed children playing in the park across the street, with their mothers nearby keeping a watchful eye. I thought to myself, *This is where my boys should be, swinging on the swings, laughing, having a good time.* All I wanted was that kind of normalcy, without the fear someone was waiting to do them harm.

I quietly sat down in the back of the church, hoping to go unnoticed. The priest was performing a christening for a young couple with their newborn. As they left the church, I could hear congratulations from the priest and the laughter of their friends and family. How I envied their having the support of so many people.

When the priest saw I was not with the christening party, he came over and asked if there was anything he could do for me. I asked permission to just sit and reflect for a little while. He said, "Of course, my child, stay as long as you like. If you would like to talk, I will be in the room to the right of the lectern for about an hour. My name is Father Patrick."

I thanked him as he turned and walked away. I felt safe.

When I opened my eyes, after closing them to pray, and looked up at the altar, there was a beautiful stained-glass window behind the altar, depicting Jesus surrounded by small children and animals. To the right of that was another stained-glass scene, the Crucifixion, the sacrifice Jesus was asked to make by his heavenly father.

My head was awash in thoughts in the midst of a storm, but the one about adoption kept forcing its way in: *Is this what I am being asked to do? Do I have to love my children enough to make some kind of sacrifice to keep them safe?* I tried to keep adoption from cascading back in my head but was unsuccessful. *If I keep my boys close to me and something happens to them, can I ever forgive myself?*

My mind was on overload. As I walked out of the church I kept saying to myself, *Deborah, this is not about you. This is not about your wants. This is not about your needs. It is your job as their mother to do whatever it takes to keep your boys safe. Move out of the way, Deborah, and do something.*

Driving home, I began to recognize that I could not come up with any other solutions and would have to reach out to the only person who seemed to have one. But first I had to locate the crumpled piece of paper Bob had given me with the woman's name and contact information.

When I arrived home, Mom was beside herself when she saw how I looked.

"Honey, talk to me. You never told me what you and your brother talked about when he came to the house. He said that you would have that conversation with me when you were ready."

I knew I had to give her some answers. "Mom, I am not ready yet and just need some time."

"Is it George Sr.? Is he pushing you to do something you don't want to do?"

"No, and if there is anything going on with George Sr. or any change in our relationship I will let you know, OK?"

"OK, but I would still like to know what is going on."

"You know, sometimes I think you forget that I am a grown woman with two small children. I feel you still are treating me as if I were a child. I know you love me and are concerned, but you are smothering me. I am asking you to trust me and let me figure things out on my own. Can you do that, please?"

"Why can't you tell me now?"

"Mom, you are doing it again! When I have worked things through, I promise you will be the first to know, but for now please give me some time."

She knew by the tone of my voice that the end of my rope had been reached. Meanwhile, I knew very well where the crumpled piece of paper was, but I could not bring myself to retrieve it. Procrastination became a friend, and procrastinate I did.

I kept hoping and praying that another way would shine a light on how to move forward. Another week went by before I went in the den on a Monday morning, my blood turning to ice, sat down at my mother's desk, and removed the paper from my robe pocket, then smoothed it out till the name Sarah D. and a phone number became legible. I kept telling myself, *You can do this,* because after all, I was only calling to get information. I picked up the phone and, after misdialing several times, finally got through to the right agency and heard a friendly voice at the other end of the line say, "Good morning. Boston Children's Service. May I help you?"

"Yes, could you tell me about your agency?"

"Basically, we are an adoption agency," the woman replied. Before she could continue I thanked her and hung up. I paced the room, wondering why my brother had not told me that it was only an adoption agency. I wanted to call him and give him a piece of the dark side of my mind. My brother probably knew me better than anyone else in the family. He knew that if and when I made a decision to call I would follow through no matter how angry I might be with him. He also knew that when I calmed down I would recognize it was indeed my decision and mine alone to make. And that is exactly what happened.

* * *

IT WAS LATE in the afternoon before I found the courage to pick up the phone again. This time when the person at the other end announced who she was, I asked if I could speak with Sarah D. My hands and voice were shaking. The operator returned and informed me that Sarah D. was not in and asked if I would like to leave a message. I asked if she would be in tomorrow and when the answer was yes, I said I would call then. I felt relief but knew there would be little sleep for me that night.

I immediately went into the next room and drank in the smell and sight of my two boys, who at that moment were definitely being boys. David was exploring everything he could get his hands on, and George was playing with his cars, trucks, and soldiers and conversing with each of them. Every thought that came into his head came out of his mouth. The interaction with his soldiers and the fact he was telling them all to be good boys because their mothers were watching brought a smile to my face.

We had not taken our walk for the day and even though it was late and very cold outside I bundled them up and off we went. When we returned,

George wanted hot chocolate. It was his favorite. He was always asking for anything chocolate.

"Hot chocolate, Mama, please, with the white on top, please?"

Whenever George asked for something, he always added, "David too." However, by now David was getting old enough to make his own wishes known, and he would look at George and then to me and say, "No, Mama, no hot chocolate."

I told George it was too close to suppertime to have hot chocolate and reminded him that if he had too much chocolate, his eczema would come back and make him itch.

"George, have you had your quota of chocolate today?"

He looked up at me with those big brown eyes and said sheepishly, "Yes, Mama."

By ten o'clock the next morning, when the boys were in the living room playing, I reluctantly headed into my mother's den once again to make the dreaded phone call. After being connected with Sarah D., I gave her my name and asked if she recalled talking to my brother, Bob.

"Yes, I do remember and would love to talk with you, but I do have a meeting scheduled. Are you available later on this morning?"

"Of course," I replied.

I gave her my number and went into the kitchen for my fourth cup of coffee. The phone rang around 11:30 and, after a few pleasantries, Sarah D. asked how she could help. I asked if my brother had explained my situation and she said he had but that she wanted to hear it from me. After I went over all my information, she suggested I set up an in-office appointment for the following week. I thanked her but said I did not want to do that until I knew she could help. "I am not interested in adoption if that it is all your agency has to offer."

"Well, you are right. The main function of this agency is placing babies for adoption, but on occasion we do work with older children and try to find solutions for families who are in crisis. In your case, I think it might be helpful for you to go over some areas you have not thought about, and I would work with you to find a solution you are comfortable and can live with."

That sounded reasonable to me, and we went ahead and set up an appointment for the following Wednesday morning at 10:30. As I hung up I felt a renewed sense of hope that everything was going to work out.

CHAPTER 12

A Journey with No Maps

I WISH I could find the right words to explain what was happening to me the first time I climbed those stairs to the adoption agency. I have no recollection of what the building looked like, the name of the street, the office, what the weather was like, the day of the week, the month, or any of the other details about how I got there. What I do recall are feelings. I remember feeling like a stranger walking into a place that was completely foreign, like I was in another country and people were speaking to me in a different language. I kept asking myself, *What am I doing here?* The only way I could give any rational answers to anyone who asked me a question was to keep telling myself I was there because of George and David. The one thing I knew with absolute certainty was that I needed to put my own feelings away and stay focused.

I also remember being introduced to the lady I had talked to on the phone, who was pleasant enough, but everything else about her—what she wore, the color of her hair, everything but her name—is a complete blank. I remember, too, her asking me many, many, many questions about why I was there, questions I already had gone over with her when we talked on the phone. Finally, I interrupted her and asked if she knew of any options other than adoption. Her answer was "No, I do not." My immediate reaction was to ask myself, *Why am I here, then?* as she continued explaining what I already knew only too well: that our society was dealing with a climate of extreme prejudice and hate toward the black race and that it was not going to change for many years to come. It was her suggestion, she said, that I begin to think seriously about adoption as a means of keeping the boys safe.

Her answer devastated me. I remember telling her how disappointed I was that she had no other solutions but that I did appreciate her honesty and was pleased that her focus was on George and David. I do not remember anything after that, because I was still trying to process what I had just been told. She suggested I make an appointment to go over the details with one of the social workers at the agency.

I told her I wasn't ready to make that decision yet but would think about it and get back to her within the next few weeks. I was trying my best to stay in control, but she told me that the longer I waited the more difficult it would be for the boys to adjust, and I knew then that my answer would have to come soon, whether I was ready or not.

I was totally exhausted and drained emotionally as I headed to the subway. I was in a daze. I remember thinking as the train headed back home how my actions would affect all of us and, if I chose to go ahead with adoption, how the journey would be laden with hurts, tears, broken hearts, and misunderstandings. I couldn't shut my mind off from thinking, *Is adoption the only choice I have?*

How does a mother find a way to go against nature, knowing she will never see her babies again? How does one prepare for a journey when you know there are no maps and you are totally ill-equipped to find your way forward?

I had to find tools that would allow me to go down this path of no return. I knew there were challenges in life that no one could prepare you for, and this certainly was one of them. I had to find a way to keep my personal feelings at bay so I could make intelligent decisions on where the adoption process should go. I had to take control because I was the only one who knew what I wanted for my boys.

The following day I went to church, got down on my knees, and prayed for a cool head, clear mind, and good judgment. With the boys' future hanging in the balance, I decided that the only way I could get through this was to surround myself with walls so high that it would be impossible for anyone to penetrate or break them down.

I finally got enough courage to call the agency and set up an appointment and was told I would be seeing a social worker by the name of Catherine G. When I walked up those stairs for the second time, adrenaline was rushing through my body. We were scheduled to meet at nine thirty, but I was a half hour late, and it seemed she too was running behind. I was kept waiting for another fifteen minutes, which was OK. It gave me time to shake off the negative feelings, to calm down, let my heart rate slow down, and get my thoughts together.

When I entered Catherine G.'s office, I found a woman who reminded me of the librarian back home, who was an extremely conservative, no-non-sense, mind-the-rules type of person. Catherine G. looked to be in her forties and was wearing a loosely fitted navy-blue blazer with a white blouse. Her hair was dark brown and pulled back in a bun at the nape of her neck. The tortoiseshell glasses she wore seemed to match her persona.

Her desk was pristine, along with the rest of the office. She introduced herself and asked me to take a seat. I was not sensing much warmth as she leaned over to shake my hand and said, "Well, let's get started."

She began by going through all the information I had already provided, which I understood was necessary in an adoption, but I began to grow impatient with questions such as "Do your parents know you are here?" "How did you get to the agency today?" "Where are you living?" "Do you have brothers and sisters?" "How many people live in the house?"

It became clear after another half hour that we were not connecting. It felt like I was being talked down to and talked at. She seemed to have a preconceived idea of who I was and why I was choosing adoption. The relationship ahead did, in fact, prove to be a turbulent one, but over the next few months I became convinced she had the boys' best interest at heart. This was a woman who followed through and was committed to whatever she had agreed to. I was extremely impressed with her thoroughness.

Catherine G. spent a great deal of time explaining to me that adoption had a process and that it was going to take some time. There would be paperwork to fill out, documents to be notarized. There would be physical exams as well as psychological exams for both boys. She requested detailed information on their father and all the medical background, not only on his side but mine as well. She asked if I had informed him of my intentions to put the boys up for adoption. I told her that I had written a letter to him explaining all of the circumstances and why adoption was the only choice. She interrupted me and asked if he agreed. He said he had no objections, I told her. I began to explain how his letter had affected me but was quickly cut off.

"We will talk about that at another time," she said.

She sent me home with forms and material to read over and fill out. "Be sure to bring them in the next time we meet," she said, instructing me to make another appointment on my way out for two hours in three weeks.

CHAPTER 13

Telling Mom

WHEN I RETURNED from the agency, I knew there was no putting off informing my mother about my plans for George and David. I struggled with how, where, and when to tell her. I knew that whatever venue I chose, her reaction would be one of disbelief and devastation once she heard the word adoption.

Shortly before the weekend I suggested we go out for lunch.

"Is this about what has been going on with you?"

"Yes."

"Why can't we do it at home?" she asked.

"I think it would be best if we did not talk about this particular issue in front of the boys."

She agreed and said Saturday would be the better day for her.

"Fine," I replied.

My dad agreed he would look after the boys for a couple of hours. Of course, they wanted to go with us, but Dad told them he was going to make a special lunch after we left.

Kidding, I said, "I hope it's not your concoction of cereal, molasses, honey, and fish oil with a few walnuts and raisins thrown in."

He laughed and said, "Why, you don't think they would love it?"

"No."

"But it would be so healthy for them."

Dad promised the boys they could work with him in the yard after lunch, picking up some of the debris from winter. He had a way of convincing both of them that he really could use their help.

As Mom and I headed out the following Saturday, we commented on what a beautiful, sunny day it was, not a cloud in the sky. The crocuses, forsythia, daffodils, and even a few tulips were blooming in abundance along with all the greenery that had been asleep for the winter. Mom looked forward to warmer weather, and the warmer it got the better she liked it. I knew our conversation would change the mood, for not only this day, but many days, months, and possibly years ahead.

"Mom, do you have a preference on where we have lunch?"

"No, as long as they have pecan pie."

I told her about a new restaurant called Cozy Corner that had just opened up in the next town and probably would not be as crowded on a Saturday morning as some of the other, better-known spots. We agreed that if it wasn't what we were looking for we could always leave.

As we pulled into the driveway, the restaurant looked more like a house, painted pink with brown shudders. There were only three cars in the parking lot. The smell of bacon and fresh baked goods filled the air as we opened the front door.

Everything about the decor said welcome. There were fresh flowers on each table and cute pink curtains on the windows, accented by dark brown valances. A waitress welcomed us with a big smile and a cheery hello.

"Please make yourself at home and sit wherever you like."

I spotted a corner booth and, as we headed over to sit down, we both said at the same time, "This is delightful."

As soon as we were seated, the waitress asked if we would like coffee.

"Coffee would be great," we both said in unison.

My mind was taking flight, noticing every little detail I normally would not have paid any attention to, trying to avoid the conversation that was about to take place. Mom looked tired and had that worried look on her face that I had come to recognize when she was concerned about one of her offspring.

After we ordered lunch she started the conversation.

"OK, you have been avoiding me long enough. I know something is going on. Please, let's stop talking about how beautiful the day is and how cozy the restaurant is and get down to why you have been so upset these last few months. What is going on?"

"Mom, this is not easy for me, because I have been struggling with making a huge decision regarding George and David. I have prayed over it, agonized over it, mentally exhausted myself, but have come to the conclusion I need to find an environment where the boys can be safe. As their mother I cannot give them the skills to live in our society that is so full of prejudice, hate, and bigotry."

"What in the world are you talking about?" she cut in. I could see she was already getting upset.

"Please let me spell it out for you. George will no longer go to Sunday school, because of the episode I have already told you about, and neither one of the boys has any friends. In other words, no one to play with. George will be starting school soon, and I don't want him subjected to all he is going to have to deal with. He will be socially ostracized. He will be ridiculed and be called all kinds of ugly names because of the color of his skin."

"So what are you saying?"

"What I am saying is that I have been looking into and dealing with an agency that possibly could help me find a family with the same background as the boys ... who could give them what I cannot."

I will never forget the look of disbelief and horror on my mother's face. She slammed both hands down on the table and with defiance in her voice said, "Are you saying you are giving up George and David? No daughter of mine is going to give away her own flesh and blood. Is this your idea? Is this what you and your brother have been doing, going behind my back?"

"No, Mom, I only talked to Bob once a couple of months ago, and he made it perfectly clear it was my decision and my decision alone. He asked me to think it through before I did anything. This is not about me. It is about what is best for the boys, and neither you nor I can fight the way the world is now. Please try to understand."

"No, I don't understand. The boys are your responsibility."

"But, Mom, it is also my responsibility to keep them safe."

"This plan of yours is unbelievable and unthinkable. I cannot sit here any longer and listen to any more of this nonsense."

With that she got up and stormed out of the restaurant. I sat there with my head in my hands, thinking. I had known her reaction would be strong, but I never expected the tornado of emotions that spilled out and flooded the table. I looked up when the waitress began putting our lunch order on the table.

"Is everything all right?" she asked.

"No, not really," I replied.

Rather than getting into a lengthy explanation, I said that Mom was not feeling well and we had to leave. Apologizing profusely, I paid the bill and walked out.

We rode home in silence. Mom was in emotional agony, but at the moment there was nothing I could say or do that would make her feel any better. I knew that. I also knew she was a mother before she was anything else, and that fact extended to her grandchildren. All her protective instincts were coming out in full force.

I was picking up her hurt and was overwhelmed by her emotional bleeding. Between that and my own emotional pain, the only response I knew at the time was to shut down. I had not looked forward to breaking her heart, but I could not allow her emotional reactions to influence my decision regarding the boys. I could not allow that to happen.

When we arrived home David was taking a nap, and George wanted to go out for ice cream.

"As soon as your brother wakes up, we will go out for a walk," I told him.

"No walk, Mama, ice cream."

"Honey, how about if we do both?"

"I go wake David up."

"Can you tell me first what you grandfather fixed for your special lunch?"

As he started to recount all that had happened, he heard David's voice and stopped right in the middle of a sentence and ran into their bedroom and shouted, "Get up! Let's go! Time for a walk and ice cream!"

I thought to myself, *Life goes on, ready or not.*

After the boys were put down for the night, I was sitting on the back porch thinking about the day's events when Mom came out and sat down beside me.

"We need to talk," she said. She began by asking, "Is there any chance you and George would be getting back together, and if you did, would that make a difference in your decision regarding the boys?"

"Mom, I am sorry, but it looks like it is not going to happen. If he were to come up with a plan, I certainly would listen, but he has shown no interest in the last few years, so it is not even worth speculating."

"I think you know I will never be a party to this. I will not allow it."

From the moment she said "I will not allow it," I knew I had to set some boundaries. I was determined to make my point. I started by asking how she would feel if something happened to either of the boys.

She responded in a loud voice, "Nothing is going to happen to them as long as I am alive" and repeated several times, "You should have greater faith in God, you should have greater faith in God."

I can't remember my mother ever being so adamant and aggressive about anything in my entire life, even the day my brother, at the age of eighteen, decided to drive to Florida on his own. She pleaded with him not to go and was brokenhearted when he would not back down, but not the same way she was reacting to me. Her posture and the stern, grim look on her face were showering me with confusion and, yes, guilt. I knew her reaction was coming from the thought of losing her grandchildren. I pulled out all of my adult courage and said to her, "Mom, it is not your decision to make. I know they are your grandchildren and you feel you have a right to be part of this decision, but we are on two different paths on what we think is best for the boys. I am not going to sit here and tell you that I don't know my choice is killing you and your heart is breaking, but so is mine. I am their mother, and I do have the final say. I am so sorry, it is what I feel I have to and need to do."

Again, the look of disbelief, of disappointment, of bewilderment that her younger daughter could contemplate such an act. Without another word, she got up and walked away. I wanted to call out to her, "OK, Mom, you win. I can't do this to you." However, my instincts told me that if I was going to stay the course I had to emotionally divorce myself from her and do what I thought was best. That was the only way I was going to get through this. I kept telling myself, *There is no way you can get caught up and enveloped in her pain*, because I didn't know if I could survive my own pain.

It would have been nice if we could have found a way to support each other. Instead, we locked each other out.

CHAPTER 14

The New Parents Must Be Black

WHEN I ARRIVED at Catherine G.'s office for our second meeting, it was right down to business. Even before I had an opportunity to take a seat, she was asking for the papers I was supposed to have filled out. When I told her they were not completed, she chastised me like I was four years old, and I felt like a four-year-old being chastised. I kept telling myself she was only doing her job, but I knew it was a sign of her need to be in control.

She asked how I felt the boys' best interests could be served by her and the agency. With all of the aplomb I could muster—shoulders back, sitting straight up in my chair, looking her in the eyes—I calmly stated my case, "I would like the agency to find a loving family, an educated family, and a Christian family. I insist the boys stay together and must not be separated under any circumstances. It is imperative they not be adopted down south. I would request the agency locate a family who lives in the Northeast or on the West Coast. I also am adamant that the couple be black."

As I was laying out my conditions, there was a look on her face I could not quite figure out, but it appeared to me to be twofold: she was not used to a mother making her wants known, and she realized she was losing some of her control.

The next question she asked angered me to the point of my almost getting up and walking out. "Why do you insist upon a black couple?" she asked. "And why would you not consider a white family?"

I told her I had already gone over every detail with the woman I first spoke to at the agency, including why I would never consider a white family.

"Well, tell me again," she said. It was all I could do to restrain my frustration with Catherine G. I wanted to send a sarcastic remark across her desk, but I was in my logic zone and was not going to be derailed by her putting unthinking questions on the tracks. Once again I had an uncomfortable feeling she was forming her own opinion as to why I was putting the boys up for adoption. I was learning how to stand up, react, and fight for what I needed to do for my boys. So as I was beginning to answer her questions, I thought to myself, *If she wants answers, I will talk until she is tired of hearing the sound of my voice*, and once again I went over all the reasons I had requested certain conditions and concluded with "And why would I even consider a white family when it is the white community that is displaying racism, hatred, and bigotry towards my boys? If you cannot, or the agency cannot, commit to what I feel is best for George and David, then I need to know so I will not waste any more of your time or mine."

"Please calm down," she said. "It is important for you to know I will do everything I can to find the kind of family you are looking for. It is my job to give you options, and it is also my job when I disagree with you to go over those reasons with you. Now, once we decide on what you want, I will make sure George and David will be placed in the kind of a home you have requested. It might take me a while, but I can promise you I will adhere to all your wishes."

As she continued talking, I thought to myself, *This is a woman who does not make promises she is unable to keep. This is a woman who is committed to her job, and I should let her do her job.*

When she finished I told her, "As long as we are on the same page regarding the boys and their best interests, we can continue." It did not matter how she felt about me. All that was important was for her focus to be on George and David.

She wanted to know if I had talked to my mom about the adoption. She wanted to know in detail why I felt adoption was the only solution for the boys and whether there was anyone in our family who might be willing to parent them. What was the relationship between me and their father?

The questions continued and soon she was asking how things were at home and whether there was tension in the family because the boys were black. I responded loud and clear, "No, there is not."

"I know some of my questions might seem invasive, but I am trying to get a complete picture of what is going on in the boys' lives and yours."

After all of her questions had been answered, she explained that the next three months would be filled with appointments. George and David would be tested by a psychologist at the agency. However, it would be my responsibility to have them physically examined by a doctor who was approved by the agency. I would need to get copies of their birth certificates back to the office. The boys would also have to be observed by a qualified therapist together and individually. All of these things were mandated by Massachusetts law. Then when all of that was completed and we had all the paperwork in place, the process of looking for appropriate parents would begin. She concluded by asking if I had any questions.

"What about these tests the boys are going to be taking?"

"Would you like to see where they are going to be given?"

"Yes, I would."

I followed her down the hall and she pointed to a room with all kinds of toys, a desk with paper, coloring books, crayons, books to read, colorful paintings on the wall, lots of stuffed animals, and a small rocking chair with a big, orange pillow for a seat. There was a blackboard on one wall.

"The therapist will first let the boys explore the room," she said, "and then engage them in conversation and give certain tests that will seem like games, and then she will talk to them one at a time."

"How long does this testing take?"

"About two hours."

"Can I watch?"

"Sorry, it is against agency policy."

I would soon learn that agency policy was to become my nemesis.

When we were back in the office I asked, "Will I be able to meet the adoptive parents?"

"No, because this is a closed adoption, and, by law, once you sign the court papers, you will give up all legal rights as a parent, and there will be no further contact either with the boys or the adoptive parents. The adoptive parents will receive general background information about you and your parents, like education, socioeconomic background, if you have any brothers or sisters, and what part of the country you are from."

I wanted to know if the adoptive parents would have a way to get in touch with me about problems that might come up. Her reply was an emphatic no and a reiteration that all contact would be severed.

As I started to get up to go I said, "I cannot believe that severing all contact between me and the adoptive mom can be in the best interest of George and David."

"As I stated before, all contact will be severed."

I asked if I could call her if I had more questions, and she said to keep them for the next appointment, which, she instructed, I should make for three weeks on my way out.

As I exited, it felt like every cell in my brain was exploding. The realization of what was ahead for me and the boys was just beginning to sink in. I almost didn't make it to the ladies' room before whatever I had eaten earlier that day made clear that it was not going to stay with me.

As I walked down the steps out front, I was aware that my negative attitude towards the social worker may have been a little over the top, but I had a feeling that something just wasn't right and wished I could have requested a different contact person. I learned much later that I did have that option, but it was never mentioned.

CHAPTER 15

The Lawyer

I CONTINUED TO be a problem for the agency, canceling appointments with Catherine G., arriving late, dragging my feet about returning paperwork. It felt like I was being pulled in a million different directions. I had my mom telling me that if I went ahead with the adoption it would affect her health. Over and over she would say, "How could you do this to me?" I tried so hard to make her realize this was not about either one of us, but no matter how many times I repeated it, she did not hear.

All the tension that built up between us seemed to affect the boys. Their schedule had been disrupted and they both knew something was not right with their world. When George was under stress his eczema would flair up and he couldn't stop scratching. With David, I began to notice he had stopped playing with his brother. He was not eating and was shutting down, staying to himself.

When I brought the problems I was having with the boys up at the next meeting with the social worker, she said emphatically that I was responsible for the chaos at home because I was not getting all the paperwork back to her on time. The longer I put it off, she lectured, the harder it was going to be, not only on my mom but on the mental and physical health of the boys.

She repeated that we could not move forward with placing George and David in a foster home until I signed and returned all the necessary documents.

"Do you have any questions?"

"No," I replied, trying to hold back tears. I knew she was right.

For the next three weeks I was on automatic pilot, trying desperately to take care of the business at hand. Everything the agency requested was soon in their hands. Now we just had to wait for George Sr. to send back the papers allowing the adoption to proceed. The beginning of the end had begun.

Within a month after the paperwork was sent in I received a call from Catherine G. informing me the agency had located a couple, the Henrys, who had taken in foster children for many years and had a small baby who would only be with them for a short time because she was about to be adopted into a permanent home.

They would be happy to have George and David as part of their temporary family and wanted to make an appointment for the following week so the boys and I could meet with them. There was a long pause.

"Are you still there," she asked, "and can I set up that appointment? I know this is difficult for you, but we need to move ahead."

"Go ahead and make the appointment and get back to me with directions."

* * *

THE NEWS THAT the boys would be leaving soon had the predictable effect on my mom. The silence that followed filled the air with a toxicity that forced us further apart. There was a whirlwind of foreboding that sent us each into our own cocoon of safety. We were trying to survive in any way we could.

In the midst of all this turmoil, I started to receive letters along with money from George Sr., whom I had not heard from in almost a year. In one of those letters he stated that he was having second thoughts about the adoption, and when the final papers came for him to sign, he decided to hire a lawyer.

I immediately called the agency to find out if they had heard from him. Catherine G. said she was planning to call me, because the lawyer George had hired had already set up an appointment and was requesting that I meet with him in his office in a week's time. However, she had not heard from George directly. I was also informed there would be no meeting with the Henrys until all of this had been resolved.

I was relieved to learn George had hired a well-known black lawyer by the name of Edward Brooke, who, at the time, was married to an Italian woman, and they had two children. *OK, good,* I thought to myself, figuring it would help him understand my circumstances.

All the different explanations for what George was doing went around and around in my brain, so by the day of my appointment with his lawyer, my curiosity was at a fever pitch. Yet nothing added up. Why had he started to send me money the last few months? Why all of a sudden this interest in the boys? Why did he want to stop the adoption when, originally, he thought it was a viable solution? Did he have a plan for the boys? Did he want to get back together? All his actions over the past few years indicated we were not important to him. Why now? I hoped I would find answers to my questions when I met with his lawyer.

The day of the appointment I headed for Boston on the 8:00 a.m. train to make a 9:30 appointment. I had made arrangements with a woman from church to babysit the boys. First impressions are important, so I had dressed accordingly. It was around 9:20 when I entered the building where Brooke's office was located, which was close to the statehouse. It was magnificent, with granite floors and a lobby that could have encompassed a one-bedroom house. When I got on the elevator, I started to think for the first time about what conditions I could accept if George persisted in blocking the adoption.

I got off on the second floor and as I opened the door to enter Brooke's office, I was shocked to see my mom come around the reception desk. We passed each other like strangers. She did not acknowledge me nor I her. What was she doing here, and how did she know this lawyer? The first thought that went through my head was that she was there pleading her case to him, which she had every right to do. That was who my mother was. Once she believed she was right, she would do everything in her power to make it so.

The receptionist asked me to have a seat and said Mr. Brooke would be with me shortly. A few moments later she called me and led me down the hall into his office. As I entered, the smell of paper and books reminded me of a high school classroom. The receptionist asked me to take a seat until Brooke arrived.

Along the walls were rows of law books and many framed degrees along with what appeared to be awards of some kind. In front of me was a beautiful mahogany desk with leather inserts on top and brass handles. When Brooke entered the room, he introduced himself with a warm smile followed by a firm handshake. He was of average height and his complexion was very light. He was good-looking and soft-spoken, and his charm made me feel immediately at ease. Once he opened his mouth to speak, his intelligence was beyond question.

He asked how my trip had been and how far I had to come, then apologized for making the appointment so early.

"I know you must have a lot of questions as to why you are here," he said, "but first I would like you to tell me a little bit about yourself. For example, where did you meet your husband, and what has brought you to the point where you feel adoption is the best solution for your boys?"

I asked whether everything I shared with him would be confidential, seeing as I was not his client. He assured me it would be. I asked if that was true for everyone he met in a situation like mine. He smiled slightly and said, "Yes, it is."

I then started from the beginning and told him everything I could remember since George and I first met. He listened intently, stopping me occasionally to ask a question. He wanted to know if I was pregnant before we were married. I answered no.

"Did you and George talk about how difficult life was going to be as a biracial couple?"

"Yes, we discussed the pros and cons for months."

"Can you give me some details on why the marriage broke up?"

"From my perspective, the marriage had become toxic, and his inability to communicate, on any level, as to how to solve problems we were having was a major factor."

"Do you feel you have an open mind to solutions other than adoption?"

"Mr. Brooke, I have been over and over in my mind again and again trying to figure out another way. If their father had been involved and had shown any interest in their welfare we possibly could have worked something out."

He then thanked me for the information and apologized for having to leave but said he had a court appearance with another client scheduled. He asked if I could return that afternoon at 2:30. I said I could. He suggested I go have some lunch and said the receptionist would provide me with a list of places to eat. "I look forward to seeing you this afternoon," he concluded.

After I left the office I walked down to the Boston Common, a large park nearby, where I could sit and think. It was a cool, crisp day and the leaves were just beginning to turn colors. The Common is right in the heart of the city, with spacious lawns, a playground, and a pond that is turned into an ice rink in the winter months. It is usually busy with pedestrians, runners, tourists, and people eating lunch or stopping to rest. There are many historical monuments scattered about the Common, along with Boston's famous Swan Boats.

All of those things were completely invisible to me on that day as I sat down on one of the benches. I was focused on the children with their moms, playing and having a great time. There was one little boy who had fallen down and ran to his mother. I said to myself, *I am going to be losing all of that in a very short time because my boys will be running to someone else for comfort.*

My own pain, coupled with confusion over seeing my mom at the lawyer's office, was starting to overwhelm me, and I could not hold those emotions back any longer. I wanted to run to her and beg for her forgiveness. I needed my mom to walk with me and support me, but instead I found her walking out of Brooke's office and again it appeared she was overstepping her boundaries.

I had not noticed that an older woman was now sitting on the bench beside me, and as the tears started to flow she asked if there was anything she could do to help.

"Would you like to talk about whatever it is that is breaking your heart?" she asked.

Wherever I was, that brought me back to reality. I looked up and thanked her for her concern but said, "I am fine."

She gently smiled and said, "I know you are *not* fine, and it isn't my intention to intrude, but whatever you are going through I have been through tenfold, and I can feel your pain, but please know this, too, will pass, and God has given you nothing you will not be able to handle. Let him walk with you and give you strength."

I thanked her again for her concern then explained that I had an appointment and needed to go. She asked if she could give me a hug. By this time I needed all the hugs I could get, and as she reached out her hands I could feel strength surge through me like a wave that would carry me through the rest of the day. Was I being blessed by a guardian angel?

As I walked back towards the building I felt dazed and light-headed. My body was telling me I had not given it any fuel and that I better get something to eat. I eyed a coffee shop on the next corner and stopped and had a hot chocolate along with toast and peanut butter, which was my particular comfort food. As I left I got a candy bar, paid the cashier, and headed back for my 2:30 appointment.

Once I arrived, the receptionist immediately led me into Brooke's office. He asked me to take a seat, then paused a moment before asking whether I would want to speak with my husband directly if I had the opportunity. He then said, "I have heard both sides of your stories, and I really think you two should have a conversation with each other and try to find a solution that is in the best interest of your children."

"I don't know how that is possible when he is in another state. Are you suggesting we talk on the phone in your presence?" I asked.

"I believed it was important to bring your husband here, so you could talk to him in person."

With that, he instructed his secretary to bring George into the room. I was totally unprepared for what was happening, but as I look back now I have to say the lawyer handled the situation with finesse and a great deal of insight.

As George entered, we acknowledged each other, and Brooke asked him to sit down. He asked if either of us had a problem with going into the anteroom and trying to work something out. We both agreed. In a strange sort of way, I was hoping George had done a turnaround and really cared what happened to his boys and might even have some constructive input that would prevent the adoption from happening.

As the door closed behind us, George asked how I was doing.

"Under the circumstances, not so well."

"Are you aware that I am now living in Washington, D.C.?" he asked.

"I think the agency might have mentioned it, but I honestly don't remember."

The rest of the conversation went very much like the one we'd had in New Jersey. I would ask him questions and he would not answer. It was very frustrating. Finally, I asked, "Why are you here?" When he didn't answer, I said, "George, is there any way you would consider setting up an apartment, now that you are living in Washington, D.C., and become involved in the boys' lives?"

He looked at me for a very long time and finally said, "No, I cannot do that, but I would like you to consider moving there with me permanently without the boys."

As I looked at this man whom I had loved, I saw a perfect stranger and could feel anger beginning to rise up once again.

"You know there is no way I would ever consider such a move," I said, ready to lash out at him, but just then I heard a knock on the door. Brooke entered and asked if we had come to an agreement. "No," I said, "we have not."

What happened next was another shock. Brooke spoke to George in a very authoritative voice, using words I did not understand, almost like another language, but I understood he was chastising him. George had his head down and reminded me of George Jr. when I had to scold him. I almost felt sorry for him.

Brooke said something about the agency and fulfilling responsibility, then asked George to leave the office. He turned to me and said, "I am sorry, but you needed to witness that."

None of it made any sense to me. Why would a lawyer treat a client like that unless he was not really the lawyer's client? Had our conversation in the anteroom been overheard? I had so many questions and no answers. I raised a few with Brooke, but each time he invoked client privilege. I felt numb, muddled, and cold all at the same time. Brooke asked if I would like to lie down in the other room. I said no and asked if I could just sit for a few minutes so I could get myself together.

"Of course you can," he said. "Take all the time you need."

The day had been one shock after another and I quickly realized, as I sat alone in Brooke's office, that I was not going figure it out there and then. I needed to go home. As I got up, Brooke came in and asked if I was all right. I said yes and explained that I was going to head home. He asked which way I was going and I told him, "North Station."

"I am headed that way and would be happy to give you a lift."

We sat silently in the back seat of his car, driven by a chauffeur. When we arrived at North Station, he reached out and put his gloved hand on my forearm and wished me good luck. I thanked him for the ride and left.

On my way home I decided I was not going to mention anything about the day unless my mom brought it up, but I've often wondered, in the years since, who initiated that meeting with Edward Brooke. George did not have the finances to afford an attorney of Brooke's caliber, and if Brooke had been George's lawyer, he would have spoken to him in private. I knew it wasn't the agency; they would have had their lawyer there representing my interest. So, did my mom hire him as a mediator to try to get George and me back together? That was hard to imagine, since she had tried to get our marriage annulled. However, that was before there were children involved— her grandchildren.

Now, all I have is speculation. I told myself many times that I would ask Mom at some point, because she seemed to be the most likely candidate, but the more time passed, the less important the answer became. Many times in life we are left with only questions. For me, this was one of those times.

CHAPTER 16

The Foster Parents

THE DAY HAD left me emotionally drained and physically exhausted from all of the unexpected encounters, but when I woke up the next morning and saw my two boys, it rejuvenated my anguished soul. I looked out of the window and saw what another beautiful fall day it was, then asked the boys if they would like to go out and rake some leaves for Grampa after they had breakfast.

"And then could we play in them?" George asked.

"Of *course*. Isn't that why we rake leaves?"

I knew the social worker would be calling to inform me whether George Sr. had signed the release papers, and I wanted to be out of the house so the ringing of the phone would fall on deaf ears. I needed time to recharge before I could deal with whatever his decision was.

Later on that week I learned George had indeed signed the necessary papers, so our appointment with the foster family would go ahead as planned. Catherine G. informed me that we should meet at the couple's home, in Everett, a suburb of Boston, at about 11:30 a.m. on the following Friday.

"Who should I tell the boys these people are?"

"Just tell them they are friends of yours. It is important to see if this couple will connect with the boys and the boys with them. It is also imperative you are comfortable with the surroundings and see for yourself how this is going to play out. Let's take this one step at a time."

For the very first time, she and I were in total agreement.

I needed to inform the boys we would be taking a trip. George loved going places and meeting new people, so he was psyched; David not so much.

David did not like change, and I reminded Catherine G. he had to be watched very closely whenever this transition took place. She assured me the agency would be in touch with the Henrys by phone and make frequent visits to be sure things were going well. She also said I would be able to see the boys at least once a week, or every other week, depending on how things went. Her mantra had become "One step at a time." She added that whatever questions I had would be answered, so there would be no surprises.

In preparation for the meeting, I laid out what the boys would be wearing the night before, because I knew I would be too nervous to make any judgments the next morning. I chose typical playclothes but struggled over whether to dress them in corduroys and decided against it because it wasn't cold enough and neither one of them particularly liked corduroy pants. I told the boys to bring something to play with in the car because the drive would seem long.

In order to proceed with some sense of normalcy, I had to live one moment at a time and not allow my mind to play out the what-ifs. I had to measure every step the agency took and decide if it was the best thing for my boys and not just accept what *they* thought was best. Meeting the Henrys would involve extreme scrutiny on my part, and if they did not match what I was looking for, I was ready to inform Catherine G. we would have to look elsewhere.

As we pulled up to the address she had given me, I could see right away it was a typical home and neighborhood. There was a nice big backyard with swings and a seesaw, along with lots of toys. The house itself appeared to have been recently painted brown with light beige shutters and a wrap-around front porch.

George could not wait to get out of the car and ran up the steps, where Catherine G. greeted him and asked him to wait for David and me. When we walked in the front door, George immediately eyed a bassinet and asked if he could go over and see the baby. I asked him to wait until he met Mrs. Henry and to then ask her permission.

Mrs. Henry approached with a gracious smile and welcomed us into her home. I was happy to see she immediately introduced herself to the boys and told them they could call her Mrs. H. and that Mr. H. would be down shortly. I was so proud of George when he said, "Well, my name is George, and I am happy to meet you, and you can call me George." He added without hesitation, "May I have permission to go see the baby?"

"Of course," she answered. "Her name is Susan, and she is only four weeks old."

"I will talk softly because my brother was a baby once," George replied, and Mrs. Henry looked at me with a knowing smile.

Just then Mr. Henry came down the stairs, and as I looked at him I felt my knees buckle and my heart beat a little faster. His persona was similar to George Sr.'s, with the same physique and stature. Would he bring back bad memories for George?

That fear did not materialize, though, because he immediately engaged both of the boys by asking if they would like to go downstairs to see the train set. He added that they could start the engine and watch it go through tunnels, pass farms, and hear the horn blow. Their eyes lit up, both nodding their heads in the affirmative, and off they went.

Catherine G. had prepared me with good advice when she told me not to ask any personal questions but to concentrate on whether I would be comfortable with the boys staying with this couple for a short time. Did I like how they interacted with the boys? Did I like the surroundings? Concentrate, she said, on how the boys were reacting to them. And if, indeed, I was happy with this family, she could answer all of the personal questions I had at our next meeting, she explained.

As the day progressed it became obvious there would be no alone time with the Henrys. My instincts would have to guide me. So instead I focused on every nuance, every detail, my eyes and senses could take in so that I could get a good idea of who these people, the Henrys, really were.

Their home gave off vibes of peace filled with joy, love, and warmth and had a lived-in feel to it, not a place meant to impress those who entered. The toys in the living room meant it was not off-limits to children. The smell of baked muffins filled the air. All of this could not be manufactured. It had to reflect the people who lived there. There was no mistaking that.

Mr. and Mrs. Henry both talked to the boys in a calm respectful tone. They showed a loving attitude towards each other. Mr. Henry told George and David he had to change the baby's diaper and asked if they would like to help him, which told me they shared responsibility. George immediately answered yes, but David ran over and sat in my lap without saying a word. By the time we left, both of the boys were engaged with Mr. H., who also showed them different kinds of knots using a single piece of string.

Catherine G. interrupted the flow of things after an hour, telling us it was time to go. The boys wanted to know if they could stay longer, and I said we could come back and visit another day. I was not surprised when George ran up and gave Mr. H. and then Mrs. H. a hug. She had asked me ahead of time if they could each have a cookie when they left and I had said, "Yes, that will be fine." Both of the boys thanked them again. I was so proud of their manners.

On the drive back George and David sat in the back talking about what a good time they'd had, while I thought about how much I liked Mr. and Mrs. Henry and wondered why I wasn't feeling any jealousy. The overwhelming feeling was one of relief. This was what I wanted: a loving family, a mom and a dad who could give them what they needed to survive in a world where they would be safe.

Catherine G. had told me to go home and think about what had transpired, then give her a call in about a week to set up an appointment at which we could go over everything and proceed from there. That night after supper my dad asked after I put the boys to bed if I would come in the living room because he wanted to talk with me.

As I sat down on the sofa, he began by saying, "I am glad your mother is in Florida visiting your sister so we can have this talk, but I want you to promise me that what I am about to say to you will never go beyond this room."

I did agree and I have kept that promise all these years, but now I think his words need to be repeated.

"I just wanted you to know I support your decision and honestly feel it is the right thing to do for the boys, my grandsons. There have been many times I have wanted to speak up, but with your mom feeling so strongly, I knew it would have been counterproductive. I will be heartbroken when the time comes for them to leave, but I know their lives will be more normal than they could ever be in this community. I am sorry your marriage didn't work out, and I also wanted you to know that the road ahead is going to be devastating for you, but I am asking you to be strong. I know how hard it has been for you to go against your mother, and it breaks my heart to see you being torn in so many different directions. OK, I'm done. No more said."

At that very moment I wanted to crawl into his lap and have him hold me, but I knew it would be too much for either one of us to handle, so instead I reached out my hand to touch his and said, "Dad, you will never know how much those words mean to me. Your support and concern will help carry me through the next few months. I love you. Thank you."

I got up to leave with tears streaming down my face and heard my dad say, "I love you too, honey."

I called Catherine G. the next morning to set up an appointment for the following week.

CHAPTER 17

Going Ahead with the Plans

MY MOM HAD returned from Florida, and the tension at home began rising between she and my dad. I was surprised to hear them arguing one night about why he had not tried to convince me that my decision to put the boys up for adoption would have serious repercussions not only for the boys but also for me. Like many men, my dad did not like confrontation, and he knew with my mom he had to end it quickly. He replied by saying, "It is not our call to make. Our daughter is doing what she thinks is best for her boys, and I am sure you are right, there will be all kinds of consequences for her to face, but it is the road she has chosen, and I will not interfere."

There were only two other times growing up that I can remember my parents arguing. The first was when my mother insisted my brother, who had polio, be treated like everyone else and be taught there was nothing he could *not* do or achieve. My father's approach was to teach him his limitations.

The second was when he slapped my sister on the bum because she was talking back to my mom. My mother's brisk response was instantaneous. "You are never to use any form of physical punishment on any of the children ever again," she said to my dad.

He replied, "Well, I can tell you when I was her age my father would have given me the strap for the way she behaved, and I believe my actions were appropriate."

"There will be no physical contact when it comes to punishment in this household ever," she repeated. And there never was.

So, yes, I was shocked to hear him speak up, because he had stopped arguing with her a long time ago. The next morning Mom informed me she had heard, from my dad, that George had signed the release papers. My plans for the boys to be adopted had not changed. She then asked that I let her know what day they would be leaving, because she could not handle being in the house. I told her, "I promise, when I know, you will know."

I was surprised when she added, "I also heard from your dad you are doing a good job looking out for the boys' interests, and I would expect nothing less of you even though I disagree with your decision."

* * *

WHEN I WALKED into Catherine G.'s office the following day, my adrenaline level was spiking in anticipation of what lay ahead. I had written all the questions down I needed to ask. She threw me off guard when she commented that I looked different. I asked if she could be a little more specific and she said I did not look as stressed. Without breaking a confidence, I told her about the positive conversation I had had with my dad and how my mother seemed resigned to the fact the adoption would proceed as planned.

She asked how I felt about that, and I told her the environment at home seemed to be less toxic and that, yes, indeed, the stress level there had improved.

"I know this is difficult for all of you," she said and then asked about our visit the previous week with the Henrys. I listed all the positive things I had seen and said that if she could answer each of my questions I would be comfortable leaving the boys in their home on a temporary basis. She told me to go ahead and ask the questions.

"Can you add anything to my assessment of Mr. and Mrs. Henry before I begin?"

"In all the time they have been taking in foster children," she said, "there has never been one complaint. I think you will be more than happy with who we have chosen to place your boys with. They are very much like the adoptive parents you have requested the boys be placed with permanently."

"Thank you. That is good to know. My first question is, what will their sleeping arrangements be?"

"Together in the same room with bunk beds, or you can request a room with twin beds."

"Will they be going to church on Sunday?"

"Yes."

"How do they discipline?"

"They do not believe in spanking, and when discipline is necessary, they will be sent to their room for a short time, and then a conversation will take place about what behavior is acceptable and what is not, or a privilege will be taken away for a day or two."

"Do they have any set rules to be followed?"

"They believe in giving children as much freedom as they can handle. The Henrys have been doing this for quite some time, and they pick up from each child pretty quickly what their limits are. However, they would like as much information from you as possible as to the boys' strengths and weaknesses, along with any idiosyncrasies they might have."

"Are there other children in the neighborhood to play with close to their ages?"

"Yes."

"Are there trips to the library?"

"Yes."

"Can I request they say prayers before bedtime?"

"Yes."

"Will they be read to?"

"Yes."

"Is there a park nearby?"

"Yes."

"Is there a limit to the number of foster children they can have in the household?"

"Yes. The limit is three at one time."

"How much notice do I have to give before I can see the boys?"

"One day."

"Will I be informed if they are not adjusting?"

"Yes."

She answered yes, but I learned much later, after I located the boys, that was not completely true.

"Can I communicate with the Henrys directly?"

"No. Everything has to be OK'd by me. It is agency policy."

"What if she has questions that only I can answer?"

"I will get in touch with you and get back to Mrs. H." She then added, "If you do not have more questions, we need to think about moving on and making plans for the boys to be placed with the Henrys so the search for a permanent home can begin."

"I do have one more question: How long will the boys be living with the Henrys?"

"Ordinarily it would only take about three months, but because you have very specific requirements on who you would consider to be appropriate parents and the fact they are biracial, it might take longer, possibly six months, but I cannot give you a specific time frame."

I told her to go ahead with the adoption plans, but with my emotions banging at the door, wanting to flood my thoughts of life without the boys, I needed to take flight and asked to be excused, then headed for the ladies' room. As I was telling myself to stay focused on why I was here, there was a knock on the door. "Are you all right?" asked Catherine G.

"I am fine and will be right out."

Once again I draped myself in the robe of reason and put all my emotions back in place. When I reentered the room, I told Catherine G. I was ready to proceed. She handed me some papers and told me to look them over later. "When you leave here," she continued, "I want you to go home and make a list of all the things you want the Henrys to know about the boys, for example what foods they like, what are their interests, do they have any allergies. Describe their personalities. They have a camp and would need to know if either one of the boys has any fear of the water, do they sleep well at night, any idiosyncrasies, do either one of the boys take any medicine, and anything else that you can put down that you might feel would be helpful."

She added that I should be getting together any favorite toys, books, and stuffed animals the boys would like to take with them. "I need you to provide clothes for a week, and buy a couple of pairs of pajamas, along with new socks and underwear. Pack any winter coats, sweaters, or jackets."

She reminded me to go over the papers I'd been given and told me that if I had any further questions to give her a call. She said I should plan to make the transition with George and David by the end of the month. I nodded my head, trying not to let her see my vulnerabilities.

On the drive home I was still trying to hold my feelings at bay, but sadness continued to wash over me like waves taking me out to sea, and the only thing keeping me afloat was the sense of relief in knowing that both George and David would be safe. It was imperative that I stay strong.

CHAPTER 18

"What Do I Tell the Boys?"

I HAD CONCERNS about how I would explain to the boys what was happening, so I called Catherine G. and she told me to make an appointment so we could talk it over and kept repeating her mantra over and over: one step at a time.

Our meeting was scheduled for the following Monday morning. I went over different scenarios and believed I had come up with the gentlest way possible to prepare the boys. However, it wasn't long into our meeting before her thinking came into conflict with mine, and soon we were locked in total disagreement.

She recommended I tell George and David that they would be spending the summer at the Henrys' and to give them as little information as I could.

"What if they want to know why? What do I tell them?"

"You tell them the truth, which is, you need to find a job. From my experience, this approach has worked and I do not see any reason to change it now."

"I respect and value your input," I said, "but all children are different, and I feel I know my boys better than anyone else. Would you at least hear me out?"

I knew from past experiences she did not like her decisions challenged, so I give her credit for reluctantly agreeing.

I told her that I wanted George and David to be part of the decision, and my plan was, yes, to tell them they were going to the Henrys' so Mama could find work but to ask them what they thought about it. Was that something they would like to do?

She immediately cut me off. "David is too young, and to give George a choice is not, in my mind, the right way to go. What if they disagree?"

"Both boys have been asking to visit with the Henrys," I said, "so I don't think it will be a problem. I do respect the fact you have dealt with many children over the years, but just the fact you're telling me David is too young to understand raises questions in my mind that you are judging him as a typical three-year-old, when he is not. David is a sleeper, and, yes, I know he will look at you with those big brown eyes like he does not understand and say nothing, but I know my son, and I can tell you he does. If you are evaluating him on those tests you gave both boys, I know George did well and I know his brother did not. David is shy, and it takes him a while to trust people. However, he is my son, and I know he is far ahead of any three-year-old. If he is not on the same page with his brother, this move is not going to work. David needs to be included in this decision, and his voice needs to be heard."

"Well, if you feel that strongly about it," she said curtly, "I would suggest you do it your way, but I am going on record by saying I disagree with your approach. Children that age need to be told what to do."

I think I was still under the illusion at that moment that I was in control and would have further input in my boys' lives. I was their mother; why wouldn't my input be important? This should have been my wake-up call. It was not.

Before the meeting ended I asked if I could have a copy of the tests the boys had taken with the therapist. She said it was agency policy to keep those tests in-house. She also said they were just to make sure the boys were adoptable.

"And I am assuming they were?"

"Almost 100 percent."

She then reminded me about the list I needed to compile for the Henrys.

"Of course," I replied as I got up to leave.

* * *

I BEGAN TO notice over the next few weeks that my dad was spending more time with George and David. The popular kids' show *The Little Rascals*, also known as *Our Gang*, would play every night before supper. The boys would plunk themselves down on the floor, George to the right of Dad's chair and David to the left, and as I prepared supper I could hear them all laughing. Sometimes, when waiting for things to finish cooking, I would join them. It seemed the only way each of us could survive what lay ahead was to live every moment and treasure it as a miracle that would and could dissipate at any time.

The second week after my conversation with Catherine G., I finally was able to find the courage to write a very detailed list to the Henrys about the boys' personalities along with their preferences in food. I explained in a cover letter that I hoped the information that I had enclosed would be helpful in their transition and if they had any questions to please get back to me through the agency.

INFORMATION ABOUT GEORGE AND DAVID

George likes to eat oatmeal, peanut butter and jelly, toast with butter, pancakes with syrup. He has a good appetite and will eat most foods but is not shy about telling you what he does not like. Eggs and fruit are not some of his favorite foods. He will break out if you give him too much chocolate, tomatoes, strawberries and salt because of his eczema.

David also has a good appetite. He likes to eat much of the same food his brother does and has no restrictions. He is hesitant about trying food he hasn't eaten before and will spit it out if does not like it. He loves anything that is sweet but will shy away from fruit. David has no allergies.

The tricky part with David is giving him food George can't eat. For example, if I give David ice cream in a dish, I will put a little chocolate on the bottom and cover it with strawberry or vanilla or both. George can have vanilla and/or strawberry. They both love hot chocolate and toast at night before they go to bed, so I tell George ahead of time his hot chocolate is going to be mostly milk, and after he sputters a bit, he will be fine with that.

Neither one of the boys are on any medication.

George's Personality

George is a normal 4 year old little boy who loves to be active. He is extremely verbal and sometimes is impulsive, wanting to try things he is not ready for. He adores his brother and feels it his job to protect him. I have been able to provide him with all of the normal experiences, but there is one area he has not had the opportunity to experience and that is socializing and playing with his peers. I am hoping you can take him places where he will have the opportunity to play and socialize with other children his age. He needs this in his life as any child would.

Please be aware and I cannot stress enough if George sucks his fingers, DO NOT TRY TO STOP HIM. He suffered a traumatic event with his father regarding finger sucking. He has gotten better, but if he feels insecure or threatened in any way the fingers will automatically go to his mouth. Nothing you can do will stop him.

My suggestion would be just to hold him for a few moments and it will pass.

David's Personality

David is much more passive than his brother. He is extremely sensitive, soft spoken, and a thinker. He loves to look at books, magazines, and likes to be read to.

He likes board games, word games, and playing with cards. He is patient with his brother and will engage in physical activity when George encourages him to do so. Once they get started playing ball or swinging on the swings he seems to be very good at it and enjoys it. Like his brother, he has not had an opportunity to socialize with other children his age and what I have suggested for his brother I would suggest for David.

David will not let you know what his needs are the way George will. At about the age of 2 he was not talking as much as his brother, so I made some flash cards to help him learn some words. He amazed me when he went through those cards and knew every single word and could pronounce them correctly. He learns by listening and watching.

He will not come up and sit in your lap like his brother, so I have to take time to be sure I give him the attention and affection he needs. In other words, I constantly have to anticipate his needs.

David sleeps well at night but sometimes his brother will wake up crying. I will hold George for a few minutes and he will go right back to sleep.

Both of the boys love watching TV while I am cooking dinner.

That completes the list. Please let the agency know if there is anything else you would like to know.

CHAPTER 19

Goodbyes

I COULD NOT put off a conversation with the boys much longer about what lay ahead. They kept asking to visit the Henrys, so it would have been an easy topic to bring up, but I still resisted until the social worker called and asked if we had talked. I resented the intrusion but told myself, once again, she was just doing her job. I thanked her for calling and told her I would get back to her by the end of the week.

In the past few weeks I had tried so many times to bring up the topic of visiting the Henrys, but I knew once I had that conversation with the boys, their excitement would take over and I would have to move on it. Tomorrow, I will bring it up, tomorrow.

The following night, right after supper, the boys mentioned going to the Henrys' again. Taking a deep breath, I asked if they would like to stay overnight. George answered right away: "Oh, could we?" David had a quizzical look on his face until George mentioned the train set, and as he enthused more and more, David finally warmed up to the idea as well.

I called the agency the next morning to inform Catherine G. that the boys had been told and were looking forward to seeing the Henrys. She seemed relieved and said, with my approval, that she would like to make arrangements for the following Saturday at 2:00 p.m. Fine, I replied, and then asked if she had passed on my list with the cover letter, and she answered she had. Catherine G. then wanted to know how I was doing.

"Not well."

"Would you like to come in and talk about it?"

"Not at this time, but thank you for asking."

"I know how difficult this is for you and would encourage you to make an appointment to talk with me at a later date."

How could she possibly know how difficult this was for me? I am sure she understood intellectually, but unless one has given a child up for adoption, there is no way emotionally anyone can fully understand.

Still, nothing about this whole process sat right with me. I had requested several times to be part of the transition but was told it was against agency policy. The feeling of being locked out of the process was frightening, but I had to stay focused and find a way to work within a system and let the agency do its job.

* * *

THE NEXT STEP was to inform my mom when the boys would be leaving, and once I did, she wanted to take them out for lunch. I told her, "Of course. The day they leave I will be at church praying for all of us."

"I know you believe you are doing the right thing," she said, "and I pray to God it is, because the sad part about all of this, you will never know."

At the time she made that statement I thought, *Good, she is placing the responsibility where it belongs, on me.* As I write this now and relive her statement, however, I realize my mother was trying to tell me that not knowing how the boys were doing was the cross I was going to have to carry, and indeed she was right, because there has never been a day that has gone by since the boys were adopted that that cross has not gotten heavier.

* * *

OVER THE NEXT few weeks I went into the boys' room at night, watching them sleep. I remember their laughter and how I would watch them at play, trying to burn into my memory each and every scenario so I could replay it in my head when they were no longer there. I remember reading them stories at night, not just one, but reading until they would fall asleep. I also remember how hard it was trying to keep everything as normal as possible so they would not pick up on all of my self-doubt and self-loathing.

The night before we left, the boys helped me pack. As we put their new pajamas into the suitcase, I thought about the day when we all went shopping, how both of them were beginning to form their own ideas on what they liked and did not like. Previously, when I bought a shirt or pants for George, I would purchase the same for David. When George wanted to get a pair of pajamas with red, blue, and yellow trucks, I encouraged him to look at other patterns, but he was emphatic that these were the ones he wanted. "David too," he said, but his brother shook his head no. After David looked at the different styles, he finally picked a pair with yellow stars and a white moon spattered all over a royal blue background. George tried so hard to change his mind, but David kept shaking his head no and gave him that look. It was not going to happen.

As I smiled to myself, watching this back-and-forth between the boys, the realization hit me that this was the last passage I was going to experience with the two of them. I was overcome with sadness that swept through my whole body.

After the boys went to bed that night I went downstairs, sat on the sofa, grabbed a pillow, and didn't move until my dad came in and said I should get some sleep. I told him I would be up shortly. I never did make it to bed, though. The next thing I remember is the boys waking me up and saying, "Is it time to go yet?" For the rest of the day, I was on automatic pilot. The day of departure was here, whether I was ready or not.

While I fixed breakfast I told the boys they could go in the living room and watch cartoons with Grandpa. When I went in the living room to call them, I noticed there were tears in my dad's eyes. I said nothing. I had never seen my dad cry before, and my heart ached for him.

When the time came for us to leave, Dad kissed the boys and told them to be good.

"Promise me?" he asked, and they replied in unison, "Promises made are promises kept." He had taught them to say that because he liked it better for their age than the infamous "Cross my heart and hope to die."

The scenario that followed was very much like the first time we all visited the Henrys. The social worker was there waiting and never left my side. After they boys settled in, I told them I would see them next weekend and to please be good, followed by hugs and kisses.

As I walked down the front steps with Catherine G., I managed to get up the courage to tell her that this practice of not allowing me to speak to the Henrys or be more involved in the transition until the adoption took place was ludicrous. I said I didn't think it was a healthy process for any of us and that I felt I was being dishonest with the boys. Her response was, "You might be right, but all of us have to work within the system, and if you want what is best for your boys, I would strongly suggest you find a way to work with us."

Well, she was right about one thing: I did want what was best for the boys and if it meant working within the system for their future, I had no choice but to comply.

CHAPTER 20

The Visit

WHEN I ARRIVED home it was about five o'clock and the house was empty. I ran upstairs and buried myself under the covers and did not come out for three days. The feeling of emptiness, that something had been ripped out of my womb, was overwhelming.

When I finally was able to pull myself out of my cocoon, Mom informed me that Catherine G. had been trying to get in touch. When I reached her she said it was imperative that we meet before I saw the boys the following weekend.

"Is everything OK?" I asked. "Have you seen them?"

"No, but I have talked with Mrs. Henry, and she reported George and David were adjusting well."

Adjusting well? *What did that mean?* I decided it was just a common expression, so I did not pursue it. We set up an appointment for the following day at 2:00 p.m.

The next morning, no matter how many cups of coffee I drank I couldn't seem to get it together. That afternoon when I entered Catherine G.'s office I must have looked worried, because the first thing she asked was "Is there anything you would like to talk about?"

"No."

She then told me in an upbeat tone that there might be a great family interested in adopting George and David.

"This family is exactly what you wanted for your boys, and I know you must be excited for them."

"I am, but did not expect it to happen so quickly."

"But surely you understand that the sooner they are in a permanent placement the better it will be for their transition."

That statement made perfect sense to my intellectual reasoning, but not to my dysfunctional emotional reasoning.

"Do you plan to see the boys this week?" she asked.

"Of course I do. Nothing could keep me away."

"Well, then, we need to go over some ground rules. First, you will not be allowed to take the boys outside. The Henrys will be in the house, but not in the same room. Your time will be restricted to one hour. Please do not bring any food, but small toys are allowed."

I could feel anger beginning to rise deep within me.

"I know by the look on your face," she said quickly, "you are not happy with this arrangement, but if you want to go ahead with the adoption you have to follow the rules."

She then added that she was obligated to inform me before we moved forward that if I wanted to change my mind, now was the time, because once the process began, there would be no turning back. "Try to keep your focus on what you want for the boys and control your emotions. Do you think you can do that?"

"Yes, I can do that."

"Good, then let me do my job, but in order for me to do that, I need your complete trust I want you to understand, when I ask you to do something, it is always in the boys' best interest."

Since I knew there was no other choice, I told her we were on the same page.

"Please don't forget you can me call anytime, and be sure to remind the boys that after your next visit, you will not be able to see them for another two weeks."

I looked at her and said what I needed to say, and that was, "I will."

As I walked towards the door I heard her wish me good luck.

"Thank you," I replied, but thought to myself, *Another dumb rule.*

* * *

IT HAD BEEN raining all day when I drove in to see George and David. I thought of how the weather was reflecting what I had been feeling the past week. The rain was my tears, which continued to fall. The sound of lightning and thunder represented the ominous storms I would have to face. I prayed I was strong enough to survive.

I was anxious and scared at the same time. I had been told by Catherine G. the last time we talked that Mrs. Henry was doing a good job of answering the questions George was asking and again she repeated that David was too young to understand.

As I went up the steps to the Henrys' home, I was met by Mrs. Henry. I hoped to have an opportunity to speak with her, but as soon as she greeted me, she disappeared. Both of the boys ran up to me as I went in the door and gave me big hugs. George pulled on my sleeve, wanting to show me his coloring book. "See, Mama, how good I stay in the lines?"

They both looked well and happy. George would get very hyper when he was excited and did not stop talking until I asked him to sit in my lap for a few moments. I just held him close until he calmed down. David, I had to go over and pick him up. He snuggled close to my chest until I asked if he had anything he would like to show me. He slid down, took my hand, led me over to the window, and pointed to a red tricycle.

"Want to see me ride?"

I told him it would probably not be a good idea, seeing as it was raining out. "Are you riding all by yourself?" I asked. "Mama is so proud of you, and the next time I can watch you ride, OK?"

He looked up at me and said, "OK, Mama, I show you."

I could not believe, when Mrs. Henry entered the living room and pointed at her watch, that my hour was nearly up. I was dreading telling the boys that I would not be seeing them for another two weeks. When I started to explain, George said, "It's OK, Mama. Mrs. H. told us how you needed to find work and we were going to be here a little longer."

David did not say a word. I was surprised when he held up his arms, wanting me to hold him, which was unusual. I picked him up and said, "I love you, David."

"I love you, Mama."

I was trying hard to hold back tears, not wanting him to pick up on my sadness, so I quickly changed the subject by asking if they had made any new friends. Before they had a chance to answer, Mrs. Henry walked in again and reminded me it was time to leave. There was a fair going on at their church and the boys were looking forward to seeing what it was all about after they had lunch. I gave them both a surprise grab bag as we said our goodbyes. That was followed by lots of hugs and kisses. We waved and threw more kisses as I walked down the steps.

To see the boys so happy and adjusting well brought me a huge sense of relief. I had so many questions I would have liked to ask Mrs. Henry. The next day I called the social worker and she was able to answer most of them. So instead of fighting the rules I was learning how to work within them.

The next day at breakfast I told Mom the boys were doing well. She thanked me and said, "I am happy to see you are not running for cover like you did last week."

My confidence in Catherine G. was beginning to grow, the trust not so much. She'd been right about some, but not all, things regarding how the boys would react under certain conditions. I fully realized that as time went by, she was going to be my only lifeline to them. I believed her when she continued to say she had the boys' best interests at heart.

CHAPTER 21

A Family Is Found

MY THINKING AT the time was that things would get easier each time I visited George and David, but that thinking proved to be flawed. I sensed they were getting restless, and I was not surprised when Catherine G. called me the following week and said, "The boys are acting out after you leave, and Mrs. Henry has asked me to inform you that visiting once a month might be easier on them. It is not unusual for this to happen, because they are beginning to recognize something is changing. I have gone through this many times and know it would be better for everyone if you would be willing to reduce your visits to every four weeks."

"Better for everyone" kept reverberating in my head. Not for me it wasn't. It was becoming more apparent that our lives were taking on a whole new dimension. It was as if I were swimming upstream without a life jacket and there was no help in sight.

Sleep was my way of escaping until I could see the boys once again. Crawling under the security of my blanket I would imagine bringing them close to me, telling bedtime stories, until we would drift off into a world that was filled with only love and peace. Another form of escape was to get away from the house, with all of its memories, and walk for hours, and when I could not take another step, I would head home and fall into a dreamlike state of sleeping once again. I remember my mom telling me at one point that nothing she said or did was registering with me. She described it as my "zombielike stage."

Finally, when I was just a few days away from seeing the boys again, I received a phone call from Catherine G. asking me to set up an appointment ASAP.

"Did anything happen to the boys? Are they all right?"

"They are fine. Is there a possibility you could get in to see me today, say at 3:00 p.m.?"

"Yes, of course."

When I sat down in her office, the first thing she said was "It looks like we have found a family for the boys. They are everything you have asked for: well-educated black couple, Christian faith, and in a part of the country you have requested."

"Are there any other children?"

"No but lots of relatives and cousins, about the same age as the boys."

I went stone cold.

"Are you OK? Would you like a glass of water?"

"No, but I would like something hot, anything hot. Just give me a moment to catch my breath and I will be fine."

She left the room, which gave me a few moments to pull myself together. After she returned with hot tea, I thanked her and she told me more about the prospective adoptive couple.

"We are in the process of checking them out, and it looks like everything is coming back positive. We think it is a good match. You will be happy to hear the boys are doing well and have improved in every way."

I asked her what she meant by that last statement. She said she didn't think I realized how the tension between my mother and me had affected George and David. *Oh, great*, I thought. *Now on top of everything else, I am being showered with more guilt.*

"I tried so hard to keep it away from them," I said.

"I am sure you did, but children do pick up emotions that are going on around them."

She continued: "After going over everything with the staff who evaluates where the boys are when the time comes for them to be adopted, we all have come up with the same conclusion, and that is, you need to explain to George he is going to have a new mommy and daddy."

After I took in a long big-woman's breath I said, "What about David?"

"We still feel he is too young to understand what is happening."

I did everything I could to change her mind, but she would not budge. I heard myself begging to let me explain to both boys what was going on.

"No, it is not a good idea," Catherine G. said firmly, then reminded me the staff members all had degrees in social work and were more than qualified to make this decision.

I wanted to shake her and say, "But I am his mother. He needs to hear it from me." However, I knew by the look on her face that I would be talking down a well, so I backed off in defeat. "I know: rules are rules," I said with disdain.

Realizing I needed to come back to reality very quickly, I asked, "What are your thoughts on how we are going to arrange this meeting with George?"

"Well, here is my plan," she said. "I will pick him up and drive to where you are. You can pick the place, but it should be no more than a mile from the house. How does that sound?"

"Is this something I will be able to do without your being present?"

"Yes, I will leave you two together and will come back in about half an hour. You can take him to the park or take him out for hot chocolate."

Only half an hour, I thought. That seemed insensitive to me, and then to suggest I take him where there would be other people around. I don't think so. Finally I said in a controlled voice, "If I only have half an hour, I would rather talk to my son in a more private place. We will stay in the car."

"Fine."

Did she really have any idea how traumatic that conversation was going to be for both of us? Maybe that casual attitude she was projecting was just a facade. I'll never know.

"I am due to see the boys in a couple of days," she said

"So what day were you planning for me to see George?"

"Is Thursday good for you?"

"I am due to see the boys this coming Saturday, so I am assuming you mean the following Thursday. Is that correct?"

"Yes, she replied. "By the way, there is a parking lot right beside the playground, or you can park along the street opposite the playground."

"I prefer the street versus the parking lot."

"I will meet you there around 2:30 p.m.," she said.

On the drive home, traffic was heavy and I had plenty of time to think about how I was going to try to talk with David alone. If that meant going against Catherine G's advice, then I would take that risk. I kept telling myself to follow my instincts as a mother: *You will know when the time comes what it is you have to do or not do.* My thoughts drifted to the realization I would be seeing the boys together on Saturday for the last time.

When I pulled into the driveway, I just sat there. I did not want to go in the house, where my mom and I were trying to deal with our own emotional journey, each in her own silent chamber. I thought of how comforting it would be to have each other as support, but that was not going to happen. I knew that.

Please, God, walk with me, guide me, and protect my beloved George and David.

CHAPTER 22

The Big-Boy Talk

THREE DAYS LATER I had my final visit with George and David together. Before I headed out I asked Catherine G. to switch the location from inside the house to the front porch and sidewalk since we were only allowed an hour. She agreed and said she would let the Henrys know. When I arrived, the boys were excited to see me and looked healthy and happy. David was a little aloof but finally came over to give me a hug. He was eager to show me how well he was doing on his tricycle. George wanted me to push him on the swing and kept chattering away about how he and his brother had gone to church on Sunday, how they were making new friends, and how he loved going to the park.

"And, Mama, I get to watch cartoons with David and Mr. H., but we miss Grandpa."

"I know you do, honey, and he misses you too."

Mrs. Henry kept coming out of the house to check on us. Did she think I was going to try to abscond with the boys or make a scene because this was my last visit? I wanted to ask her but knew she would just smile and say, "You know I can't answer that."

I treated this visit like any other, not fully accepting the fact that this would be my last, until Mrs. H. came out on the porch and pointed to her watch.

I ran up ahead of the boys, hoping to have a moment to tell her how much I appreciated her kindness towards George and David, but she called them to come in and then went quickly back into the house.

I followed them inside and was still saying goodbye, telling them how much I loved them, giving them extra hugs and kisses, when she came into the living room again pointing to her watch.

The memory of pleading for more time is still fresh in my mind, how the nod of her head from side to side was like a punch in the solar plexus. Somehow I did find the strength to get up off the floor and ask the boys if they would walk me to the car. As we were going down the steps, Mrs. Henry did not make a move to stop us but rushed down behind us. When I opened the door and gave the boys their last hugs and goodbyes, I ignored her piercing look of disapproval. The last visual memory I have of the boys together was them walking back into the house with Mrs. Henry, turning around, and waving goodbye. I don't know if there are any words to describe what I was experiencing at that moment, but what I do know is more of my heart and soul died that day.

As it turned out, I was never able to find an opportunity to talk with David because of watchful eyes on me every minute. He should have been told.

* * *

IT WAS A cold, rainy day as I headed out that following Thursday afternoon to meet up with Catherine G. and George. After she drove up and parked behind me, she brought him over to my car. I could tell he was confused and upset. All of my motherly instincts came rushing out, and as he came towards me, I opened the car door, pulled him in, and gave him a big hug.

When he finally settled down, I told him that Mama needed to have a conversation with him.

"Why couldn't David come?"

I explained that I needed to talk with him alone because this was a big-boy talk and his brother was not quite a big boy yet. I asked if he had enjoyed staying at Mr. and Mrs. H.'s house. He told me he liked being around people who looked like him and his brother. As I think back about it now, I am surprised that he would make such an observation about race, but at the time I was much too tense to think anything about it.

He continued on, telling me how he and David had made lots of new friends and talking incessantly about things they did and places they would go and added, "But, Mama, Dave and I miss you so much."

"Me too, honey," I replied. "Me too."

After we talked a little while longer, I asked if he would like to have a new daddy. He looked up at me with those big brown eyes and said he would love that. I told him that with a new daddy there would be a new mommy. When I looked down his bottom lip had started to quiver. He raised his head, looked me straight in the eye, and said, "I want a new daddy, but I don't want a new mommy."

His head fell on my lap, and he started to cry. I sat him up and pulled him onto my lap and said, "George, I am going to ask you to look at Mama and listen very closely to what I am about to say. Can you do that? Mama needs you to stop crying and be a big boy."

After he calmed down I asked him if he was ready to be a really big boy. He said he could be a big boy but stated loud and clear he still did not want a new mommy. I told him I understood.

"Do you know Mama loves you? Do you know I would never ask you to do anything that was going to hurt you?"

His head went up and down.

"Mama had to make the most difficult decision about you and David and that is to keep you both safe. I love you more than anything else in this world, and no matter what happens that will never change. What I am about to ask you is because I love you."

To my surprise, he said in a very calm voice, "Is this because of all the bad people who don't like us and want to hurt us?"

I looked at him and said, "Yes, honey, it is."

I then told him that a new mama and daddy were waiting for him and David, with lots of cousins and aunts and uncles who would love and take care of them just like I had.

"I am asking you to be a very big, grown-up boy and do this for Mama so I will know you will be safe."

When he looked up at me it seemed like he was reaching into my very soul and said, "I can be a very big boy, Mama, and I will take care of David. I love you, Mama."

I lost it and started to cry and pulled him close to my chest, and we just sat there and held each other.

"Don't cry, Mama. I will be fine. I promise. Remember, a promise made is a promise kept."

I was supposed to be comforting him, not the other way around. A passage from the Bible ran through my crowded brain: "And a child shall lead them."

Just then there was a tap on the window and, sure enough, it was Catherine G. I was hoping she would give us a little more time together, but rules were still rules.

"Do I have to go now?" George asked.

"I think it is that time. Remember, George, I love you forever."

As he turned to get out of the car, he said, "I love you forever, Mama."

After that I could not move. I have no idea how long I sat there, but I wanted my babies back. Suddenly, all of those thoughts I had shut off in a compartment of my brain came pouring over me and would not cease. All of the guilt, the shame, the pain I had caused my parents, the anger towards the agency and its damn rules, the anger at the people who had deserted me, the anger towards George Sr., the anger towards the police who would not protect me, the anger at the man who threatened to hurt my boys, the anger at society for being intolerant of anything or anyone who was different, the anger at myself for not being able to find another way. What mother would give up her children? I hated who I was.

When I finally arrived home my mom was not there. She was still visiting my sister in Florida and would not be home until tomorrow. My dad was at a Masons meeting.

I ran in the house and filled the tub with steaming hot water. I thought if I could cause enough pain on the outside of my body it would relieve the pain I was feeling inside my body.

It was not working, so I grabbed a pair of scissors and stabbed myself in the thigh several times. That did not help either, and I was bleeding profusely. I cleaned myself up, put bandages on my wounds, and went to my room and cried myself to sleep.

Those scars and the emotional roots of those scars, I knew, would be with me for a long time, if not the rest of my life. More than anything, I wanted to exit this world. It seemed the only way to end my loathing of someone whom I could no longer live with. I will call what happened next a dream, because that's the only way I can rationalize it.

I was reliving the whole nightmare of what I had been through again, but in the dream I was experiencing it for the first time. Both boys wanted me to know they had been given angels to watch over them, and I was not to worry. They told me they had asked if I could be given an angel to watch over me, and their wish had been granted. As they disappeared in what appeared to be angel dust, I began running after them. A bolt of lightning woke me, and as reality began to seep in, I wanted to go back into whatever sphere I had come out of so I could see my boys once again, but I could not.

CHAPTER 23

Coping

THREE MONTHS WENT by and I was calling Catherine G. every week to see how the boys were doing. I was told they were both adjusting well. There were no other avenues to go down to double-check, so I took what I was told as fact. The system was not set up for any birth mother to know if the information she was receiving was accurate. In this particular case, what the agency was telling me was not the complete story. I learned much later that the boys had not been adopted by the couple I'd been told about and remained with the Henrys for quite some time.

Meanwhile, my whole body was trapped in a place where taking a flight into oblivion seemed to be a viable option. Before I could go down that path, however, I needed to write a letter to George and David explaining all the circumstances surrounding their adoption. After three days, all I had to show was a floor covered with crumpled-up paper.

Self-loathing was preventing me from seeing the bigger picture, but it was my attempts to write a letter to the boys that made me realize I did not have the luxury of taking my own life and leaving them with the legacy of a mother who did not have the courage of her convictions nor the strength to carry on. I had to find a way. I fell on my knees and asked for guidance. It was in that moment that I came up with a plan: when the boys turned twenty-four and twenty-five years old I would find them. That was my redemption, the only thing that made it possible for me to find an opening in the space where I was trapped. So one moment at a time, one hour at a time, and one day at a time, I made the opening a little wider by keeping the vision in sight and reminding myself that someday I would see George and David again.

My mom was pressing me to stop hiding in my bedroom and suggested I see someone to help me through this. I told her she was right but to please give me a couple more weeks, and I promised that, one way or another, I would move on.

CHAPTER 24

Abyss

THE NEXT FIVE years were full of poor choices, falling down, getting back up, falling down, and getting back up again. It seemed I was repeating the same mistakes over and over. Intellectually, I knew that in order to move forward I would have to let go of the past, but the power of loss and grief and the thought that I might never see my boys or learn where and how they were doing threw me into an emotional abyss that separated me from my intellect. The days that followed turned into months, during which my emotions and intellect were constantly battling each other. I was in a place where I trusted no one. Everyone I respected and loved had turned their backs on me. I was told again and again to get on with my life, that I would forget, would marry, have other children. *Get married?* I thought. *Never!*

I knew I had to do something, and something was to build a wall so thick and so high no one would ever be able to hurt or get close to me again.

I was living back home at the time and needed to tell my mom I would be moving out in the near future. Her reaction was predictable, an attempt to keep me under her wing. However, I assured her I had a plan and that she need not worry.

The first thing I had to do was find a place to live. I heard about one in Boston called the Franklin Square House, or just the Franklin House, so I called and set up an appointment for the very next day.

The building was huge, made of brick, and when I entered through the double-thick doors, it felt more like a rundown municipal building or an old school that had been renovated than like an apartment building. After introducing myself to the receptionist, I was given an application to fill out and proceeded to wait and wait for my interview with the director. I was not getting a warm, friendly feeling at all.

When I was finally called in, I was met by woman who reminded me of my sixth-grade teacher, who used to walk up and down the aisle with a ruler in her hand and slap it down on your desk when it was your turn to answer a question, and if you didn't know the answer she would slap the ruler even harder and make you go in the coat closet with your book in hand until you found the correct answer. She was a disciplinarian, and I could see the director of the Franklin House was cut from the same cloth.

The thought ran through my head that my sixth-grade teacher's cloth was woven with colors much brighter than those of the woman sitting on the other side of the desk from me. As she read over my application, she commented that at least I was not illiterate and my references looked good, but she let me know in no uncertain terms she was going to check every one of them. She then asked, "Are you pregnant?"

"No, I am not pregnant."

"Well, let's not waste any time. I will go over the rules at the Franklin House, and I want you to listen very carefully. If you have any questions do not interrupt me until I am finished.

"One: no drinking, no smoking, no pets. Two: no men allowed in your room, and if you have a date, he must check in at the desk. They will call you, and it's mandatory that you come downstairs and meet your guest in the lobby. You must sign out. Is that clear?"

I smiled sweetly and nodded my head.

"Three: all doors will be locked by 10:00 p.m. Four: no food or drink allowed in your room. Five: you are to keep your room neat and clean at all times. Six: there will be random checks of your room at any time. Seven: no radios allowed. Eight: cafeteria opens at 6:00 a.m. and closes at 5:00 p.m. If you break any of these rules, a notice will be left in your room and you are to return the keys immediately and leave the premises. Once a decision is made for a person to leave, there is no recourse. If you agree to these rules, please sign your signature below."

By now I was intimidated, but, yes, I did have a question, which I, unfortunately, asked: "You mentioned the cafeteria closed at 5:00 p.m. What if you don't get out of work until five thirty?"

Immediately, I was sorry. I could tell by her demeanor she was irritated.

"You *realize* these cafeteria workers have families and need to get home to take care of them," she said in sort of a half question. "Let me repeat: the cafeteria is open from 6:00 a.m. and closes at 5:00 p.m." Then she asked again, "Do you think you can obey our rules here at the Franklin House?"

I assured her I could. I needed a place to live and this was the only one I could afford, plus the subway was just down the street, so I signed the application.

When I first saw my room it seemed more like a long closet with a bed, bureau, and a rod for hanging clothes. *OK*, I thought, *at least a place where I can find solitude.*

The biggest problem was the bathroom, which was shared by five other young women. It was a good thing most of us on that floor were young and our bladders were strong, because there was never a time when I needed to use it that someone had not gotten there before me.

The very next day job hunting was on the agenda. It seems that people who had typing skills were in demand at the time, so I was immediately hired by a magazine company in Boston. After filling out the necessary paperwork, I reported for work the following day. It turned out my responsibilities were extremely boring, involving filing and lots of typing, and when my mind wasn't wandering and wondering about the boys, I thought I was doing OK.

The people at work and at the Franklin House tried to reach out to me, but I was having none of it. They would invite me to go out for a drink or a party, but I always refused, claiming I had other plans. I would go to the library and pick up books to read but never finish them. My mom was concerned about my health and wanted to know why I didn't come home more often. She wanted me to think about going back to school, getting involved with my music again, but it all fell on deaf ears.

This went on for six or seven months. I was going through a routine like a robot, sleeping a lot. One morning I slept through the alarm. I was going to be late for work, so I left in a hurry without making my bed, skipped breakfast, and off I went. The person who checked rooms reported to the director that mine was in complete disarray. She also said there had been other days when my bed had not been made, but she had not reported it because she didn't want me to get into trouble. That was a lie, but when I returned that evening there was my notice on my bed ordering me to be gone by morning.

I returned my keys the next morning and left, feeling this must be what it's like getting out of prison. That same day I rented a room in a private home near my job. However, there were more surprises waiting. When I went into work the next morning, I was told my services were no longer required. It seems I was making typing errors and not correcting them along with not following through on assignments.

In the next two years I had many jobs and kept losing them for the same reasons. Finally, I concluded I should take a position where very little was required of me and got a job as a receptionist at General Electric. They were looking for someone who had a pleasing voice. I honestly believed I could handle it.

I also found a new apartment closer to work and roomed with two other girls, who were secretaries. They accepted me and never questioned that I was anything but a young woman looking for a place to settle in. I continued protecting myself with iron gates so high no one could get in, nor could I get out. Things went fine at work for about four months. However, I was not sleeping well, so at night I would get up, rent a car, and go down to

Cape Cod, which is a good two-hour drive, then come back the next morning. I never gave a second thought that my roommates might be wondering or questioning where I was.

My boss was a gentleman by the name of Mr. Smith. He called me into the office one day and asked, "Is there anything you would like to discuss regarding your job here at GE?"

"No."

"Is there anything in general you would like to talk to me about?"

Again I said no.

"Are you happy working here, and do you like your job?"

"Yes, I do."

"Are there any problems with your colleagues?"

"No."

"Is there a reason you are always late getting back from lunch, and are you aware that you're taking more time than is allotted at breaks?"

"Sometimes I do lose track of the time, and I will certainly try to do better in the future."

"You are doing a good job when you are here, but there are other people in the office complaining that you are not reliable. I would really like to keep you on, but if you continue this pattern of not showing up on time, I am going to have to let you go."

Apparently my pattern continued, because once again I was called into Mr. Smith's office.

"I am afraid nothing has changed," he said, "and I have no choice but to let you go. I know you are suffering and obviously you choose not to talk about it, and I respect that, but I am wondering if you will do something for me."

He caught me off guard when he then presented me with a book written by Jimmy Piersall, who was a baseball player for the Boston Red Sox at the time.

"You need to read this. Can you promise me you will?

"Yes, I will."

I thanked him for his kindness and left with the feeling I had let him down. This was the first time since the boys left that I had felt anything for anybody else. I recognized he had an office to run and my actions were disrupting the flow of that well-oiled machine. He had been more than patient with me and somehow his kindness had made a crack in my iron-gated wall.

By now it was about three o'clock in the afternoon and I decided to walk back to the apartment. When I arrived, there was a note on the dining room table saying the girls needed to talk to me and would I please wait before I disappeared into the night. *Strange phrase*, I thought.

CHAPTER 25

The Hospital

I WAITED FOR my roommates on the steps outside of the apartment. As I saw them approaching, I could sense by the look on their faces this was far more serious than I had anticipated. I wondered, *What have I done?*

We all went inside and the girls sat down on the sofa and started by telling me they had talked it over and decided I needed to leave. They could tell by the look on my face I was shocked by what I had just heard. Tears began welling up in my eyes, but I got the courage to ask why. They looked at each other and said, "She doesn't have a clue."

Their expressions softened a bit and one of them added, "It was not an easy decision, but we have been worried about safety issues."

"Safety issues?" I asked. "What in the world are you talking about?"

"Well, let's start with this morning. Do you realize after you used the ironing board you did not turn the iron off and within the last two weeks you left the apartment three times and did not lock the door? We cannot go to work and worry about having to come home at lunchtime to check and see everything is in order. We also worry about being burglarized. Do you realize these are serious safety issues?"

"Of course I do, and I hope you don't think I did any of this on purpose."

"We didn't know what to think. And we also didn't know what to think when we asked you to join us, whether it was to go bowling or out to dinner you always refused. We began to wonder when you disappeared at night where you were going and what were you up to, because you never offered any explanation. You never joined us for dinner nor offered to make dinner. You never did your share of housework. We know nothing about you or your family, and you were never around on the weekends. We wanted a room-mate, not a boarder."

As I sat there and listened, it felt as though they were talking about another person, but nothing they were saying could I refute. I quickly recognized there wasn't anything I could do or say that would change their minds, and through my tears I asked if I could stay at the apartment that night and leave the next day. They agreed and added, "We are sorry it didn't work out."

I needed to go out for a walk to clear my head. The meltdown was coming. I could feel it as I walked out of the apartment. I had just lost my job, again. I no longer had a place to live. And the knowledge that I truly did not remember doing any of those things brought an added sense of vulnerability.

It was still light as I stepped outside and began walking up the street, but my tears prevented me from seeing where I was going. I found a bench and sat there as the tears continued to flow. I shook uncontrollably. A stranger passing by asked, "Is there anything I can do for you? Are you going to be all right? You know, it is getting dark, and it probably would be safer if you found some place to go, because sitting here alone is not a good idea, especially in your condition."

"Thank you for your concern, but I am just waiting to hail a cab."

Without another word she sat down beside me and waited until one came. She wished me well and made sure I was safely inside before she left. The driver asked where I wanted to go and, for whatever reason, I said, "The hospital."

"Which one?" he asked.

"I don't know. The closest."

When he dropped me off he said, "Good luck, lady."

I walked inside and up to the front desk, still feeling out of control. I asked if I could see a doctor. The man behind the desk looked more like a football player than a nurse. He asked me to take a seat in the lobby and said he would send someone over as soon as he could.

Some things happen in life that will leave an indelible imprint on your consciousness, and the following episode, with the doctor, was one of those events. I remember every nuance, every detail, like it was happening right now.

When the doctor appeared, he sat opposite me in a wingback chair with his ankle over his left knee. He wore a typical doctor's white lab coat. I remember he had reddish hair and blue eyes that seemed to stare into my very soul. He first asked if I was on drugs. By now my adrenaline was running wildly and I could not stop crying. I tried to answer his question, but nothing came out, so I nodded no.

"Why are you here?"

The tears kept coming and now my whole body was shaking. I have no idea how long it took me to calm down, but I knew that if I didn't respond, I was not going to get any help, so I told him I had gotten kicked out of my apartment and lost my job and had no place to go. I asked if I could sleep at the hospital that night. He answered with an emphatic no. "Do you have any idea where you are?"

"I am at a hospital."

"Do you know what hospital this is?"

"No, I do not. I just asked the cabdriver to drop me off at the nearest one."

"Well, my dear, you are at the Boston Psychiatric Hospital."

I was exhausted and just wanted to lie down somewhere. I asked again if I could stay the night and again he said no. He asked why I didn't go to a hotel, and I told him I did not feel safe in my condition and did not have any money.

I finally got up nerve enough to ask why it wasn't possible for me to stay. In a very authoritative voice and in great detail he explained, "This is a psychiatric hospital and there are two wards, one being for patients who are out of control, need to be medicated, and are up and down all night, talking to themselves or to the walls, some walking around naked, and if I had a bed you could have tonight they would steal the clothes right off your back. The other ward is far more serious, filled with patients who have raped, murdered, or who are criminally insane, and putting you in there is out of the question."

If it was his intention to frighten me, he had succeeded. The cobwebs in my brain were starting to clear and I began to realize I was walking down a road where there was no detour.

He told me he needed to get back to his patients. I said I understood but asked if he had a few minutes. Reluctantly, he replied, "What is it now?"

"In your opinion, do you think I need psychiatric help?"

"You are the only one who can determine that, and because you have not shared what is really going on, you probably should consider making an appointment at the clinic next door for an evaluation."

He left as abruptly as he had come, saying, "You need to leave."

By now it was very late, and as I sat there thinking about the terrors of the night and where I was going to go, I apparently fell asleep. It was about seven o'clock in the morning when a male nurse gently woke me up. I apologized, got up, and left.

I knew the girls would not be leaving for work until about eight thirty, so I went to a nearby church and just sat there looking at the altar. A phrase came to mind: *be not afraid, be not afraid, be not afraid.*

I called my mom and asked her to come pick me up at the apartment and told her I would fill her in on the way back home.

CHAPTER 26

Aha Moment

WHEN MOM PICKED me up, suitcase in hand, one of the first things she said was that I did not look well and was too thin. She had been worried sick, she added, and as I listened to her many legitimate concerns, I began to understand the ripple effect my actions were having on her.

"I know, and I am sorry my life has been crazy lately, but could we talk about this a little later, because right now I am mentally and physically exhausted."

I heard her say, "I understand," then sleep refused to wait any longer.

After we arrived home, I felt she was entitled to an explanation, so we talked about what had happened at work and the apartment. I needed to sugarcoat everything quite a bit for her not to overreact. When she noticed after a half hour that I was getting tired, she offered to continue our conversation later after I got some sleep.

"I am just happy you are safe."

And sleep I did, off and on for the next three days. Home was a haven of comfort and love. However, my responsibility, I knew, was to reassess and clean out the dust and confusion of where I was and where I was headed. Mom and I had several conversations in the weeks ahead, and in one of those conversations she asked why I was so angry with her when she was only trying to help.

"Sorry, it is not you I am angry with."

I did still hold some hostile feelings because of the way she had treated George Sr. However, it was because of those conversations that I finally came to understand that my mother never stopped being a mother. And that was how our healing process began.

There were many days I went out and just walked around the neighborhood. As I went past the park one day, I remembered when I was young and how, after much pleading, my mom would allow me to take my sled there on snowy days. I would stay until hunger took over. I remembered watching squirrels in the fall gathering nuts for the winter and how they would scurry about looking for places to bury them. I remembered how that same park would burst into colors with the onset of autumn and I would sit under the oak tree and do my homework. I also remembered as I went past the candy store how grown up I felt when Mom said I was old enough to walk down there all by myself. There was a certain peace I found in reminiscing about all the good times when I was little. However, there were other days when I would just walk as if I were brain-dead and not realize I had strayed so far away from the house.

One day I informed Mom I planned to head down to the Cape because I needed to be near the ocean. I knew she would understand because she loved the ocean as much as I did. I also assured her I would return home before dark.

The roaring of the sea always had a calming effect on me. I would sit for hours on the dunes watching the waves rolling in and out and thinking of the people who had walked on the seashore over thousands of years. There were many times the thought of just walking into the ocean and never coming back crossed my mind.

As I drove home, my thoughts were about the boys. I wondered if they would ever know how much they were loved.

Then there were days I would find a church just to sit and feel the presence of the Deity and the comfort of knowing this was a house of God and here I would not be judged. Sometimes, if the priest or minister was there, he would remember me from singing either at a wedding or funeral and would ask if there was anything he could do for me. I would ask permission just to sit for a few moments, and the answer was always yes.

And so it went for several weeks, which then turned into months as I tried to break out of the prison of fear in which I had put myself. As I chastised my nonaction, I prayed again and again for the courage to move on.

In one conversation I had with my mom, she was concerned about my moving back to the Boston area. Somehow I had to allay her fears, but I knew it would take some time.

"Mom, I will not go until I feel I am able to take care of myself, and what happened in the past will never happen again."

"How are you going to do that?"

I promised her I would reach out for help.

"But you haven't done that yet."

"You're right, but it is next on my agenda."

"Will you let me know when you do?"

"Of course I will."

I followed through the next week by calling the outpatient clinic at the Boston Psychiatric Hospital and setting up an appointment for one month later. Mom asked why so long, and I told her it was the first availability. She wanted to go with me and ordinarily I would have said no, but because I could sense the pain and anguish I had caused, my answer was "Yes, of course, you can come with me."

I think she probably did not trust me to follow through, and certainly I had earned her distrust from all the broken promises I had racked up in the last few years. About that time I finally picked up the book my former boss had given me. I wasn't particularly interested in baseball, but I heard his words reverberate in my head—"You need to read this"—and when I started to immerse myself in the pages of *Fear Strikes Out*, it became clear to me why

Mr. Smith, in his wisdom, had asked me to give him my solemn promise that I would follow through.

With the help of sportswriter Al Hirshberg, Jimmy Piersall writes about his battle with mental illness. Page after page—217 of them, to be exact—I was enthralled and finished it in three hours. In order to fully comprehend the complexity of his illness, however, I had to read it several times.

I was trying to figure out his weird actions, his mood swings. There was much less known in the 1950s about mental illness. Doctors at the time reported that Piersall had had a mental breakdown, but if they were diagnosing him today, they would say he was bipolar. He was acting out on the ball field and could not control his emotional outbursts. In 1952 he was demoted to the minors, but when his bad behavior continued, on and off the field, he entered a mental hospital. With excellent treatment and the support of his doctors, wife, family, fans, and the Red Sox team, he eventually returned to the major leagues and became one of the top players in baseball.

There were many symptoms he experienced that I could not relate to, like his antics on the field, and his manic behavior, his emotional outbursts, but there were other actions I definitely could relate to, and it was scaring me. He was taking flight; I was taking flight. He couldn't sleep; I couldn't sleep. He was losing weight; I was losing weight. He couldn't focus; I couldn't focus. There were other incidents for me. I was losing jobs and moving around a lot. I had socially isolated myself and was putting myself in jeopardy by forgetting fundamental rules for safety. In other words, I seemed to be headed for a mental breakdown at a breakneck speed that would soon be out of control. And if I continued, I feared I, too, might be taken away in a straitjacket.

I'm sure you're familiar with the idea of a lightbulb going off over your head when a thought comes to you. However, for me it was multiple illuminating lights all going off at the same time, so many, in fact, that my brain could not assimilate the brightness all at once. Some people use the expression *aha moment*. Well, my aha moment became a tsunami aha moment, causing the billions of cells in my head to crash into each other, all wanting center stage to bring out what I should've recognized and put into action long before now.

After reading Piersall's book I understood that I had looked at myself as a victim. Yes, it is true, like so many others during the 1950s I was a victim of a social injustice that I had no control over, but what I did have control over was how I would face and deal with my depression after losing the boys. I needed to find meaning in what I had been through and choose a different path. There was no way around it. Remaining locked in the past was not going to bring the boys back. And taking flight was no longer an option. If I had a nervous breakdown, my dream of seeing the boys again someday would die. So, once again, the boys became an impetus for me to regain control over my life.

The second thing I recognized was that I had allowed the people who had treated me in a negative manner to win. I could not do anything about the hate and bigotry that were destroying so many people's lives at the time, but I would be damned if they were going to continue to crush mine. I began to realize, too, that I was multiplying my pain by judging myself over and over, that somehow I had to turn my pain and suffering around to work for me instead of against me. I didn't care how long it would take me. Finally, I could see that I needed to accept that the boys were gone and that there was nothing that could be any worse than what I had already been through.

For the first time in a long time, my head was clear and my thoughts were focused on the future. I didn't quite know how I would get there, but there was no question in my mind that I had to take control, that no one could do it for me. I wanted to thank Mr. Smith for opening the crack in my iron gate. I wanted to thank Jimmy Piersall for writing about his heartbreaking journey and how it had impacted my life. Instead I thanked my higher power for sending me those two angels when I needed them. Again the phrase that kept coming back to me was "Be not afraid, be not afraid."

CHAPTER 27

Evaluation

I HAD A week to prepare before heading in for my psychiatric evaluation. The words of the doctor I had talked with when I had my meltdown kept reverberating in my head—that I had not shared with him what was really going on, and that the only way I was going to get through this was to hold nothing back and be completely honest. *Keep remembering that, Deborah. Be completely honest and hold nothing back.*

I kept trying to convince my mom I had turned a corner, but I knew it was going to take some time to rebuild the bridges of trust I had damaged over the last several years. I hoped the psychiatric evaluation would bring her some comfort. It was important to me that she not have to live with fear and uncertainty about me when I moved out. I owed her that.

In the meantime, I had set my future in motion by making a few phone calls and arranging appointments to look for a place to live in Boston. At this point I was the only one who knew my head had cleared, my confidence was back, and my indulging in self-pity was at an end. My job now was to convince whatever doctor I was going to be talking to, and my mom, that I was going to be OK.

Finally the day of the evaluation arrived. As we drove into Boston, Mom asked if I was nervous.

"No, not at all," I said.

Who was I kidding? The jumping beans in my stomach were having a field day. I was keenly aware my future was in the hands of one person and that how I handled myself would determine whether I would be able to follow through with the appointments I had set up for the following day.

I had paid extra attention to how I looked. I tried to dress conservatively with a little flair and spent extra time putting on a bit of makeup. After signing in at the reception desk, I filled out the necessary paperwork and answered the questions as honestly as I could. I kept reassuring myself, *You can do this, Deborah. You can do this. Whatever it takes, whatever questions he asks you, you can do this.*

When the nurse called my name, I looked at Mom and smiled. She smiled in return. I got up and dropped the magazine I had been trying to read, then nearly tripped over the person sitting next to me, who had his feet sprawled out in front of him. The nurse called my name a little louder. "I am here," I answered.

I followed her into what I assumed would be a doctor's office. Instead, it was a large room with seven doctors sitting in a circle. I was greeted warmly by another doctor, who was standing. He introduced himself, then led me to an empty chair and asked me to please sit down. He pulled another chair next to mine and then explained that each doctor would be asking me questions and that I was to answer to the best of my ability. It was extremely important, he added, for me to be honest at all times. "Do you have any questions?"

My first reaction to this setup, with all those doctors, was terror, but I also was starting to feel frustrated because I had not been informed ahead of time how I was going to be evaluated. If their purpose was to throw me off guard, they had succeeded.

As a singer I was used to putting on a good performance and that is exactly what they were going to get today, not a good but a great performance, an honest one. I quickly slipped into my singer's robe, where I had a better chance to control my nervousness and would not be easily intimidated by the questions they asked. I took a deep breath and said that I had no questions.

"Let's get started," the leader said and, with clipboard in hand, he got things rolling. "Tell me a little about yourself."

I then talked about my childhood and what a great family I had. I talked about my love of music and some of my goals. When I began to explain the darker period of my life and all of the difficult decisions I'd had to make regarding George Sr. and the details of George and David's adoption, I could feel myself losing control. *Losing control is not an option*, I screamed to myself. *They can see your vulnerability, but do not lose control.* I stopped talking for just a few seconds, asked for a glass of water, took a deep breath, and continued on. When I finished, the doctor with the clipboard thanked me and asked his next question: "Why are you here?"

"I am here because I want to move on with my life and feel I have learned from my mistakes, and I need a positive evaluation to do that."

Now the other doctors started to fire questions at me, one right after another.

"How did you know you were in trouble?"

"I should have recognized I was in trouble long before the episode with my roommates, because I had lost several jobs and had moved several times, but I was too busy running from myself. However, it was the day they informed me I would have to leave because they were concerned about some safety issues. It seems I was forgetting to lock the door when I went to work and had left the iron on several times, and it frightened me, because I did not remember any of it. It was on that same day that I had a meltdown and was told by a doctor, at this hospital, I should seek help here at the clinic. It was then that I realized I needed help."

"Did it make you angry when they asked you to leave?"

"No, I was hurt but understood their concerns, and as I have said, it frightened me that I did not remember."

"Who are you angry at?"

"Why would I be angry at anyone else but myself?"

"Why are you angry at yourself?"

"Because I could not find another way to protect my boys, other than adoption."

"Did you ever try to commit suicide?"

"Yes, once."

"What stopped you?"

"My boys. I made a vow on that day that when they were twenty-four and twenty-five I would find them."

"How do you intend to find them?"

"I will cross that bridge when they are twenty-four and twenty-five."

"What turned you around?"

"There is certainly more than one thing, but it is when I read a book by Jimmy Piersall the baseball player and learned if I did not turn my life in another direction, I, too, would have a mental breakdown. And, frankly, I would call reading his book a wake-up call. Another wake-up call is when I became aware of the effect my actions were having on my family, especially my mom."

"What plans do you have in place to move on?"

"I plan to move back to Boston, find a job, and decide if I want to go back to school, become a social worker, and get back to living a productive life. I know it won't be easy, but I will take one step at a time."

"You came in the hospital four weeks ago looking for help and the report we have from the doctor is you were distraught and out of control. You had been fired from your job and had no place to live. Can you explain how in four weeks you now feel ready to be on your own?"

"Yes, you are absolutely right. It has been only four weeks. However, in those four weeks I have had time to reflect. I have had time to understand I was in denial by not accepting the fact that George and David had been adopted. I have had time to understand why I was taking flight. I had time to understand what my family, especially my parents, were going through because of my inability to deal with my particular issues. I have had time to understand I was allowing myself to become a victim, and because of all those realizations, I feel I have made a passage to understanding what lies ahead."

The questions kept coming and I tried to answer each one with a message of hope.

One of the last questions they asked me was "What have you learned from your experiences?"

"I think one of the biggest lessons I've learned and still am learning is the past is a part of me, but not all of me, and if I get stuck in my emotional grief I cannot move on. I've learned I need to pick up the pieces of my life and make those pieces work for me instead of against me. I've learned if the present keeps quarreling with my past, I can have no future. I've learned the hope of connecting with the boys one day depends on my determination and ability to make some kind of success of my life. There is no question in my mind that the lessons I have learned will propel me to succeed in the future."

As I was answering the last question, I did not notice but my voice rose with enthusiasm and passion. When I finished there was absolute silence. That frightened me. Even though I knew I had not lost control, I feared that they thought I had.

The lead doctor thanked me and said I could go. However, I timidly asked if I could ask a question first and he replied, "Of course."

"When will a determination be made regarding the evaluation?"

"In a week or so."

I then rose further out of my timidity and asked another question: "Would it be possible to talk to my mother before we leave and give her a summary of the evaluation—whether it is positive or negative?"

His answer surprised me.

"If you are willing to wait a couple of hours, the other doctors and I will put our heads together and make a decision."

"Of course we will wait, and thank you."

I went back into the waiting room and looked at my mom. She had desperation written all over her face. When she saw me approaching, she lit up and asked how everything went. I suggested we find a place to have lunch and then return so that the doctors could talk to her. We walked several blocks, but there were no restaurants close by and I could see Mom was getting tired, so we headed back to the hospital and ended up having lunch in the cafeteria. The surroundings were not conducive to any kind of a private conversation, so I suggested we walk down to the lobby and wait there. She agreed.

She again asked me how things had gone with the doctors, and I told her I had no idea. I also promised I would abide by whatever decision they came to, whether positive or negative, and I expected her to do the same. Mom went into what-ifs. I asked her please not to do that, because before we made any decisions or plans we needed to hear the results of the evaluation.

We went back to the waiting room, and two hours started turning into three. Finally, Mom was called in. I thought to myself, *What in the world am I doing here?* and swore that, no matter what happened, I would never, ever put myself in that position again.

When Mom came out of the office I could not tell by the look on her face what had happened. Knowing that we needed to get home before the traffic became insane, we avoided the topic till we were out of Boston. Finally, I asked what the doctor had said.

She began by saying she didn't totally agree with his assessment but, per our agreement, she would abide by their evaluation.

"Mom, can you be a little more specific?"

She explained that the doctors would be submitting a written evaluation in a couple of weeks, but they all agreed that I was going to be fine. "They told me I should not worry about you. However, they did suggest you should consider seeing someone on a regular basis."

I asked if that would relieve some of her anxiety when I moved out.

"Absolutely," she said.

My strategy had paid off. Now I could focus on my dream of one day reconnecting with George and David.

CHAPTER 28

The Apartment

MOVING ON AND making plans for whatever the future held became my top priorities. I looked at this as a new beginning and was determined to focus on the positive.

First on the agenda was finding a place to live in the Boston area. I had arranged to look at four apartments that fit the location and price range I was looking for.

By 4:00 p.m. the following day, I still had not found anything and was beginning to grow impatient. With the first place, I was not happy with the neighborhood; the second, there was no transportation available; and the third, I was uncomfortable with the lack of security. There was one more possibility for the day. When I finally reached one of the tenants, whose name was Ginny, she informed me there would be five other people living in the apartment but added, "Please don't let that scare you. Our place is exceptionally spacious, beautifully decorated, and I would encourage you to at least take the time to see for yourself."

"I will be over in twenty minutes, and by the way, my name is Deb."

The first positive was that the apartment was in an excellent neighborhood near Boston University, and the subway was nearby. As I approached the building, I was impressed with the security measures. You could only get in the building through the front door, which had enormous visibility from the street, and as you continued into the foyer there were only numbers on the mailboxes. I followed the instructions Ginny had given me to push the button below mailbox number 102, and when I announced who I was, she pushed a buzzer to let me in and greeted me with a cheery "hello." We chatted for a few minutes, then she proceeded to show me around.

The spaciousness of the apartment was indeed impressive. I liked the way the bedrooms were separated from each other, one being in front and the other two off a long hallway that led to the back of the apartment. There was a huge kitchen to the left and an oversized living room to the right, along with a large TV and a stereo. It was all decorated in a fashionable, contemporary style. She explained there were two people to each bedroom. Even with two twin beds, the rooms were more spacious than mine at home.

As we continued, I noticed there was only one bathroom and asked her how in the world, with six females, that could possibly work. She smiled and said, "Sometimes it can be tricky, but for the most part it seems to work out because three of the girls work in hospitals, as nurses, one works in a lab, and the other one is attending Boston University, which means we are using the bathroom at different times of the day and night. If you are interested in the apartment, you should also be aware of what will be expected of you. We have teams of two, working together. The cleaning of the apartment is on a rotating basis, and at no time does any one team have to clean the bathroom and kitchen at the same time. We all pitch in for food expenses, and the shopping is done in pairs of two. I have lived here for three years, and I couldn't be happier."

I was greatly impressed with the organization and logistics these young women had put in place and was drawn to her enthusiasm. We talked for a long while and finally she asked if I was interested in the apartment.

"Yes, I am very interested."

"You will need to make an appointment to meet the other girls. I will get back to you with a time that is convenient for the rest of the tenants."

I received a phone call the next day and Ginny said she'd talked to her other roommates, they trusted her recommendation, and I could move in by the first of next month.

Now I had to gently inform Mom of my plans and invite her to come and see where I would be living and meet the other girls. She asked many questions and was satisfied with the information I provided her regarding safety. I also, in line with our agreement, made an appointment to see a therapist the week before I was scheduled to move. "I am pleased you followed through," she said.

I promised I would let her know how things went.

The Boston Psychiatric Hospital had given me a list of doctors, and I chose one close to where I would to be living. My first appointment did not go very well. I suppose you could say the connection was dysfunctional right from the beginning. Within the first fifteen minutes the doctor did most of the talking and very little listening and told me I should take some pills he was going to prescribe for me.

That did it. I wanted to get up and walk out of his office, but instead just sat there until my hour was over. I then smiled sweetly and said, "Thank you for your time," and left.

I worried that I had overreacted, but my instincts told me I was doing the right thing. Later, I called my mom and told her what had happened. After much discussion, I promised her that if I needed help or someone to talk to I would go back to the clinic.

Next on the agenda was finding a job. This was going to be a little tricky because in my other, mixed-up life, I had managed to fall down a flight of stairs, damaging my coccyx bone. My family doctor had advised me to find a job where I did not have to sit eight hours a day. I went on several interviews but was unsuccessful in finding anything full-time, so I decided to take a part-time spot at Radio Shack to tide me over for the time being.

After many interviews I finally landed a position as office manager with a company out of New York called Wells Television. It had set up a satellite office in Brookline, just outside the city, that provided and serviced televisions for hospitals and hotels in the greater Boston area. The job was challenging enough to keep me sane and allowed me to move around; I had purchased a special cushion with a hole in the middle for when I needed to sit down.

By then I had settled into the apartment, and things seemed to be working out just fine. I was still concerned about the bathroom situation, but learned quickly that the girls only used it for their basic needs. They washed their hair in the kitchen sink, dressed and put their makeup on in their bedrooms. I was still amazed that it all worked out without our running into each other.

It had been several years since I had last seen George and David. I continued to wonder how they were doing, what they looked like, whether they were happy. I prayed for them every night. The vision that I would see them one day kept me focused, but how I wished I could make a phone call to the adoptive mom and dad. The adoption system at that time was tightly closed. How much easier it would have been for all of us if we had been able to stay connected.

CHAPTER 29

John

THE RELATIONSHIP WITH my family had taken on a new veneer. In short, we were trying to bury the past by never talking about it. We lived in an era in which unpleasant things were rarely discussed—things like spousal abuse, incest, prejudice, child abuse, mental illness, unwanted pregnancies, divorce, sexually transmitted diseases, just to mention a few. All of the above became secrets that would come back to haunt many of us.

For me, the return to some kind of normalcy was a relief. I was becoming a functioning person once again, and the routine of holding down a job was a strong stabilizing factor in my life.

I was taking advantage of everything a big city had to offer. The Boston Public Library was one of my favorite places to go when I wasn't headed home for the weekend. I would spend many hours reading and enjoying the solitude of this impressive facility. At the time I was not aware that the library, which is located in Copley Square, was one of the best in the United States. I also began attending concerts at Symphony Hall, which filled a void in my soul that had existed for a long time. Symphony Hall was then and still is among the three best-sounding concert halls in the world. I could only afford the inexpensive seats, but no matter where I sat, there was absolutely no differ-ence in the quality of the sound that filled that magnificent auditorium.

However, there were certain entry points into my soul that remained locked, graced with signs that said, DO NOT ENTER. I was great at listening and helping other people with problems they might be having, but whenever they would ask any personal questions, I became very good at changing the subject to avoid answering.

The door to dating had also been slammed shut a long time ago. Janice, with whom I shared a room, asked one day, "Why do you get angry when someone asks you out?"

"Thanks for bringing that to my attention," I replied, "because I was not aware that I came across as getting angry when someone asks me out. Looks like I am just not ready to start dating yet. I really do enjoy my free time on the weekends and not having to answer to anyone." She seemed satisfied with my answer. "Is there anything else you would like to talk about?"

"As a matter of fact there is," she said. "The girls wanted me to mention that we are having a get-together in a couple of weeks and we all have friends we would like you to meet. What do you say?"

"Of course, I would love to."

I really had no interest at all, but I was trying hard not to repeat the mistakes of the past, like not joining in and interacting with the other girls in the apartment.

Meanwhile, my job was a haven of responsibility where I could go every day and get lost in the minutiae, keeping my mind from wandering and wondering how my boys were. The general manager, Lenny Gibson, who was in and out of the office, had explained that it was my job as office manager to ensure that everything ran smoothly, and because it was a one-person office, my duties ran from secretarial to billing to scheduling and anything else he asked me to do.

One of my duties was to file a report with the New York office each night after the three troubleshooters who rented out and took care of the televisions checked in at the end of the day.

Sometimes, if they did not act in a businesslike manner, I would just hang up. I was quickly tagged "No Nonsense Deb," which was fine with me. There was one troubleshooter named John who always behaved professionally and never kept me on the phone longer than necessary. One night when he reported in, he asked if he could ask me a question not related to work. *Oh boy*, I thought to myself, *here it comes. He's going to ask me out.* Much to my surprise, he wanted to know my thoughts regarding President Kennedy. I told him I was still waiting for Henry and Phil to check in and needed to keep the lines open but would be happy to discuss this another time. Several weeks passed without John mentioning it again.

It was mid-February and we had just had a serious nor'easter snowstorm that had shut down the whole city. I missed a couple of days of work. Once I could finally get in to the office, we were all trying to catch up, and there were some roads on the outskirts of Boston where the servicemen were still having a hard time getting through to the hospitals, which meant we were all working late into the night.

I decided to go in the next day, which was a Saturday, to take care of some unfinished details. I knew the office would be closed and there would be no interruptions. As I was walking up the stairs the following morning, I heard the hum of what sounded like a vacuum cleaner. When I opened the door, I was surprised to see John cleaning the office and a girl who I assumed was his daughter sleeping on the floor, covered in what looked like a sleeping bag. When he shut down the vacuum, she immediately woke up, looked up at me, smiled, and said, "Hi, my name is Denise."

"Nice to meet you, Denise, and how old are you?"

Without any hesitation she replied, "I am almost four, but right now I am three and a half." She then asked, "How old are you?"

"I am probably around the same age as your dad."

"Dad, how old are you?" she asked.

"Are you asking too many questions?" he replied.

"You told me it is the only way I am going to learn."

Because I could see John was becoming flustered, I wanted to change the direction of the conversation and asked, "So, Denise, what do you like best about school?"

"Everything," she said. "I like reading, but we don't read that much because there are only two of us who know how, but sometimes when everyone has gone home and I am waiting for my dad to pick me up, Mrs. Gill will give me books to read and take home."

And from that point on she talked nonstop. I learned all eight of her classmates' names, what they looked like, who she liked, and who she didn't like. Once she started telling me about what her teacher wore every day, her father interrupted, saying, "Denise, I think Deb came into the office to work today and I think it would be nice if you let her do that, don't you?"

"OK, Dad, but is it OK if I ask one more question? Please, just one more?"

"Just one more, but that is it."

"Are you married?"

"No, I am not married."

I could see John was smiling but could tell he was embarrassed, and when he started to say something, I stopped him: "John, it's OK. She is just being who she is, which, by the way, is amazing. You have one articulate, bright, precocious child on your hands."

"I sure do," he said. "I sure do."

John then explained that on the weekend he cleaned a couple of banks around the area, along with our office, and that he would be through in a couple of minutes. By this time Denise was sitting at my desk having a great time with the coloring books her dad had brought to keep her busy. John and I chatted a bit about his daughter, who, he told me, was in a private preschool during the day.

"Sounds like your life is extremely busy," I said.

"I like busy," he responded.

I smiled and said, "Well, I think I better get to work."

"Me too."

As he was finishing up, I began working at my boss's desk and could not help but overhear the chatter between father and daughter. Denise continued talking, but John never lost patience with her barrage of questions. It was clear that the connection between the two of them was special.

Realizing I had not gotten back to him about President Kennedy, I interrupted their conversation and began to apologize, but he said, "I would still like to have that conversation about JFK. Would you be willing to do that by phone?"

"Of course. That would be fine. When would be a good time for me to call?"

"After I put Denise to bed, so I would say any evening after 7:30 p.m."

He wrote his number down and I told him that I would call the following week. As they left the office I was filled with thoughts about the bond between the two of them but was also overcome with sadness that George and David never had the same connection with their dad. On the other side of the coin, hopefully they were getting that now.

It was very unusual in the early 1960s that a man would end up with custody of a child. I was curious about the circumstances that had brought that about. Soon my attention turned back to work without my recognizing that it had been the first time in a very long while that I had taken an interest in anyone else other than the boys and my family.

CHAPTER 30

The Party

I KEPT PUTTING off calling John, telling myself I did not have to follow through, but the motto my dad had taught the boys, "Promises made are promises kept," and the fact that I had been brought up with the understanding that your word is your bond, made it impossible for me not to make that call. Finally, I found the courage to pick up the phone the following week and was relieved when John answered and said, "I have been running late because of the snow and was just finishing up reading Denise her bedtime story. Can I call you back in about fifteen minutes?"

"Of course."

I gave him my number without any hesitation and thought to myself, *That was easy*, because up to this point no one had my number except my family and my boss, Lenny.

The first thing John did when he called back was to apologize. I told him there was no apology needed. "By the way," he said, "I really appreciated the way you handled my precocious daughter last week at the office."

"Not a problem," I responded. "She certainly is one special little girl."

"Yes, she is."

The conversation that followed was filled with information about his family: the fact that he'd been born in Springfield, Massachusetts, and had three sisters and a brother; that he was attending Newman Prep in Boston. As I began to feel a little more comfortable, I asked, "So why Newman Prep?"

"Well, when I graduated from high school there were no finances for me to attend college, so my dad sent me to trade school, and when I applied to Northeastern, I was told I did not have the necessary credits to attend. So I am going to Newman Prep for a year to acquire credits in math and English. My goal is to continue on at Northeastern and eventually get my degree in engineering."

"Where do you find time for everything?" I asked.

"No big deal," he said.

He makes everything sound so simple, I thought.

"So, John, how can I help you?"

"Well, during this past election I was unable to vote because when I moved from Springfield to Boston I neglected to register. But even if I had, the fact that I didn't know enough about either candidate would have prevented me from casting an educated vote. So, what I am attempting to do is learn as much as I can about President Kennedy's plans for the future and what he hopes to achieve in the next few years. I tried talking to Lenny, but he wasn't much help and suggested I talk to you. If I am being presumptuous, please let me know."

"Lenny gives me more credit on being knowledgeable in this area than I am, but I am happy to share with you what I know so far."

"That would be great. I'd love to hear it."

"During Kennedy's campaign he promised to deal with unemployment in depressed areas, which he has done. He promised to improve education, medical care, and is putting some initiatives together to present to Congress. He promised civil rights for the nation's black minority and is working on legislation now. He encouraged more scientific development and has followed through by expanding the space program. He promised to set up some kind of Peace Corps and did that three months after he became president. Right now that is all I can remember. Is that the kind of information you were looking for?"

"That is exactly what I was looking for. Thanks so much for your input and taking the time to share. And now I will say good night, Deb."

"Good night, John."

Interesting person, I thought.

* * *

FOR THE NEXT three weeks, the routine at the office remained the same: Lenny trying to figure out problems with the equipment that the troubleshooters had been unable to resolve; Henry, John, and Phil calling in their reports at the end of the day, always complaining about how maddening the traffic was. When John reported in, the conversation would always end with a question like "How was your day? Did you get stuck in the snow?" I was learning quickly that he had an exceptional sense of humor, because when he asked about the snow, for instance, it was June. He made me laugh. I began to feel comfortable and at ease around him because he never asked any personal questions, never pressured me or asked me out.

One day he mentioned that his last call was at a hospital near the office, so from then on he would be dropping off his reports every Friday in person. After he did, he would stay for a little while and ask if I was looking forward to the weekend, was I doing anything special. I found myself asking how his daughter was doing and how school was going. We would chat a little while longer until he had to leave to pick Denise up at day care. In the back of my mind I was aware this was one special, unique, caring guy, but the information had not found its way to my conscious brain yet. It was lying dormant, waiting for an event to open the door a little further.

* * *

IT WAS TIME for the get-together at the apartment to take place, and I was not looking forward to it. My roommate informed me I could invite two or three people, and she was hoping they would be of the opposite sex. Thoughts of taking flight occurred to me, but having gone down that road with my former roommates, I decided to stay the course.

I figured that if I invited Henry and John, at least there would be someone there I knew and could talk to. I asked John first and he wasn't sure he could make it, because of his daughter but said if he was able to get a babysitter he would definitely be there. That night when Henry called in to give his report for the day, I invited him also and he accepted immediately. I made it clear it was an invitation from all my roommates.

From the preparations the girls were making for the coming Saturday, it quickly became apparent it was going to be a genuine party. I had no objections to that, but why, I wondered, did they call it a "get-together"? I had learned by now to go with the flow and not question the small stuff. I warned the girls that I did not drink. The taste of hard liquor, beer, or wine made me sick and I asked the girls to not tease me about it. They all said they would never do that. I was learning to be honest and up front with people. This was better, I had begun to realize, than leaving them to wonder and speculate.

Ginny had taken over as the party organizer and had given each of us a task to make sure everything ran smoothly. The morning of the party some of us were preparing food and others arranging the apartment with a few balloons and putting out glasses, napkins, putting flowers around, making sure everything was spotless.

"OK, Ginny, we are ready for your inspection," we all said in unison.

As she looked over our apartment, she made the comment, "Well it looks like we are in good shape. You all did a great job, but just remember, girls, the next time it will be someone else's turn to do the organizing."

As the time for guests to arrive approached, Janice kept reminding me I needed to get ready.

"You look fantastic," I replied. "Is there someone special coming tonight?"

"Don't change the subject, Deb, because I will be back in ten minutes and you better be changed, dressed, and ready."

When she returned I said, "OK, Janice, I am changed and dressed. What do you think?"

"Much better, Deb, much better, but are you ready?"

I assured her I was, but certainly did not feel I was ready.

I felt even more uncomfortable as the night progressed, walking around with a glass of cranberry juice as Ginny introduced me to her friends. One was a guy named Tony, who began following me everywhere I went. I was getting more irritated by the moment. The more he drank, the more obnoxious he became.

When I noticed Henry and John coming in, I excused myself and went over to welcome them and showed them around the apartment, introduced them to Janice, and asked her to take good care of them and introduce them to some of her friends.

"Please make yourselves at home," I told them.

I kept moving, going in and out of the kitchen, replacing hors d'oeuvres, but could not shake Tony. Somehow he backed me into a corner and was trying to fill my glass with wine. I refused by putting my hand over the glass. He became more aggressive, putting his arm around my waist. I pulled away and asked him to stop following me.

"I have told you several times I am not interested."

"Why, is there something wrong with me?"

"No, there is nothing wrong with you, but how many more times do I have to tell you that I am not interested?"

By the look on his face I could tell he was not about to back off. I noticed John was heading towards us. He asked if everything was all right. I smiled and shook my head slightly from side to side. He then asked if I would like to dance.

"Of course. I would love to."

Tony piped up: "I saw her first."

That did it. I was about to lose it when John said, "I think you should respect Deb's wishes and back off, cool down, and find someone else you can charm with your good looks."

Tony walked away in a huff and muttered something under his breath. I was relieved by the way John had diffused that situation and thanked him. He then asked, "Would you like to go outside and get some fresh air?"

"Yes," I said, "I would like that."

I grabbed a sweater and as we walked down the front steps, we both commented on what a beautiful night it was. The air was clear, and even though we were in the city, with bright lights, you could see thousands of stars in the sky. I again thanked John for coming to my rescue.

"No big deal," he said. "Glad I was there."

We decided to walk for a little while and John admitted that he too was uncomfortable at parties and the only reason he came was because I had asked. He said he also was not a drinker but did like a nice cold glass of beer on a hot summer day. I mentioned how good it was to get away from the loud music and he agreed. That led to a discussion about the type of music he liked.

"I think I know more about what I don't like. I do not like rock 'n' roll, and I am not sure about the names of any of the groups out there, but I do know I like the sound of Peter, Paul, and Mary, along with the Kingston Trio. I also love certain types of jazz."

"Are you at all interested in classical music?"

"I don't know, because I have never listened to it, but when I have more time and my life settles down, I certainly would like to learn and make sure Denise is exposed to the world of not only music but the art world as well. She is almost four, and Boston is one of the best cultural centers on the East Coast, and we need to start exploring."

When we headed back into the apartment, the music had softened, and John asked if he could have one more dance before he left.

"I think you certainly have earned it."

I was surprised how comfortable I felt in his arms. As we said good night, he thanked me for the invite and especially for the dance. I think something happened that night, but at the time it was not obvious to me that my resolve had softened.

CHAPTER 31

A Door Opens

A COUPLE OF weeks after the party John asked if he could call me at the apartment because he had something he wanted to discuss with me and it did not relate to work. Up to this point he had been respectful, never crossing barriers, and I could not find any reason to say no.

We talked the following night. Apparently Denise had been asking about me. He said they were going to Lake Pearl that coming Saturday and asked if I would like to spend the day with them.

"Where is Lake Pearl?" I asked.

"It is southwest of Boston in the town of Wrentham and about a forty-five-minute drive from where you are. We have never been there before, but Henry tells me it is has picnic tables, plenty of trees for shade, and a beautiful, clear lake," he said. "We were thinking about bringing a lunch."

I was totally unprepared, completely out of my comfort zone. Panic set in and a feeling of inadequacy ran through me. I took several breaths and found the strength to pull myself together.

I asked if I could call him back, saying I had to double-check with my mom to be sure we didn't have plans and would get back to him by the next morning. He said that would be fine.

I then spent half the night trying to figure out what to do, what road to go down. It wasn't until I calmed down that I finally came up with an answer. John was not asking me for a date, only to spend the day with him and his daughter. If I decided to accept, I would need to tell him a little more about myself and explain that I was not looking for any kind of a relationship but would like to develop a friendship. I enjoyed his company, and God knows I needed a friend.

Bright and early the next morning, I called and said, "John, you hardly know anything about me, and before I accept your invitation I want to tell you that I have been married before."

His reply was, "What has happened in the past is over, and unless you need to talk about it, it's of no consequence."

"But I also need you to know that I am not looking for a relationship other than friendship."

"Good, because neither am I."

"Then I would be happy to spend the day with you and Denise."

"Well, that's settled," he said. "I'll say goodbye for now."

John and Denise picked me up around 9:00 a.m. the following Saturday. The weather could not have been better, with only cumulus clouds and the temperature in the low eighties. Once we arrived and began to settle in, Denise asked, "Dad, can I go in the water, please? I need to go in the water. Deb, do you like to swim?"

"Love to swim, Denise. Just give me a couple of minutes and I will join you. Can you do that?"

"OK, because Dad won't let me go in by myself," she replied.

I looked at John to get his approval. "Go ahead," he said. "I will put up the umbrella and join you later."

A half hour went by and no John. When we came out of the water Denise ran up to him, dripping water on his stomach, and said, "Dad, wake up. Is it time for lunch? I'm hungry."

John flung his arm out to the side and there was a strange look on his face as he sat up, but his recovery was instantaneous.

"Sorry about that," he said. "What time is it?"

"Time for lunch, Dad."

"No, not yet. Let's take a walk and do some exploring. Deb, would you like to come along?"

"No, I think I'll pass."

As they walked away I wondered about the strange look on John's face when Denise tried to wake him up but decided it was more out of embarrassment that he had fallen asleep.

As we headed back to my apartment, after a delightful day, I thanked John and Denise for inviting me and as I started to open the door Denise gave me a big hug and said, "I think I like you a lot."

"Thanks, Denise. Does that mean we are friends?"

"Yup. OK, Dad?"

"OK, Denise."

The warm memories of day were still with me as I opened the door to the apartment.

Over the next few months, I accepted John's invitation to go to the playground with Denise. Another Saturday we went out for ice cream, and another day to a Walt Disney movie at the outdoor drive-in theater, where after a half hour John fell asleep. Denise and I were in the backseat, and she looked up at me and said, "Sometimes I get to stay up late because Dad is always falling asleep. He does that at home all the time."

"I heard that. I am not asleep. I am just resting my eyes."

We laughed as Denise reached for my hand.

As I watched her play and interact with us, I would wonder what the boys were doing.

The phone calls from John began to come once a week, then twice a week, and after three months he was calling me almost every night. We discussed politics, ethics, philosophy, education, religion, relationships, commitment, civil rights, the Peace Corps, the space program, the Cold War, art, movies, television, literature, and other topics that we found interesting. We talked a lot about civil rights and the injustices that existed in our country, because I had to be sure of where he stood on those particular issues before our friendship continued. We learned from those conversations that we were in agreement on most issues.

During the next three months, things began to change. I could sense from John he wanted more than a friendship. He told me Leonard Bernstein's *West Side Story* was playing in Boston and asked if I would like to go. Apparently he remembered when I mentioned Leonard Bernstein's *Young People's Concerts* on television and how Bernstein made classical music fun and exciting. I told him I didn't know if Denise was too young for the program, but it might be a good idea to check it out.

"No, it is an evening performance, and would be much too late for her to be out."

Teasingly I asked, "John, are you asking me out on a date?"

"You can call it whatever you want as long as you accept."

"I would be happy to accept as long as we can go dutch."

"Not an option," he said, laughing. "Are you trying to destroy my ego?"

"Wouldn't dream of it," I replied.

"Then I will pick you up at 7:00 p.m. on Saturday, with my ego intact, agreed?"

"Well, if you put it that way, I agree."

It had been a long time since I had been to the theater with anyone. I was excited to be going there with John. On the appointed night, when the usher escorted us to our seats—first balcony, first row—I was thrilled. *Great seats*, I thought.

During the last act I felt John's hand reach over and touch mine. It all seemed so natural, but frightening at the same time. As we were driving home we talked about the performance and what a difference it makes to hear and see music live in a concert hall. He stopped in front of my apartment and said, "Could we talk before you go in? I have something I want to say to you."

"Of course," I replied. "Is everything all right? You seem anxious."

"Yes, anxious and concerned how you are going to take what I am about to say, so I will just put it out there."

"Deb, you need to know that I am falling in love with you and would like you to consider being my wife."

With his anxiety obvious, he continued: "Please don't say a word, but I just wanted you to know how deep my feelings were, and unless you tell me there is no chance at all, I am not going anywhere."

I closed my eyes and breathed hard for a moment and said, "John, I know we enjoy each other's company, and I have sensed our friendship is turning into something I am not ready to deal with right now, so I am going to ask you to give me some time. Can you do that?"

With obvious conviction he said, "My love for you is not going to change, and however long it takes, I will be waiting. I know you have been hurt, but remember, Deb, so have I. I needed to move on, and you need to do the same. We have talked about our goals and dreams, and I'm convinced we have the foundation for not only a *successful* marriage but a *wonderful* marriage."

"John, I do not question the fact that we are compatible in our goals and what we want from a marriage, but this is all happening so fast. I think I need to take some time off from work to sort out my feelings. I will inform Lenny on Monday I will be taking my two weeks' vacation along with an extra week."

* * *

ONCE AGAIN, THE Cape was my destination, and while driving down, I was thinking how different my state of mind was from the last time, when taking my own life was an option I considered. I sat for hours on the beach watching the ocean and wondering how John had broken down my barriers. Was it his patience? Was it his honesty? Was it his lack of pressure? Was it his respect for me? Was it his ambition? Was it the way he treated his daughter and the fact he had custody of her? Was it because he made me feel safe? Was it because he listened? But the big question was, do I love him? My heart was telling me yes, but my intellect kept saying, *Don't go there. You can't take another hurt.*

By the second week, all the pros and cons had been considered, and even though there were more advantages than disadvantages, I was still undecided. In another week I was due back in the office, so I wiped my mind clear of all thoughts and prayed I would be given a sign that would guide me down the right path.

The week passed and I returned to work with my feelings still in limbo.

When it was time for John to report in, that first day I returned to work, I received a call and an unfamiliar voice informed me he was filling in for John. I asked my boss what was going on. He said Denise had had a fall the day before and John had needed to take her to the emergency ward and was taking a few days off. As I was walking out of his office, I heard, "Oh, by the way, he left a message for you and asked me to tell you that she would be fine and not to worry."

My reaction when I did not to hear John's voice surprised me. That was my sign. I knew immediately that I did not want to live without him and Denise in my life. I knew that the very next thing I needed to do was make that phone call and tell him that my answer was yes.

"Never doubted it for a moment," he replied. "You think now we could have that first kiss?"

Another door had just been opened.

CHAPTER 32

"What Is Your Heart Telling You?"

THE NEXT STEP in our journey was to introduce each other to our future in-laws. John had three sisters, one brother, and a large extended family, all of whom he was anxious for me to meet. I had a small extended family of aunts, uncles, cousins, nieces, and nephews, in addition to my brother, sister, and parents.

My mom and dad already knew about John and Denise, so it was no surprise when I brought them home. It took my mother a while to get used to John's sense of humor, but I could see she and my dad both genuinely liked him. When we announced our engagement in the fall of 1962, they both seemed to be excited and happy for us. Once we set the date, we explained to our families that the wedding would be small because our finances were limited. It seems my mother had other plans.

"I want you to have a traditional church ceremony, so please let it be our gift to you."

I talked it over with John, and we decided we would gracefully accept her offer. If that was something Mom wanted, I decided, fine, I wouldn't question her.

She planned two surprise wedding showers and helped me with the guest list, the reception, picking out my dress, picking out the invitations, the flowers, and managed all of the other details. I included Denise in as many of the activities as she was able to handle. I wanted her to enjoy all the excitement and anticipation of what was about to happen. She had already asked me if she could call me her mother.

"Would you like that?"

"Can I start now?"

"I am going to love being your mother, and, yes, of course, you can start now."

She looked up at me, her eyes sparkling with delight, and said, "Hi, Mama."

"Hi, daughter," I replied.

That made me wonder what George and David were calling their parents. I was quickly brought back to reality when Denise asked when we were going to be shopping for *her* wedding dress.

We had found an apartment on the second floor of a two-family house in Medford, right outside of Boston and only fifteen minutes from where we both worked The owner lived on the first floor. There were two bedrooms, a large kitchen with a small pantry, and, down the hall, a living room. It was perfect but needed a lot of work, and because John was willing to bring it up to date by painting, wallpapering, and redoing the floors, the landlady reduced the rent.

By the time we got married, John had not only finished the work, but had moved all of his furniture in, plus our new bedroom set. Everything was in place for the wedding. My sister was to be my maid of honor. I had picked four of my roommates to be bridesmaids, and the soloist would be my cousin Doris.

Because we were being married in January, I chose rich, dark-blue velvet bridesmaids' dresses to offset the off-white lace dress I would be wearing. My mom suggested I have my lace dress lined with beige. It was the thinking at the time that a bride should not wear white if she had been married before.

A few days before the wedding, the urge to take flight arose, mixed with impulses of fear, doubt, confusion, and uncertainty about what was to take place. One of my bridesmaids wanted to know, "What's going on, Deb?"

I shared my concerns and she assured me that it was not unusual for either the bride or the groom to have fears and doubts before walking down the aisle.

"My brother experienced it before he got married," she said, "and my sister also before she married her husband. I'm going to ask you the same question my mother asked each of them: What is your heart telling you? Put everything else that is running around in your head somewhere else and focus on and answer that one question."

I thanked her and said I needed a few moments alone. I had already answered the question she asked me, and my heart was telling me that marrying John was the right thing to do. After I told "flight" to never visit me again, the one feeling that remained was that I was not worthy and did not deserve happiness. As I had done so often in the past, I got down on my knees, closed my eyes, and asked for guidance. My mind went absolutely blank, and then there was one thought that kept repeating itself over and over and over again: *John chose you. John chose you. John chose you.* I got up off my knees feeling calm and was now looking forward to joining our two lives together and becoming a family.

* * *

I WAS ABOUT to walk down the aisle with my dad. I was listening to my cousin sing Schubert's "Ave Maria." I wanted the church to be filled with this piece of music, one of the most beautiful ever written and one that I felt represented the joy of what was about to take place but also the loss I had experienced. This was a song I had sung at many weddings and funerals. It had a very special meaning for me because I had seen how, at funerals, it touched people who were grieving and yet, at weddings, it expressed new life filled with expectations, hopes, and dreams. As the music filled the church and my soul, all doubts dissipated and the bright light of a new beginning was in the air. My dad squeezed my hand, telling me it was time. He leaned over and whispered in my ear to take his arm and to keep my eyes on John. This day, January 26, 1963, I was blessed in holy matrimony to become Mrs. John Joseph Blanchard.

CHAPTER 33

Settling In

THE TRANSITION WAS much easier than I expected. We both continued to work at Wells TV, and Denise stayed in preschool. Our dream was to buy a house, but at the time we did not know exactly how that was going to happen. John came up with the idea of placing three one-gallon jars around the house, with every bit of change we had at the end of the day going into those jars. Every Sunday we would sit at the kitchen table and cut out food coupons and make note of all other items on sale. For the next year and a half, we took our own coffee and lunches to work. Instead of buying Christmas gifts, we gave everyone something homemade. John was now working for a company called Unitrode, which made semiconductors. They also paid for his tuition at Northeastern and provided a great health care plan.

After a year of renting, we started to look into where we wanted to live. Because Denise would be entering first grade the following year, it was important that the school system have a good rating. We began looking in areas southwest of Boston, which meant an hour and a half drive each way to work for John. Every weekend the three of us would head for the real estate office, where Mr. Casey, our Realtor, would aid our quest to become homeowners. One Saturday he asked if we would like to look at some foreclosures, warning us that some were in pretty bad shape.

"Yes, of course, we would," John said.

Some, it turned out, were so damaged there was no way we could move in right away. However, there was a ranch-style house in Franklin, Massachusetts, where the damage was minimal, and with the money we had put away, along with Federal Housing Administration backing, we were able get a bank loan and purchase our first home in 1964. So with a rental truck and the help of John's brother-in-law, one of our dreams came to fruition.

John continued to attend Northeastern at night, which meant commitment, hard work, and sacrifice. He had a way of making everything look easy, never complaining, keeping his mind focused on what he wanted to accomplish. There were some nights, especially in the winter, when he didn't get home until midnight.

Our marriage was happy, productive, and very busy. I was falling more in love with John every day but knew that until I was able to share my secret with him, there would always be a part of me that was closed off to him. I looked forward to the time when he would know everything about me, secrets and all.

That is not to say *everything* went smoothly, because in marriages there will always be challenges to overcome, problems to solve, and mountains to climb. Because of past failures and my artistic nature, I kept looking for things to be perfect. I knew there was no such thing as perfection, especially dealing with an overactive five-year-old, a working husband who was in school three nights a week, settling into suburbia, and all the nuances of being a mother and wife. Still, I felt I needed to prove myself every minute of every day.

The first two years, John was very patient with me. Apparently I was displaying extreme trust issues. Every Saturday Denise would go to a dance class in Milford, two towns away from Franklin. John and I would go out for coffee, then head back to watch the last half hour of her class. One Saturday, however, after we dropped Denise off, John said he had some questions to ask me and that I should not take them personally. He was trying to find some answers, he explained, so he could help me.

"Help me? Why? What am I doing wrong?"

"Nothing major, just something you should be aware of."

Soon after the wedding he had figured out that I felt threatened, he said, reminding me we had agreed to talk to each other when things came up and find an answer together. He lovingly put his arm around me, which made me feel safe enough to let him go on.

"I need your help so I can understand why it is you question everything I do. If I tell you I am going to the hardware store to pick up some quarter-inch nails, you want to know why I need them. If I am headed out to the bank, you will ask why and want to know when I will return. And the last few months, it has gotten worse. The other discussion we need to have is your inability to talk about your feelings. You talk around them a lot, but I feel you never get to the heart of what is bothering you. I don't want you to answer me now. I just want you to think about it, and we can talk later Can you do that?"

"Of course I will," I replied.

For the next two weeks, I paid close attention and tried desperately to break the pattern. The real question was, why was I questioning everything? I knew part of it was my past. I had been transferring my insecurities onto John, and that needed to stop. The last thing I wanted to do was to push him away. The talk we would later have was one of many during our marriage, but it was that first one that set the precedent of honesty, openness, and comfort that has prevailed ever since.

It happened on a Sunday night, after Denise had gotten her bedtime story and was fast asleep. I approached John and said I was ready to have a conversation. We settled down in front of a roaring fire in our living room with hot chocolate in hand. I explained that I had given my brain a good workout over the issues he had brought to my attention a few weeks earlier and asked if he had noticed any improvement. He smiled and nodded his head yes. I told him I suspected my actions—all the questions and avoidance—were a repercussion from the past and that I was transferring my insecurities all over the place, especially onto him.

"I knew that is what you were doing," he said, "but I needed you to recognize it, and now you have. Problem solved."

"John, sometimes there are subjects I would like to discuss with you but can't seem to find the courage to start."

"OK, then it is my job to make sure you feel secure enough to take that leap. We will continue to work on that one together."

He then reached out, pulled me close, and wrapped his arms around me, and the evening played out in the warmth of our love.

CHAPTER 34

A Surprising Twist

BEFORE JOHN AND I were married, I told him I would not be able to have children. It was not an issue for him. Nevertheless, I often fantasized about what our child would have been like. I knew from the start it was a fairy tale that would never come true. However, one afternoon I saw a doctor on public television talking about a new procedure for women who were having difficulty getting pregnant. Hoping it might apply to my situation, I jumped out of my chair and ran to get paper and a pen to write down the information. In my excitement I tripped over the pile of clothes I had been folding and did not make it back in time. The next morning I called the TV station to find out what I had missed. That night after dinner I asked John if he remembered the conversation we had about my not being able to have children.

"Of course I do," he said. "Why, are you pregnant?"

I then told him about the doctor and peppered him with so many questions that he wasn't able to respond.

"Calm down, honey," he said, laughing. "I realize you are excited, but give me time to answer some of your questions and concerns."

He assured me he, too, was thrilled about the possibility of having a child together. "Can you imagine how Denise would feel about having a brother or sister? Yes, absolutely. Go ahead. Set up an appointment with this doctor and see what he has to say. You mentioned money. Please don't worry about the cost. We will find a way."

There was, of course, a larger concern. "I would like to know a little bit more about this Dr. Mulligan," John added. "What if he says there is nothing he can do for you? How would you feel if you went through with the operation and didn't get pregnant?"

I told him that I had already called our primary care physician and asked about Dr. Mulligan. She had assured me he was one of the best gynecologists in Massachusetts. "To answer your other question, honey, of *course* I would be saddened if it did not work out, but I would be going into this knowing at least we tried to make it happen and would be OK with whatever the outcome was destined to be."

John has a deadpan sense of humor, and he asked, "Deb, do you think you can handle a child who might have all my worst traits?"

"What bad traits?" I asked.

He smiled and then gave me one of his bear hugs along with a reminder to take one step at a time and deal only with the facts.

When John left for work the next morning, he wished me luck. I called the number I had been given by the station and spoke with a nurse. She asked a few questions about my tubal ligation, including why I'd had it done. I said my family doctor had been concerned that if I had another pregnancy the baby and I would be at risk because I'd had two children eleven months apart. She suggested I make an appointment to see Dr. Mulligan so he could assess whether I would be a candidate for the procedure. The appointment was made for the second week in April, only two weeks away.

Thoughts of having another child had been frozen in my brain for so long it took a while for the ice to thaw and for newer, brighter thoughts to start blooming. The possibility of new birth occurring with the man I loved was something that could not be ignored. I kept telling myself not to get too excited, but that was like asking a child not to play with a new toy he or she had just received. What if I *was* fortunate enough to have another child? Then George and David would have a half sibling. How I wished I could share that thought with my husband.

CHAPTER 35

The Doctor's Office

I WAS SURPRISED how quickly the next two weeks flew by. The day arrived, and I drove into Boston. It was one of those days in April when the bright colors of spring are beginning to blossom everywhere. The sky was cloudless, and the warm sun was a reminder that spring was pushing winter out the back door. The crocuses, daffodils, jonquils, and small buds on magnolias and other flowering trees were about to burst into bloom. *How appropriate*, I thought.

As I entered Boston proper, I was a little early, so I decided I would drive past my last apartment, on Park Drive, where one of the biggest transitions of my life had taken place and I had found my way back to some kind of normalcy. All my roommates, I knew, had moved on. Two of the girls were married, one living in upstate New York with two children and one in Chicago with three. We had all kept in touch for three years and then drifted apart, except for Ginny, with whom I was still in touch. I drove by Wells TV, the place where John and I both had worked, and was surprised to find it no longer there.

Finally, I headed to Dr. Mulligan's office. I was informed he was running late due to an emergency and the wait might be as much as an hour. I smiled at the only other person in the waiting room as I picked up a magazine to read, but my curiosity began to increase to the point where I asked if this was her first child.

"Yes and no. I have had three miscarriages, but I am now five months pregnant and, thanks to Dr. Mulligan, my dream of carrying my baby to full term is now becoming a reality. I had to stop working, but I was willing to do whatever he asked and here it is five months later and I only have four months to go. I have been praying to be a mother for five years now, and I honestly believed it was never going to happen."

As she was about to continue, the nurse interrupted, telling her, "The doctor will see you now."

"Good luck," I said as she walked away.

She turned around and smiled. "Thanks, and good luck to you."

When the nurse finally called me in, I was led into an anteroom. She said she would be right back and returned with a clipboard, then asked if I had called my doctor and given him permission to release my medical records.

"Yes, I did."

"Well, it seems they would like you to sign a release form. Some doctors' offices like to have those signed forms for their records, and others will send it out if a patient calls and requests them by phone. So if you would please sign here, I will send it out today."

I was then taken to Dr. Mulligan's office and waited a few minutes before he walked through the door and greeted me with a warm, friendly smile, then got right down to business.

"I would like to go over some of the details that you provided for my nurse when you called in, and then we will talk further. I understand you had your tubes cut and not tied after your second child was born. Is that correct?"

"Yes, that is correct."

"And that was twelve years ago?"

"Yes, it was."

"Were there any complications in either one of those births, Mrs. Blanchard?"

"No."

"Good. Sorry about these questions, but I have not received your medical records yet. We did think about canceling your appointment until I received that information, but decided that was not necessary, especially where there were no complications."

He then explained in detail more about the operation: "Mrs. Blanchard, what I will attempt to do is something called tubal reversal. It is a surgical procedure that can restore your ability to get pregnant. Basically I will be building a bridge in order to connect the fallopian tubes. In your case, where your tubes have been cut, it is a highly delicate procedure, and the chances of your getting pregnant are only 60 to 70 percent. I wish there were better percentages, but you need to understand exactly what may or may not happen regarding your having another child."

"I appreciate your honesty, but any odds are better than none. This is something both my husband and I feel we at least have to try. What is the next step?"

"I will give you a call after I receive your medical records, and we will set up a time for you to go into the hospital. Once a date has been set, the nurse will explain to you in detail what you will need to do to prepare for the operation. If you don't hear from her in two weeks, call the office and we will set up another appointment if necessary."

As I was driving home in the midst of a traffic nightmare, I thought, *There will be lots to talk about tonight in the Blanchard household.*

CHAPTER 36

The Secret Revealed

THERE WAS NO question in my mind or John's that we were going to move forward with the operation, but as the two-week waiting period drew close to an end, Mulligan's office still had not called. The day before I planned to contact his office to find out what was going on, I received a call about 4:00 p.m., informing me the doctor needed to set up one more appointment.

"Could you tell me what this is about?"

"He will discuss it when you come in," the nurse said.

I tried again to press for answers but got absolutely nowhere.

"Would it be possible for you to see him tomorrow?"

"Yes, of course."

"How about 11:00 a.m.?"

"Perfect."

The next day as I waited to see Dr. Mulligan, I tried to remain calm and not anticipate what the meeting would be about, but it was not working. Had he decided after getting my records he could not or would not do the operation? *Stop it, Deborah*, I kept telling myself, but it was like trying to stop water from running down a waterfall. My thoughts kept weaving in and out of every possible scenario.

When the nurse took me into Mulligan's office, he apologized for the wait, then explained why he had called me in. He had not received my medical records and needed to go over some other possibilities with me. "It is not a problem," he continued. "We can work around it, but is there any reason you are aware of why the doctor would not be forthcoming with your records?"

"Sorry, I have no idea," I said, shifting uncomfortably in my seat. "He has been our family doctor ever since I was in my early teens. Is it possible he is out of town or on vacation? If he is not responding, he must have a very good reason. Is it absolutely necessary you see those records?"

"No, but it would have been helpful. I have made two phone calls and there has been no response, and I needed you to come in so we could go over what the next step would be. We could go ahead and set up a date for you to go into the hospital and I could do an exploratory, which simply means once I open you up to see what I am dealing with, I would then proceed and complete whatever needs to be done all in one operation. How would you feel about that?"

"It certainly makes sense to me. I would like you to go ahead and make the necessary arrangements."

"Are you sure? Do you need to discuss this with your husband?"

"We have had many discussions and are both ready to do whatever it takes to see if getting pregnant is a possibility, even if the chances are slim. We both agree we need to do this."

"Then the nurse will have some papers for you and your husband to sign and get you set up with a hospital date, and we will proceed from there."

"I do have one request that whatever the outcome of the operation I would ask if you would inform me first so I could be the first one to tell my husband."

"I would be happy to do that," he replied.

One day in early May I entered Boston Lying-In Hospital, now known as Brigham and Women's Hospital, at 4:00 p.m. John stayed with me until the nurse informed him it was time to leave. As he leaned over to kiss me he whispered, "Remember who loves you, and I will be right here when you wake up."

The nurse, whose name was Susan, explained she would be doing some preliminary preparation at five o'clock the following morning, and the doctor's assistant would finish the procedure at 5:30. The operation was scheduled for 6:00 a.m. Dr. Mulligan would check in on me to see how I was doing and if I had any questions. She asked me if I was nervous.

"No, not nervous, just excited," I said.

"Your operation tomorrow is going to be performed by one of the best gynecologists in Massachusetts," Susan assured me, then wished me good luck as I drifted off.

At 5:30 the following morning, Dr. Mulligan asked me if I was ready and I told him I was. He smiled and said, "Well, let's get started."

I was in the operating room by six o'clock and was completely under a few minutes later. John told me after the surgery that when Dr. Mulligan came out of the operating room, he said I was doing fine and that he would let him know when I was out of recovery.

When I finally woke up, I saw the doctor standing over my bed. It looked like his eyes were moist, but I can't attest to that 100 percent, because it could have been my own eyes watering as I came out of the anesthesia. What I did see was a man who had a very serious look on his face. He smiled at me gently and said, Mrs. Blanchard, when I opened you up there was no way I could build a bridge, because there were no fallopian tubes left. It seems they were cut off right at the stubs. I am so sorry, but there was absolutely nothing I could do."

He took my hand and repeated how sorry he was.

"It is not your fault. Could I see my husband, please?"

"Of course, I will send him right in."

When John came through the door, I reached for him and felt reassured as his arms enveloped me. I then informed him I would not be able to have any more babies.

"I know how much you wanted this for us," John replied, "but what is important is that you are fine."

He held me for a very long time as I cried for the child we would never have. He then smiled at me and said, "Deb, let's look at this as another step in our journey. You took a big risk in having this operation and have done everything you could to see if it were possible to have another child, and I love you for exploring that possibility, but we both have been blessed with each other and a rich life ahead of us, so let's look to the future. We can put this to rest now. Are you with me?"

I nodded my head in the affirmative.

"Good. By the way, the nurse said I could pick you up around noon tomorrow. Also, Denise wanted me to tell you how much she misses you and asked if she could write a letter telling the hospital how sad she was she couldn't visit her mother."

"You could have told her yes," I said.

"She already knows that we make decisions together for her."

"How come you're so smart, Mr. Blanchard?"

"I married you, didn't I, Mrs. Blanchard?"

"See you at noon," he added, "and remember I love you."

As I watched him head for the door, I thought to myself, *I am so blessed.*

After he left I was alone with my thoughts about what my family doctor had done. I couldn't understand it. Feelings of anger threatened to intrude on my calm, but I had a strong sense of not wanting to become submerged in a quagmire of negative emotions and victimhood. I had a choice to make and chose the road of forgiveness. It was the only way I could move on. I knew I needed to stay strong for the family I now had and the family I had lost.

When I returned home, our lives continued moving forward, and the following ten years were filled with all of the normal challenges and responsibilities of a young family trying to reach goals and provide an environment of love and support for each other. My love for John kept growing. He continued with night school at Northeastern University. Denise was involved in dance lessons along with gymnastics. My own life was full of activities that revolved around the two of them. I also did volunteer work with the League of Women Voters, the March of Dimes, and the Parent-Teacher Association.

In the morning, when Denise was at school, I worked part-time at Sears, Roebuck in Framingham, about a half hour from where we lived, along with attending classes at Northeastern, at a satellite campus near home. I was also putting money aside in anticipation of the day when I would go looking for the boys in case I had to hire an attorney. The anxiety of never knowing how they were doing was still hard to live with, but I figured that, because everything was working out with Denise, it was also true for George and David.

Before John and I were married, I told him something had happened in my life that I could not talk about and if he thought it was going to influence his decision in any way, he needed to speak up. His answer was "If you have not taken someone's life, then there is nothing you could tell me that would change my mind."

I promised him I would share my secret when the time was right. In the fifteen years that followed, he never asked, not even once. But finally the time came for me to fill him in on all the details.

It was a Saturday morning. Denise was at her dance class and John and I were having coffee. A thousand words were causing a whirlwind inside my head. As I was getting up the courage, we were interrupted by another couple wanting to join us for coffee. I figured the conversation would have to wait another day. It had waited this long and the world does not stop because you want it to, so I joined the niceties of the day.

Our girls were the same age, both heading off to college in the fall, and we talked about how we were going to handle the next passage in our lives. After they left, the rest of the day played out as usual. Denise was looking forward to fish and chips across the street from the dance studio. The memory of that particular meal stays with all of us to this day because whatever they put in the batter was magic to the taste buds. But even more than that, it was an opportunity to share the events of the week. It was our family day.

Denise was spending the night with a friend, so later on that evening, when things had settled down and John was at the computer with Beethoven, our German shorthaired pointer, at his feet, I pulled a stool over to his desk, gave the dog some loving pats, and asked John to stop what he was doing. This was out of character for me, so the first question he asked was, "Are you OK?"

"No, I need to talk with you. Do you remember the conversation I had with you before we were married?"

"Yes, of course I do. Are you trying to tell me that now is the time?"

"Yes, now is the time," I replied.

I then went over all the details of what had happened, that there were two young men named George and David whom I needed to locate. John listened intently, and as I looked up at him, there were tears in his eyes and he said, "You mean to tell me you have lived and walked alone with this secret all these years? Why didn't you tell me?" Before I could answer he said, "It doesn't matter, Deb," then pulled me towards him, held me in his arms, comforted me, validated me, and said, "Well, what are we waiting for? Let's get started."

There were many questions after that initial conversation and many blanks to fill in.

CHAPTER 37

I Wasn't the Only One

It was 1977. Denise was off to college in Pennsylvania. George was now twenty-six years old. David was twenty-five. Although I had put aside money for a lawyer over the years in anticipation of searching for the boys, I did not have a clue about how to begin. Do I go back to the agency? Do I hire a detective?

I talked it over with John, and we decided I should go back to the agency to get help or at least guidance. Making that first call to set up an appointment, I was filled with excitement, anticipation, and fear—fear of how the agency was going to receive me, anticipation and excitement over finally setting off on a journey I had dreamed of for twenty years. I didn't have a clue as to how successful I might be.

I dialed the number and a voice on the other end said, "Good morning. How can I help you?"

I tried to respond, but when I opened my mouth, nothing came out, so I hung up. I took a deep breath and practiced what I was going to say and how I was going to say it, recalling that I had the same experience when I spoke to the agency twenty-four years earlier. Once I was in control of my vocal cords, I was able to set up an appointment for two weeks later. Those two weeks passed at glacial speed.

It seems that phone call brought back memories of another time, of a young woman who felt she had no options regarding the boys' adoption. I thought, *Don't go there, Deborah. There is only heartbreak.* I quickly shifted my thoughts around and made sure I stayed focused on finding out if the agency could help me. It was important to keep myself in the present.

I was leaving nothing to chance, so the day before my appointment, I called to confirm the time and place. The receptionist asked if I needed directions.

"No, not if you are still on Joy Street up near the State House."

"Oh no," she replied. "We are now located in an office building at 750 Boylston Street, second floor."

"Thank you," I replied and told her I would be there at 2:00 p.m.

At dinner that night, John asked, "Honey, are you OK? You seem preoccupied."

"I was surprised that just calling the agency brought me back to a time when my life was so out of control."

He looked at me with such understanding and said, "Well, that sounds normal, but I know you'll be fine, and there is no one who can ever again put you in a position you are not comfortable with. Deb, if it would help I would be happy to go with you tomorrow."

After a brief discussion we decided that this was something I needed to do alone, but it meant so much that he had made the offer.

* * *

THE OFFICE BUILDING on Boylston Street had four floors, and as I looked at the directory to verify the agency's location, I noticed that it occupied an entire floor. When I got off the elevator, there was a receptionist behind a glass partition who asked if she could help me. She then checked me in and instructed me to take a seat.

As I was waiting I began to wonder about George Sr. Had he continued on with his music? Was he still performing or was he teaching somewhere?

Did he eventually marry and have more children? If he started a search for the boys, would I want to know? Of *course* I would.

Those thoughts were put on hold when I heard the receptionist call my name, saying Margaret Boyle was ready to see me. When I got up my legs were wobbly, my head began throbbing, and as the receptionist led me down the hall, it was like walking in quicksand. I was barely able to put one foot in front of the other.

She opened the door and a woman behind a desk got up and came over and introduced herself. "Good afternoon, Mrs. Blanchard," she said. "My name is Margaret Boyle, and it is nice to meet you. Please take a seat."

She was a tall, regal-looking woman who immediately put me at ease by saying that when I came into the agency many years before, it was her first year as a social worker and she remembered the boys. She was now the director. After I explained why I was there, she seemed to understand and said, "I will do everything I can to help you. Can you tell me a little bit about yourself and what your expectations are regarding George and David?"

At last, time to tell my story, and my mouth became a very active instrument. We talked for more than two hours. She asked all the right questions, and I opened my heart, soul, and mind, telling her how I had gotten to where I was that day.

She informed me that the file on the boys' adoption was more than one hundred pages long. She suggested I make additional appointments for every three weeks, because she could only give me twenty-five pages at a time and could provide only the information that was relevant to me as the mother. She warned me that there would be passages whited out throughout the documents that contained information to which I was not privy and said that if I had any questions we could address those at our next meeting. I agreed to a set of conditions she laid out and said I was ready to go. I would have moved a mountain one rock at a time with a teaspoon to find George and David.

Just before I left her office, she handed me the first twenty-five pages of my file and asked me to read over them before our next meeting. Margaret also suggested I get in touch with a woman by the name of Susan Darke, who had started a support group called the Adoption Connection for birth parents of adoptees, as well as adoptees themselves and adoptive parents. Never having knowingly met people in any of those categories, I was eager to learn more.

I left the meeting filled with hope. As I exited the building, I was enveloped in the brilliance and warmth of the sun. I thought about dancing down the street but decided that was a little over the top. Instead I smiled at everyone on the way to the parking lot and enjoyed the feeling of the symphony of life surging into my soul.

The next day I contacted Susan and learned that she had support meetings once a month in Boston. I also learned she herself was an adoptee and, in addition, had given a child up for adoption. At my first meeting I was shocked to find out that there were six million adoptees in this country. What in the world made me think I was the only one who had ever made an adoption plan?

Susan, I would soon learn, had a genius for empathy, understanding, and for life itself. She was a light in the black forest of closed adoption. She became a lifeline for me and to thousands who were searching for information on children they had released for adoption.

I went faithfully every month to her meetings and never opened my mouth during the first four visits. I was overwhelmed by the realization that even though our individual stories differed, we had all suffered tremendous losses. We all had buried secrets. We were all learning how those secrets affected every area of our lives.

When I returned to the agency for my third visit, to receive my next twenty-five pages, Margaret informed me of an upcoming seminar on loss and grief. After attending it, I began to understand that when you lose someone through death there is a wake, followed by a funeral, and family and friends support you, but when you lose a child through adoption, the grief and loss are not acknowledged, nor are they publicly mourned. They become buried, and instead of decreasing, they actually increase over time. It all made sense to me because it was exactly what I had done.

The next time I saw Margaret, she was happy to hear that I had joined Susan's group. She asked if I had any questions after going over the files. I was reluctant to inform her I had found many discrepancies between how Catherine G. recorded our meetings and what really happened, how her perceptions differed from mine. But I sensed that she needed reassurance I was going over the information she was giving me, so I said, "Yes, I do have one question. The writings in those reports do not sound like Catherine G.'s style, and I wondered if I could be presumptuous enough to ask who wrote them."

She smiled and said, "Of course, I would be happy to answer your question. After each meeting she would give her notes to her secretary, and it was *her* responsibility to see they were typed up and put in your file and, yes, they certainly had different styles."

She then asked if I was finding the meetings with Susan Darke helpful.

"Thank you for asking," I replied. "Susan is amazing and, yes, her meetings are invaluable. Because she is an adoptee along with being a birth parent, she seems to have this innate understanding and compassion for everyone that attends. I cannot thank you enough."

"That is good to hear, and I am pleased it is working out. Before you leave I wanted to remind you I will be giving you the final twenty pages at our next meeting, which will be our last here at the office, but I will keep in touch by phone. Let me reassure you that as soon as I have any information regarding the boys I will be in touch, but please remember it is going to take some time."

Weeks went by, then months. I had no word from Margaret.

CHAPTER 38

Separated

IT WAS A Monday morning. I was drinking coffee and trying to process all the information I had been receiving over the past few months. I was emotionally and intellectually drained and taking time to reflect when the phone rang. It was Margaret.

"Do you have some news?" I asked, disappointed that she hadn't simply blurted out something earthshaking.

"I do, but it is not about the search. It's hard for me to have to tell you this, but you need to hear it before our next meeting. I have just learned one of the boys was separated from the family."

I dropped the phone, picked it up, and told her I would have to call her back.

My brain seemed unable to process what I had just heard. I don't remember how long I sat there at the kitchen table, every muscle frozen, thinking over and over, *How could this be?*

For twenty years I had believed the boys had each other. My mind was racing with questions. I wanted to call the director back but was in such an emotional state that there was no way I would have been able to speak in complete sentences. I called John. His voice and logic calmed me.

He suggested I make a list of all the questions and reminded me to be sure to ask what exactly she meant when she said one of the boys had not stayed with the adoptive family. Finally, I dialed the agency back, and when Margaret informed me that it was George who, at the age of eight, left the family, I asked, "What do you mean he left the family? Then where did he go?"

"George was placed in foster care until another family could be found."

"Does that mean he came back to Massachusetts?"

"No," she replied. "He stayed in California."

The agency had never explained to me how out-of-state adoptions work, which she quickly recognized. "Mrs. Blanchard, when we are unable to locate a suitable couple in Massachusetts," she said, "we turn to other states to see if they can find the kind of adoptive parents the birth mother is requesting. In your case, it was a California agency that found the appropriate couple for George and David. It is that agency the prospective adoptive parents work with until they have passed all of the requirements and the final adoption takes place. This is also the agency they would return to with any problems.

"The social worker at that adoption agency assured me the adoptive parents had done everything they could to help him," she continued, "but when George's behavior began to escalate, they turned to them for help. The agency suggested that they put him in foster care until another family could be found."

"What kind of behavior are we talking about? Could you be more specific?" I asked.

"I am sorry. I cannot."

Why is she being evasive? I wondered. *Keep your calm, keep your calm.*

"Then can you tell me what happened after he left foster care?" I asked.

"I can," she replied. "He eventually ended up in a group home because, it seems, whenever the agency placed him with a family who was interested in adopting him, he would display some of the behavior he had with his previous family, and he would end up back in foster care. When he reached eighteen he left the group home and was given monetary assistance until he

DEBORAH HUSE BLANCHARD

found a job and a place to live. Unfortunately, they have no current address on where he is now."

She continued: "I would suggest you take some time to process all of this information, and if you have any further questions, please call me, but in the meantime I will keep looking for George."

"Is there any news regarding David yet?"

"Not yet," she replied.

I was still in a state of confusion when I hung up and was more determined than ever to find out what really happened. My son had lost two families, including his brother. This is not what I wanted for them, and why hadn't I been told? I wanted to blame the agency, but it was I, Deborah, who had made the decision to have George and David adopted. If the boys never wanted to see me again or have anything to do with me, I would not be surprised.

With little hope for what lay ahead, I ran into the bedroom, curled up in a fetal position, and let the tears come. Finally, sleep took over.

There was only one thing I was sure of in the weeks that followed: that it was more important than ever to move forward, because the comforting image I had carried all these years of them being together had been shattered.

Susan recognized in our conversations the agony of not knowing what happened to the boys and she suggested that during this waiting period she could use some help in the office.

"I know you don't think you are ready, but working just four hours a day, three times a week, could be good for both of us. Can you start tomorrow?"

For me, what would become a long and fruitful association with Susan Darke had begun.

CHAPTER 39

Crushed

THERE WERE TIMES working for Susan when I became concerned I was not doing my job. I was unable to make decisions, sometimes breaking down in tears in the middle of a job, messing up every assignment she gave me. Frustrated, I asked her, "Susan, why do you put up with me?"

"Deborah, you are grieving, and when you come through this phase of the grieving process, you will be the greatest asset I will ever have. Tomorrow, I'm going to put you on the phones. You will be talking to people who are adoptees, birth mothers, birth fathers, adoptive parents, siblings, and anyone else who wants to know what it is we do here at the Adoption Connection. You are fine. Now go home, and I'll see you bright and early tomorrow morning."

The following day Susan reminded me that there was a meeting coming up the following Sunday at the Paulist Center, which was located near the State House, on Park Street, right in the heart of Boston.

"And by the way, Deb, you need to start sharing. I think it will not only help you process some of your feelings, but it will also help other members who are struggling as well."

"I don't know if I am ready yet."

"Well, I think you are, but let's leave it this way. Sunday I will call on you to tell your story, and if you are still not ready you can just say that you would like to pass, OK? Just promise me you will think about it."

"OK, Susan, I promise I will think about it."

It was another two months before I was able to start sharing.

When the phone calls would come in from birth parents, adoptees, and sometimes adoptive parents it was part of my job to explain what we did at the Adoption Connection. All the callers had been involved in closed adoptions and all wanted to know if we could help locate a loved one. I would explain that it might be possible to find who they were looking for, depending on the information they had. Their experiences were all different, many heartbreaking, but one thing they had in common was the trauma of a devastating loss. After sending each person papers to fill out, I would encourage them to come to our monthly meetings, where everyone could finally talk freely and feel safe in sharing secrets we all had been holding on to for years. Those meetings, led by Susan, became a lifeline for many of us, including me. I remember the time when one adoptee talked about how he had never seen a birth mother before and how normal we all looked.

One birth mother agreed when she said, "Because it was something birth parents never talk about." Another birth mother stated, "We are your next-door neighbor, your girlfriend's mother, your nurse, your teacher, and we represent the whole socioeconomic background of society."

An adoptee wanted to know, "Why did you give me away? Was it my fault? Wasn't I good enough? Did you ever love me?"

Over time, as birth mothers told their individual stories, adoptees learned that in many cases their birth mothers may not have had much of a choice, because having a baby out of wedlock at that time, no matter what your age, was socially unacceptable. Both mother and child would have been ostracized. It was also a time when mores dictated that children should be brought up in a household with two parents, and many birth mothers were convinced that adoption was the only choice in order to give their child a better life.

Birth mothers began asking adoptees questions: "Did you have a good life?" "Were you happy?" "Why did you feel abandoned?" "Do you know how much you were loved?" Birth mothers also learned that adoptees were searching for different reasons. Some made it clear they were angry. Others simply wanted to know their heritage, while some were searching out of curiosity. Then there were the adoptees who wanted to thank their birth mothers, to let them know they'd had a wonderful life. There were others just wanting to look into the eyes of the woman who had given them birth and many others who wanted to know the story that had led to their adoption.

And so it went, meeting after meeting, sharing our stories, learning from each other, and even though we were all different, there was no question the emotions ran deep, slicing into our very core.

* * *

IT WAS ANOTHER six months before I heard from Margaret regarding George. I had just hung up from talking with Susan about my taking over some of the monthly meetings. As I was sitting at the kitchen table, thinking about our conversation, the phone rang.

"Good morning, Mrs. Blanchard. I finally have some news regarding your firstborn."

I thought, *Is this a phone call of joy or sadness?* It turned out to be both.

"The good news," she continued, "is we did locate George in Southern California, but the other part of that is he is not interested in having any contact. However, he wanted you to know that he is doing fine. I am so sorry. I know how disappointed you must be."

"Yes, of course I am disappointed," I said, trying to hold back the tears. "However, I am relieved to learn after all these years that he is in a good place."

I knew, from our meetings, that George might not want to speak to me or have any contact, but I also believed that my dream had just died.

The next day, not going in to work crossed my mind, but I was determined to do my job. When Susan came in, I told her what had happened.

She stared at me for a moment then rose up from her desk, shut the phones off, and stated emphatically, "Deb, he needs to hear directly from you. How fine can this young man be when at the age of eight he was separated from his brother and family? The fact that he asked the director to pass on the message should tell you something."

I felt ambivalent, confused, and uncertain and said nothing. Susan looked at me with that determined look and said, "Talk to me, Deborah. What are you are thinking?"

"I'm thinking what we talk about at our meetings, how we should respect the wishes of the person we are looking for, and George stated clearly he was not interested in meeting me."

"Dammit," Susan said. "Stop thinking with your head and tell me what's in your heart!"

I thought for a moment, and then spoke with both head and heart: "You more than anyone, Susan, except my husband, know how long I have carried this dream in my heart, and to have it crushed in one phone call was shattering."

Tears started to form in my eyes. Susan looked at me with such empathy as she set her notepad down on her desk. "Deb, this is what I want you to do: go home tonight and begin to write a letter to George and tell him what is in your heart."

"But we don't even have an address or a last name."

"Leave that to me. Let's take one step at a time. Agreed?"

"Agreed."

"Now get back to work, and remember: everything on your desk is top priority, and I want it all today. Got it?"

"In your dreams, Susan. There is enough work for three people."

"On my desk before you leave," she repeated.

I stood and returned to my office, smiling.

CHAPTER 40

Letter to George

THE EFFORT TO write to George led to a pile of crumpled-up paper, half on the floor, half in the trash bin. *How do I start, what should I write, how much should I write?* One morning, in the midst of my inaction, Susan approached my desk. "So, Deb, how is your letter coming along?" she asked. "I would like to go over it with you when you have finished. You need to have it ready to go when I locate George."

I tried to make her understand how impossible this was for me. She explained that it was not unusual for a birth mother to resist opening up a compartment that held nothing but pain and anguish. "My suggestion," she said, "would be to think about it as if George was standing right in front of you and you are talking directly to him, and then write down what you want him to know about his adoption. I will expect to have your letter in front of me on my desk in three weeks."

As always, her advice made perfect sense. She seemed to be able to untangle any knot that prevented me from acting.

Also, the feedback I was hearing at the meetings from birth moms and adoptees who had already made contact was invaluable. The consensus was that nothing could have prepared them for that first meeting. One adoptee said, "I could not stop staring at my birth mother, and the fact I had the same interests, the same hands, same smile—I was afraid I wouldn't know what to say or how to act, but we ended up talking nonstop for two hours."

Before the reunion with my daughter, a birth mother said, "I changed my clothes five times. I wish I had lost more weight. My hair was a mess, but when I finally met her in a restaurant and saw my birth daughter for the first time, I tried to get up, but I couldn't move, and when I explained why, she smiled and said, 'That's OK. I'm nervous too. So nice to finally meet you.' Things were a little awkward in the beginning, but the meeting went well. However, it seemed we were on our best behavior and nothing of substance was ever discussed."

Another birth mom told the group how wonderful everything went until the adoptee asked her to meet the adoptive parents. "When I indicated I was not comfortable with that, she got up and walked away. She did call the next day and apologized for her actions and asked me to at least think about it."

A group discussion followed, and the birth mother added that her fear was being judged all over again, as she had been when she told her family she was pregnant twenty years earlier.

A male adoptee said, "I felt emotionally naked and vulnerable looking at my birth mother. She knows me, but I don't know who she is. I was feeling completely out of control and guilty about not wanting to hear her pain. She doesn't seem to understand what it's like never knowing your heritage or having to walk into a doctor's office without any medical information. I just wanted to know why she felt adoption was her only option."

Another adoptee said, "I am glad I was given up for adoption. I never would've survived in such a dysfunctional family."

I learned more about the emotional highs and lows and how that is such an integral part of a reunion. I was infused with a greater awareness of what might lie ahead.

These meetings were my first step toward understanding that reunions can take two to five years to stabilize and that stabilization can take place only if both parties sensitize themselves to the other's journey. We must accept others where they are and not where we would like them to be.

*　*　*

MY LETTER TO George was finally complete. The next morning I left it on Susan's desk and waited nervously for her to call me into her office. After lunch, she finally did. I sat down as she picked up the stack of pages, ten in all.

"How long did it take you to write this?" she asked.

"Too long," I replied.

"Well, you are right. It is much too long. Now that you have got your feelings out, I need you to go back home and condense this into three pages."

"How can I possibly tell George about his adoption without including the pain that went along with it? Susan, I am not sure I can do that."

"I am not suggesting you do that, but you can express your pain in one sentence and leave out the excruciating part of what happened after they left. Deb, it is much too heavy in substance for your first letter. In your second one, use both your intellect and emotions. I can see by the look on your face you get it. Trust me, it will be much easier this time."

And it was. It took several more drafts, but finally the letter was finished. In it I told George I did not want to interfere with his life, but I wanted him to know the circumstances that led to his adoption and that if he ever changed his mind the door would always be open. I closed with all my contact information. Now all I needed was an address to mail it to.

CHAPTER 41

David Is Found

It was a cold December weekend, with the temperature below zero, and John and I were out running. Even though I had always been physically active, running was not my favorite activity. When he first suggested it more than a year earlier, my response was "That is the one sport I am not friends with. Why would you even mention it?"

"Because you would really have to work hard, and it might release some of the stress you are holding close to your chest. You know, Deb, you can fool everyone else, but I know if you don't find a way to reduce your frustration and anxiety other than talking about it with your support group, it will start to affect your health."

At the end of our run, with our face masks frozen, he said, "Congratulations! You have just completed your first mile."

"That only happened," I said, gasping to catch my breath, "because the cold was biting at my derriere. I am freezing."

"Aren't you proud of yourself?" he persisted.

"I am going to smack you if you don't stop humoring me. Every step was agony."

"I know, honey, but at least you made it, and by the way, the sputtering and talking to yourself kept me entertained."

We both laughed, and I suggested we go inside, thaw out, and have a cup of hot chocolate, with the white on the top, as George used to say. How nice it was to be able to bring the boys into our conversation now.

That same weekend a nasty nor'easter blew its way in, cutting off power for two days, causing schools to be canceled, and shutting down all phone service. We were lucky we had our fireplace to keep us warm. It took another two days to dig ourselves out from the enormous snow piles and for snow-plows to clear the roads so our lives could get back to normal. We were hoping on Sunday that our phone service would be back on line by nightfall in case anyone was trying to get through to us, but as we headed out to buy groceries, we saw extensive damage—from trees that had fallen on telephone wires to streetlights blown right out of their bases—so there was no question we were going to be without service for a few more days.

As I headed out for work the next morning, I wondered whether David was dealing with the same storm, or was he somewhere where the sun was shining brightly? Maybe one day the wondering would be a thing of the past and I could stick to reality and what was not imagined.

Because of traffic I was an hour late and ran up the stairs to unlock the door. I was surprised to see Susan was already there.

"You're here," I said.

"Well, it is my office," she replied with a devilish grin on her face, "and I wanted to get here ahead of you. I have been trying to get in touch with you for the last four days. Did you have much damage? Is everything all right? I was worried."

"Everything is fine, Susan."

"Good. Get settled in, Deb, and then bring your coffee into my office because we have lots to catch up on."

I returned a few minutes later, coffee in hand. "OK, I'm back. What is so important?"

"Well, to begin with it looks like I found David, but there is a problem. I am almost 95 percent sure he is the correct person. I have an address in New York, but no phone number."

I went numb and said nothing.

"Deb, where are you?" she said as she picked up David's file and banged it back down on the desk. "Are you with me? How come you're just sitting there? I've worked tirelessly the last five months trying to find David, and I'm getting no reaction out of you whatsoever."

I squirmed uncomfortably in my chair. "Sorry, Susan. I'm just trying to keep my expectations at zero."

"That I can understand, but I need to hear what you are feeling."

"What I am feeling is scared, vulnerable, bewildered, and questioning if I even have a right to interfere with his life or his brother's."

"Stop right there," she said. "First of all, David has a choice, and as an adult he will make his own decision whether or not to contact you. At least he will know you loved him enough to reach out and explain the reasons you made an adoption plan for him along with all the information about his heritage. And, second, I do not want to hear any more of this 'Do I have a right?' business. None of us should have been completely cut off to know how our children were doing when they were adopted. You should have been informed when George was separated from his brother and adoptive family, but because of this crazy closed system you were not. Your boys have a right to know their heritage and where they came from, and you are the only one who can give them that. So let's move on, because we have lost four days of work," she continued. "We are going to have to dig in and catch up, so what I would like you to do in the next couple of days is process what we have talked about and come up with some out-of-the-box ideas on how you would like to reach out to David. Are you OK with that?"

I shook my head in the affirmative.

"Now get back to your office because we have forty messages on the phone, and I want everyone called back before noon."

"Is that it?"

She laughed and said, "No, you should be so lucky. We need to start planning for our next conference after lunch and, no, we can't afford to hire any extra help."

Our exchange continued as I headed for my office, sat down, went back to work, and smiled, knowing I would never, ever have the last word.

As I drove home the weather had begun to clear, along with my comprehension of what lay ahead. There was a sense of relief, calm, and peace as well as fear about contacting David. But he had been located and whatever happened from that time forward would be better than what had preceded it. I was sure of that.

CHAPTER 42

With Prayers, Love, and Hope

I COULDN'T WAIT to get home that evening and tell John that Susan had found David. All the way there I kept going over different scenarios of how to get in touch with him. Should I write a letter, make a phone call, send a telegram? *Think, Deborah, think outside of the box.* Nothing was working.

At 3:00 a.m. I was still struggling and John asked, "Deborah, do you know what time it is? Sleep on it, honey. Give your brain a rest. And by the way, if you are not in bed the next time I wake up, we are going to put our sneakers on and go out for a run.

"All kidding aside," he continued, "my suggestion would be to take your emotions out of the equation and think about this as if you were trying to help another birth mother."

The next morning, as I was driving in to work, the car was filled with Bach's Partita no. 3 in A Minor, which is great thinking music. I began dissecting what I was dealing with because there was a chance this might not be the right person, and sending a letter to a stranger with sensitive information was not a good idea. By the time I reached the parking lot, my gray cells were dancing with new ideas.

When I left the office after a very busy day, my need to discuss every step with Susan seemed to be dissipating. I decided to send David a telegram. I could request that it be hand delivered. In that way there would be no question he had received it. The message had to be nebulous and appeal to one's sense of curiosity, so I came up with an old saying I had heard: "If you love someone, set them free. If they come back, they are yours; if they don't, they never were." I added my contact information, stating that he could call collect. The next day the telegram was sent with prayers, love, and the hope that I would hear back, whether the response was positive or negative.

With anticipation and expectation at a high pitch, now came the hard part: the waiting. And my way of handling that was to become numb, as if I had entered a new and neutral sphere of my life. I had to keep reminding myself that if and when David called, there would be no crying, nor any gushy conversation, only unconditional love. No matter what he said, or how he said it, I would understand. And certainly if he did not want me to be involved in his life, I would respect his wishes.

There was no doubt in my mind that if he did call, I would freeze up at the sound of his voice unless I went over what I was going to say, so I memorized the words till they were automatic. I would start by saying, "David, I am not sure I have the right person, but if you would allow me to ask you a few questions to determine if you are, then we could proceed from there, but only if you are willing."

Three days after I sent the telegram, we were preparing dinner when the phone rang. Neither of us was in a position to answer it, and by the time I got to the phone, the caller had hung up. About an hour later it rang again, and it was David, wanting to find out who had sent the telegram. I felt light-headed but explained who I was. ... Nothing but dead silence on the other end of the phone.

"Are you still there?" I asked.

"Yes, I apologize, but I have to go. Can I call you back later?"

"Of course, I will be here."

I had just heard my son's grown-up voice for the first time, and I couldn't wait to tell John how David was soft-spoken, respectful, but before I could say anything more, the phone rang again.

"Answer it, Deb."

"*No.*"

"If it is David, he needs to hear your voice and no one else's."

"It's probably someone else."

"You don't *know* that. Pick up the phone."

So I did. It *was* David, and after a few questions, there was no doubt in either of our minds that he was my son. We talked for almost an hour. He mentioned that he had gone through Lowell, Massachusetts, on his way to a sports event and knew from his parents that that was where he'd been born. I learned about his interest in sports, especially football, where he went to high school and college, and what he was doing in New York. We talked about his parents, Mary and Allen Fonteno. He mentioned his mom was a schoolteacher and his dad was a merchant mariner. He seemed a little uncomfortable when I said that I had an interest in meeting them someday, so I quickly changed the subject. When I asked about the Watts riots in Los Angeles, in 1965, when David was thirteen, he said it was about that same time that his family moved to Beaumont, Texas. Finally, we made arrangements to meet the following weekend in New York City.

I had been trying hard to keep my emotions contained, but when I hung up there was nothing that could keep them from erupting. I walked from room to room crying, laughing, talking to myself, then ran outside and raised my hands to the heavens, thanking God for what had just happened. John came up behind me and put his arms around me, saying I needed to go back indoors.

"Right now you should give Susan a call and bring her up to date," he said. That conversation streamed well into the evening, and once we said good night, my need to continue talking did not cease, so out John and I went to get some hot chocolate and blueberry muffins at our favorite coffee shop.

The need to talk about the boys, after twenty years of silence, went on almost nonstop for five years.

CHAPTER 43

"Hello, This Is George"

ABOUT THIS SAME time, Susan began to turn up information about George. He had joined the navy and was stationed in San Diego, and because she was now able to find an address, my letter was finally sent. Only time would reveal if he would continue to say thanks but no thanks.

I kept my expectations low, which allowed my emotions to remain at a level I could deal with. About a week after I connected with David, George called. It was around 10:00 p.m. on a Saturday. When I answered I heard a voice that sounded very much like my brother's say, "Hello, this is George, and I would like to speak to Deborah."

"This is Deborah."

"I apologize for calling you so late, but I did not realize that California was three hours behind. Can we talk?"

"Of *course* we can," I said, wanting to sing out with joy, but I was trying hard to stay composed.

George put me at ease immediately. Like David, he was very respectful and asked all the right questions. It became apparent, once I relaxed, that my firstborn had not changed. When he was little and got excited he went on and on. I smiled to myself as he continued. How I loved hearing his voice.

He talked about the navy, some of the places he had been, what some of his duties were on the ship. He shared stories about his shipmates, what they looked like, what nicknames he had given them. He mentioned he would send pictures, which he later did. Our conversation lasted for over an hour. I was surprised when he said he would like to meet me.

Did I just hear right? Is this really happening? Yes, it was, but I had to find some courage to ask the following question: "It so happens we are going to be in California next month, because my husband, John, has an interview for a job in San Jose at Northern Telecom. Is there any possibility we could work something out?"

Immediately, I worried that I had overstepped my boundaries, but George allayed my fears. "Well, it just so happens my ship is in dry dock, being overhauled, so my schedule is flexible," he said with a laugh in his voice. "Give me the dates, and I will get back to you and let you know."

As I said goodbye, I looked over at John. He was smiling and making hot chocolate. I then called Susan. She was thrilled to hear the news. Our conversation went into overtime and I asked, "Is there anything I can do to prepare myself for meeting the boys? Because I am petrified and wondering how they are dealing with all of this."

"*That's* your answer. It is true you have not mothered them for the last twenty years, but you are still a mother, and I would encourage you to just be yourself and let those instincts take over. Just remember: the boys will pick up on your anxiety, so relax."

"Susan, how can I ever thank you?"

"You can turn up bright and early Monday morning, because there is a lot of work on your desk, along with planning for our presentation at the agency, which is next week, by the way. And don't forget, you have a newsletter to write. If your head is not in the real world, you can expect a good kick in the butt."

"Don't you mean derriere, Susan?"

"Good night, Deb," she replied.

* * *

MY FIRST MEETING with David occurred on January 12, 1980. We made arrangements to meet at the airport. I was to page him. As I wandered through the crowd, trying to find the Delta Airlines counter, I felt a tap on my shoulder and turned around. A large chest was staring back at me. I tilted my head back and saw David looking down, smiling.

"You never grew, did you?" he said.

"Well, you certainly did."

I then introduced him to John. David suggested we head over to his apartment. As we were waiting for the bus, I asked him, "Dave, do you wear glasses?"

"Yes, as a matter fact I do, but what made you ask?"

"Because I noticed how you were squinting to read the bus signs, and being nearsighted myself, I recognized the signs."

We both laughed and I felt more relaxed.

There wasn't much conversation when we were on the bus because of the noise level. John was sitting a couple of seats back; Dave and I were sitting together. He mentioned when we were on the way to his apartment that he needed to stop at the corner store to pick up some things. John was waiting a couple of feet behind us. I heard someone asking, "Are you with the FBI? What are you doing here in our neighborhood? You don't belong here. I think you better leave or we are coming after you, Mr. FBI. What's in the briefcase?"

David, realizing their questions were directed at John, turned around and, in a matter-of-fact way said, "You better not be messing with my dad. Back off." And they did. I looked over at John, who had a faint smile on his face. When we left the store, he said, "Thanks, Dave."

"Not a problem," David replied. "They were just having a little fun. By the way, what *do* you have in that briefcase?"

"Just some pictures," John replied.

David opened a pack of cigarettes he had just bought. "Do you mind if I smoke?" he asked.

"Of course not," we both said.

"As a matter of fact, I will join you," John added.

David's apartment was very small and compact, more like a studio. He asked if we would like something to drink, and we both said water would be good. He smiled and said, "Do you two always speak in unison?" After a few niceties I asked him if he had any questions about his background.

"Deb, when I first saw you at the airport, I couldn't help but notice how much George looked like you and I was wondering, who do I resemble?"

"There is no doubt you take after your father in stature, hairline, and eyes," I responded, "but your overall look is definitely from our side of the family. You resemble not only my brother, Bob, but other members as well."

He smiled and then said, "I know my mom told me that my biological father was musical but did not know much about your side."

I told him about his grandmother's many talents; that my sister had attended Boston University and was now a music teacher in the Natick, Massachusetts, school system; and my majoring in voice at the New England Conservatory. We talked for the next two hours about various topics until John reminded me that if I wanted to show David any pictures, I better get to it because our flight would be leaving soon. I sensed that David was not interested, however, and asked if he would like to look at them another time. He smiled and said yes.

He then apologized for not being able to take us back to the airport. He had to get to his job at a radio station and seemed reluctant to reveal which one but said he was going next door to use his neighbor's phone to call us a cab. As we were leaving, he promised to keep in touch and thanked us both for coming.

I stared at David for several moments as we were about to leave. I wanted so much to take him in my arms, hold him close, tell him how much I loved him, but the only thing that seemed appropriate at the time was to give him a quick hug and say goodbye. For the first time in twenty years I had just spent time with my son, and that image of him looking down at me at the airport, when we first met, will be etched in my brain forever.

* * *

JOHN AND I had made arrangements to meet George the following month, on February 6, just outside San Francisco. We flew there the day before for John's appointment in San Jose. I tried to keep myself busy by wandering around San Francisco, but nothing was working.

At dinner that night I asked John, "Why am I so nervous? I have already met David."

He looked at me with that loving twinkle in his eyes and said, "Deb, you can handle it. You have waited twenty years for this moment and now it is here. Relax."

After a restless night, morning finally arrived. We had a quick break-fast and headed to where George's ship was docked, about twenty-five miles away, over the Bay Bridge, in Alameda. He had told us to wait in the parking lot and he would be watching for us. Twenty minutes went by, no George.

"Where is he?" I asked. "He's changed his mind. He's not coming."

"Of course he is," John said. "Don't get paranoid on me."

"Did I make a mistake? Are we supposed to be in San Diego? Because that's where he is stationed."

"Deb, no, you did not make a mistake. His ship is up here to be over-hauled, not in San Diego."

Just then a man dressed in everyday clothes walked up to the car and tapped on the window. I expected to see someone in uniform. "It's not George," I said to John, becoming more panicky by the moment.

"You don't know that. Calm down and open the window."

The man tapped again and, as I opened it, he asked me to remove my sunglasses. *That's a strange request*, I thought, but did it anyway.

"Is your name Deborah Blanchard?" he asked.

"It is."

"Hi, my name is George Fonteno and I apologize, but please try to understand that in the last few hours I was beginning to think, *Am I really going to meet my mother or is this some kind of a game or a joke? I have to make sure she is who she says she is*, and now, after seeing you without your sunglasses, I am sure you are who you say you are."

"George," I replied, "being paranoid myself, and thinking you might not come, I completely understand." To myself I thought, *The apple doesn't fall far from the tree.*

"George, please get in the car and we can talk further over lunch, if that is OK with you," I continued, "but first I would like to introduce you to my husband, John."

We then drove to a Mexican restaurant George had suggested. After we made it to our table and sat down, I could not stop staring at him. It was as if I had just given birth to him for the second time. I checked his hands, his fingers, his smile, his eyes. I drank in the sight of him, as I had with David, wanting to take him in my arms, hold him close, and never, ever let go. I do not have a clue what I ordered and don't remember eating anything.

It was John who kept the conversation flowing, asking George about his duties on the ship and where his travels had taken him. George asked a few questions about what we both did for a living and told us he had been married and divorced but never asked why he had been given up for adoption. That would come later.

He was apologetic when he indicated his time was limited and he needed to return to the ship. He then slipped me a note on a napkin saying, "I really like your husband John."

Before he left, George asked when we would we be coming back to California. I told him I would let him know and he said, "Have a safe trip home."

As I got out of the car to give him a quick hug, I was surprised when he said, "I will call you in a couple of days."

He is going call me in a couple of days—really? I wondered if all of this was just a dream.

* * *

OVER THE YEARS, family, friends, and others have often asked me what it was like seeing George and David after twenty years. I usually say, "I am sorry, but there are no words in any language to describe the depth of emotion that enveloped me." However, I believe certain music can. When Tchaikovsky wrote his "1812 Overture" in 1880, it was to celebrate the ending of the war against Napoleon, and when the crashing of the cymbals reaches its crescendo, it replicates the explosion of emotions I felt when I met the boys, as well as the sense that my internal war was finally over. Beethoven wrote his Ninth Symphony in a time when freedom was repressed in Europe. Music scholars have tried to put meaning to that symphony for years, without success. What they do know, and anyone who hears it knows, is it is one of the greatest pieces of music ever written. For me, it has always and still does elevate my soul to a higher place of hope, love, and freedom. Then there is Bach's Partita for Keyboard no. 2 in D Minor. There is a happy, light, dance-like quality to this particular piece of music, and I was certainly feeling that when I met the boys as adults. My dream had become a reality. I had been set free. No more secrets. I could now shout their names to the world. There was no way of knowing what the future held, but I knew that whatever happened, it would be OK.

* * *

OUR DAUGHTER, DENISE, was due home for her college spring break and had to be informed about the boys. I was excited and, at the same time, afraid of what her reaction would be. She'd been brought up in a time when discrimination against minorities was in the paper on a daily basis, and as she had once told me, "Sometimes I feel our country is poisoned by people who just don't get it." So I knew she would have an understanding of why I made the decision to have the boys adopted. But I didn't know whether she would be angry with me for not telling her sooner.

I got out some pictures of when the boys were young, along with ones taken when they met John and me recently. After dinner one night I asked

Denise if we could have a mother-daughter talk in her bedroom. She gave me a look that meant "What have I done now?" However, she immediately sensed that something else was going on.

"What's wrong? Are you and Daddy getting a divorce?" she asked. "Are you sick? Is it Dad? Mom, you're scaring me."

"No, honey, nothing like that. Let me try and explain."

I then went over all of the details as gently as I knew how, starting from the very beginning. Denise sat there and never said a word. I thought to myself, *This is bad. My daughter has never been at a loss for words and will always interrupt to ask questions. …* Silence, nada, nothing.

When I finished she reacted the same way her father had, coming over to me with tears in her eyes and hugged me. The first words out of her mouth were, "And you carried this secret all these years? Mama, I am so sorry. It makes me sad. You found both George and David. That makes me happy, and I can't wait to meet them. I always wanted to have brothers."

There were many questions that followed, which carried us well into the night. But there was one remark that I have reflected on often. It was said with elation in her voice: "Oh my God, Mama, you're human after all."

There it was: the birth mother, always trying to be perfect, always trying to prove myself, prove that I was worthy, never recognizing the ripple effect it had on those whom I loved.

CHAPTER 44

Two Mothers

MEETING THE BOYS' adoptive parents was something I had dreamed of since George and David were placed for adoption, and now it was about to become a reality.

A few months into the reunion, I asked David if he would mind my placing a call to his mom and dad. His said he did not object. My memory of that first phone call is as vivid as it was the day I made it. When I dialed Mary and Allen's number and heard her warm, cheery voice say hello, it startled me. It was exactly like the voice I had heard many times in my head.

"Mary," I replied, "you don't know me, but my name is Deb Blanchard."

She interrupted. "Yes, I do know who you are, and I am so happy you called."

Almost from the start I was drawn to this woman, because it was obvious that her first priority was to protect her son. She wanted to find out what my intentions were. Was I going to exploit him in any way? In other words, what did I want? I loved her for that.

"Mary, if I were in your position I would be doing exactly the same thing," I told her. "My need has always been the same: to know if he was safe, happy, and loved and make myself available for any questions you or David might have."

It became clear as our conversation continued that we were two mothers who loved David. I thanked her for all she had done for him, giving him the skills he needed in a country polarized by race. We talked about how, in the mid-1950s, the civil rights movement had just begun and the struggle against racism and segregation was only entering the awareness of many Americans. We agreed that things were very different now and that we were both thankful for that. I assured her that if she did not wish to meet me in person, I would understand.

"No, Deb, I have also dreamed of meeting the mother who gave birth to our son."

She must have heard the breathless gasp along with the nonsensical words coming out of my mouth.

"Are you OK?" she asked.

"Mary, you said 'our' son."

"Deb, that is who he is, and, yes, we are talking about *our* son."

At that moment my heart stood still and my soul gained wings. I could not wait to meet this woman.

There was further discussion on how we should have been able to communicate with each other over the years and how different the boys' lives might have been if we had. That surprised me. I really believed I had put all that anguish in a place where I could deal with it, but apparently there was no such place. I think Mary, bless her heart, picked up on my pain and quickly steered the conversation in a lighter direction.

"When David stayed with you for a few days, was he neat?" she asked.

"No, not particularly."

She heaved a sigh of relief. "Oh good."

We laughed and continued talking like we had known each other forever, then ended our conversation with the hope that we might meet each other soon.

CHAPTER 45

Mary and Allen

WITH DAVID's OK, on June 8, 1980, John and I boarded a plane to Houston to meet Mary and Allen. We had never been to Texas before and were surprised when we went to pick up our rental car and were hit with extremely high humidity, as though we had just entered a sauna and a steam bath simultaneously. We then headed out to Beaumont, an hour and a half to the east, and even though the air-conditioning was up as far as it would go, my whole body reacted as if there was no cool air in the car at all.

"Well, there goes making a good impression," I told John.

I was worried what Mary and Allen might think—and not just about my attire. I looked nothing like David, who was over six feet tall, while I was not even five two. Both boys were extremely handsome and here comes this very ordinary woman looking like she just went through a car wash without out a car.

As we turned the corner onto their block, John asked if I was OK.

"No, I am not."

"Do you want to talk about it?"

"Not now. Can we talk later?"

"Of course we can." He knew when to keep his sense of humor out of the conversation.

My mouth was dry, I was thirsty, and my clothes were stained with perspiration. My legs were unsteady as I got out of the car, but I managed to make it to the front door without tripping.

"How are you doing?" Allen said, swinging the door open wide.

He was tall and distinguished looking with a trim physique and gray hair. Mary was right beside him with a smile that lit up her lovely face as she welcomed us and urged us to come in.

"Would you like something cold to drink?" she asked.

"That sounds really refreshing," I replied.

My body began to cool down and I thought, *This is where David spent a good part of his life.* There were pictures of him all around the house. I imagined him as a boy running in and out of those rooms, watching his mother cook. I wondered if he'd had a good appetite, what his favorite foods had been, whether he'd been read bedtime stories. Had he slept well at night? Did he have fun pajamas? What kind of conversations did he have with his mom and dad? What was he like as a young boy and then a young man? What had he liked to do in his spare time? What kind of trouble did he get into as a young kid? Did he go to his senior prom?

The next twenty minutes or so were just a blur. John recognized that I was floating in another dimension and came over to me to say he and Allen were going to take a walk. He reminded me that our time was limited. That zapped me back into the present. I did not want to waste a single moment.

As my emotions started to level off, my conversation with Mary remained on socially acceptable topics. We were taking the time to get to know each other, feeling each other out. At times it felt like there was an orchestra in the center of the living room, its members all playing out of tune, but slowly harmony began to take center stage. The melody of reason began rising out of discord and a foundation of trust began to take hold.

We discussed Mary's profession, teaching, and the challenges of motherhood. We came to see that our mothering skills were very similar. That brought back a recollection from when David had visited the month before. It was raining hard, and I suggested that he take an umbrella. He replied, "Deb, I don't need two mothers." Sometimes maternal instincts come out whether you want them to or not.

Mary and I bonded on many levels, but there was one thing that hung in the air, unspoken, and I knew I couldn't leave it there. I had to bring up the circumstances of George's separation from the family. If Mary were still alive, I'm sure her perception of that conversation would differ from mine, because mine was intertwined with many strong emotions: the feeling that I had no right to ask about it; the nightmare of how it may have affected David; the thought that I should not bring it up at all. It was in the past, and no amount of discussion, I realized, was going to change anything. Even with all that weighing on me, there was no way I could leave without our having that talk.

I proceeded as gently as I knew how, but Mary quickly picked up where I was headed. She told me she and Allen had done everything they could, taking George to see several doctors, going back to the agency and asking to get in touch with me to see if I had any insight into why George's behavior had become so destructive. She was told that getting in touch with me was, legally, not an option.

She then looked directly at me and said, "Deb, I went through the same agony of having to make a decision of letting him go as you did. I, too, will always feel guilty and regret we could not find another way, but he had crossed boundaries we were incapable of dealing with."

She then told me some of the details, but only after I gave my word that they would never be repeated. "You have the right to know," she added, and we looked at each other, recognizing the anguish and pain we shared. We both cried and reached out and hugged one another.

"Mary, could I ask you a question?" I said. "And if you feel I have over-stepped boundaries, please feel free not to answer."

"Ask me whatever you need to know."

"When I was informed by the adoption agency that the boys were going to be adopted, they asked me to write down information regarding the boys' personalities, the foods they liked and did not like, and any other issues I deemed important, which were several. It was made clear to me my original list would not be sent directly to you but they would copy what I had written and make sure you received it. Mary, did you ever receive that list?"

"What they provided us was a short list from the social worker giving us some information."

"Was there anything about George sucking his fingers?"

"No, but we did try many different ways to get him to stop."

She then asked me a question, which I did not hear, because I was in a daze.

"Are you OK?" Mary asked, snapping me out of it.

"I am fine," I replied, but I was not fine. I was shocked by what I had just heard. Before I could reflect on it, though, John and Allen returned and reminded us it was time to go. We had been there for five hours already. How I wished we could have stayed longer and continued our talk the next day, but that was not an option, not only because of finances but the fact that my husband was due back at work the following day.

We followed Mary and Allen back to the airport, where we had an emotional goodbye, with promises to stay in touch. The next week was spent trying to put out the fire of anger I was feeling toward the agency and Catherine G. for not passing on the information to George's parents. I needed to have a conversation with John to determine how I wanted to handle this.

After dinner the following evening, when I related all of the negative feelings I was having towards the adoption agency, John reminded me that Mary and Allen never had direct dealings with the agency here in Massachusetts, but had worked through an adoption agency in California. That agency may not have informed them about the finger-sucking episode, thinking it was not that important.

My reply was, "You know none of this would have happened if I had been allowed to communicate with that agency or the adoptive parents."

In a calm voice John replied, "I know, and that is true, but do you really want to go back there and open up those doors when there is absolutely nothing you can do to change the past? At some point you are going to have to accept the fact you will never find the answers you are looking for.

"You know, Deb," he continued, "now that you have been in touch with both George and David, I think your energies would be better spent in trying to find out what kind of a relationship, if any, they are interested in having with you, because the future is the only thing any of us have."

"I know you are right," I replied. "Sometimes I wonder if I ever would have made it through this journey without you."

"There is no question in my mind you would have made it," he said. "It just wouldn't have been as much fun."

CHAPTER 46

Susan's Meetings

WHEN I DID not hear from George or David for over a month, I decided it was time for me to get back to Susan's monthly meetings to see if I could get some input from other birth mothers and adoptees. And, indeed, there was a great deal of discussion a few days later on how the emotional trauma of a reunion affects both the adoptee and the birth mother (few birth fathers attended meetings back in those days, though later they did and definitely spoke up) and how everyone involved needs time to reflect.

One adoptee who had been found related how he finally had to ask his birth mom to please give him some space so he could process all that happened since they met because his emotions were all over the place.

Another birth mother cautioned me, "Try not to take things personally, as difficult as that may be, because your boys are just trying to deal with being found and the emotional impact that it has had on them." She added that her son told her one day that he felt like he had been hit by a runaway train after receiving her letter.

Other adoptees and birth mothers reminded me that, at a minimum, relationships take time. They had learned through trial and error that having patience, and then more patience, is the key.

I related how one moment I was elated and filled with the wonder of seeing them and the next moment I couldn't stop crying. They all agreed that was not unusual, because I was still grieving. Then someone asked whether either of the boys had inquired about their birth father.

"No," I said, "but I am still trying to locate him, because I know the time will come when they will want to know about him."

We then talked about how some birth fathers wouldn't take responsibility for the pregnancy and just walked away. And how, with some birth mothers, their parents had disowned them or forced the issue of adoption. Some of the birth mothers said that their social worker had had preconceived notions of what should be done and that they themselves had had very little input. Then one birth mother interrupted and said, "But it was the birth mother who had to sign the relinquishment papers, and I will carry that guilt to my grave."

"You are right," another birth mother said. "I think for me the fact I could and should have found another way haunts me, and that is where my guilt is coming from."

"Well, I made a conscious choice to place my child for adoption," a third birth mother said, "and know I did the right thing at the time, but I still feel more shame than guilt."

Another birth mother said, "Can you explain what you mean when you said you felt more shame than guilt?"

The first woman's voice filled with emotion when she stated, "The shame comes from society, on how they perceived young women who were having babies out of wedlock, how I and others were sent away to a relative or to a home for unwed mothers. All of that left us with shame, along with family, friends abandoning us. The shame is something that is still with me, but not the guilt, because I believed I was doing the right thing when I chose to have my baby adopted."

We talked a lot about how shame had transfused itself into our very core and that if we did not recognize it as toxic and deal with it, it would affect our relationships, along with our mental health. These were issues that many of the birth mothers, along with birth fathers, had not talked about for years. Doing so, we learned, could help us to finally release a trauma that few others wanted to hear about or understood.

For me, it was so helpful to hear how adoptees and their birth parents were genetically connected yet still strangers; how we all were trying to maneuver through a maze of emotions and find a way into the future; how this could be heartbreaking one moment and glorious the next. The group stressed the importance of open communication. I was reminded once more that relationships take time and that I needed to prepare myself for what lay ahead.

CHAPTER 47

Family

IT TOOK FIVE years for things to stabilize to the point where the boys were comfortable enough to meet, on separate occasions, my brother, sister, uncles, aunts, and lots of cousins. David met my dad, who, sadly, passed away while George was in the navy. However, he was granted leave so he could attend Dad's funeral. When he arrived he went directly to his grandfather's casket and stood there for at least fifteen minutes. I wondered if he remembered all the good times they'd had together. When I asked him about it later, on the way to the airport, he said, "I felt a deep connection to him, but, no, I don't have any memories of the past. What I do remember are voices, soft, gentle voices." David, I learned later, also had no memories of his formative years, but did remember being in foster care.

My mom passed away two years before I started my search. It saddened me that she never had the chance to meet her grandsons as young men. I only could imagine how she would have embraced them and engaged the boys in spirited conversation as only my mother could. In time I would make sure that they knew how much she loved them. Even though she was no longer with us, I felt her spirit shining down as we continued our journey.

It took another five years for George and David to feel comfortable within the journey we were on. There were many times when they needed to pull back because their emotions were running high. The silence of their voices would go on for several weeks, and I would try to prevent paranoia from taking over my thinking that I would never see them again.

During those ups and downs, I immersed myself in my work at the Adoption Connection. I had become involved in setting up panels with adoptees, birth parents, and adoptive parents for conferences we put on each year. I also wrote articles for the newsletter we sent out once a month to our members. Susan was giving me more and more responsibility along with developing and presenting forty-five-minute workshops on birth-mother stages at conferences and adoption agencies throughout the Northeast.

It was several years into the reunion before George and David began asking question about their biological father. I still had not had any success in locating him. The thought that he might have died never crossed my mind, but after depleting all other avenues, I went online and checked the Social Security Death Index. I found that he had passed away two years before I started the search. My reaction was one of sadness mixed with disappoint-ment—sadness because our sons would never meet him and, for me person-ally, because I would never have the opportunity to ask questions about why certain things happened before the boys were adopted. So now I am left with only suppositions, never knowing what really happened. It is my hope that his life eventually went in a direction that brought him happiness.

Before I shared the information with George and David, I sent for George Sr.'s death certificate to see if there was any information regarding relatives. An older sister, a former teacher, was listed as the informant. She lived in New York City, it said. I sent her a letter, explaining who I was, and she agreed to meet me at her apartment, where I also met her daughter, who looked very much like George Jr. The sister was only able to tell me that George Sr. had distanced himself from the family. In fact, she had not known before I contacted her whether the rumor that he had married and had children was true. I had hoped she could provide me with a picture of him but was told that all her family photos had been destroyed when her house burned down during a race riot down south. David made an attempt to reach out to her but without much success.

*   *   *

MY REUNION WITH my sons, George and David, has brought joy, light, laughter, and events to my life that I could never have anticipated when I began my search. For instance, John and I traveled to California to attend George's wedding on October 19, 1982, shortly before he got out of the navy. There, he was reunited with his adoptive mom, Mary, and a few other relatives.

On May 21, 1988, I attended David's wedding in Maryland, where I reunited with Allen, his adoptive dad. Mary had passed on by then, which brought the sad irony of my stepping in for her, in a sense, as she had once done for me. There was no pleasure to be had in it, though.

It has been decades that the boys and I have been in touch. Have we struggled at times? Yes, we have. Have we achieved as much as a family as I had hoped when I set out on this journey? Far more, actually. Have we gotten lost at times? Yes, of course. Have there been sad times? Yes, indeed. Happy times? Oh my, yes. And what did we gain from it? We've learned a lot—that love takes patience and time and faith, but most of all acceptance of where the other person is and that, whatever and wherever that may be, it is OK. We've learned that in all relationships growth and learning are constant. We are each intellectually comfortable with the others in our family, on many levels, but the emotional journey continues.

That is the nature of family. Continuation is the highest goal. George and David both married wonderful women—loving, beautiful, sensitive, and intelligent. Grandchildren followed, first a boy and then a girl. With my grandchildren, there was never a question of who I was. They both call me Nana and my husband Papa Jack. I have been involved in every aspect of their lives: births and birthdays, holidays, graduations, summer vacations, babysitting, and everything in between. It seems children cannot have too many people who love them.

PART II

In Their Own Words

WE ARE ALL different. Our lives follow distinctive paths, and the responses we have to the trauma and love we experience are what make us who we are. Those choices and directions form the beauty and complexity of the human experience. That is what I have tried to illustrate in the story of my journey with adoption. But there are thousands of other stories of people who sought to locate and make contact with relatives from whom they had been separated by adoption. Each story is unique. Each deserves a book of its own.

It is important that more of these accounts be heard, because many, if not all, have something vital to teach us about the human condition and familial love. What follows are twenty-three other stories of how life got in the way of maternal, paternal, and familial love.

In Their Own Words is written by adoptees, adoptive parents, birth parents, and others. But it is written *for* all who long to learn more about the love that encircles a family, whether biological or adoptive.

D. H. B.

MISSING

Jimmy Birmingham

Since I was old enough to realize, I knew I was adopted. My parents didn't hide that fact from my brother and me. This was the mid-'60s. Adoption was still not talked about or as accepted as it is in today's society. When I told someone I was adopted, I always got a look of surprise, or sometimes people looked at me like something was wrong with me because I was "different." Maybe I *was* odd or weird to them, because they knew their heritage and family history, and I had no idea of mine. It never bothered me. I liked being different. In fact, I never followed anyone. Never followed lifestyles or trends. Ever—still to this day. I've always marched to the beat of my own drum. I actually thrived on being different. I loved attention, good or bad.

By most measures, I had a great childhood. We lived in an upper-middle-class neighborhood on the North Shore of Boston. I went to a private high school (sent, actually, kicking and screaming) and graduated from two art schools. Money wasn't an issue.

On the outside we looked like the normal, American, apple-pie family. The mother and father, house with the fenced-in pool, the dog and the sibling. On the inside we were a bit different. My parents? I'll get to them in a minute. My brother? Well, maybe some reading this have experienced this sort of relationship with an adopted sibling. I was never close to my brother, who was also adopted, and as we got older we grew even further apart. I hardly speak to him anymore. We are two totally opposite people. I always compare my relationship with him to two kids plucked from different worlds, thrown together and expected to be close. How could that even happen with different likes, different hobbies, and different personalities and traits from four different parents?

My adoptive dad bought me things because he couldn't express his love verbally. I loved that man. He was a great person. Always giving and extremely unselfish. Someone I looked up to and idolized. My dad and I had a special connection. I was his favorite, and even though he couldn't tell me he loved me, I felt it. He supported anything I did, no matter how crazy, like wanting to be a rock star or wanting to have a career in art or even things he didn't agree with. He just wanted me to be happy. He always praised me, and that built my confidence and self-esteem. We continued this great relationship up until he passed away. Losing my dad in 2006 devastated me. I lost my best friend.

With my adoptive mother it was different. She had issues from her childhood, abuse and such. I always felt like she didn't want children but my dad did, so she agreed to adopt. I was now a slight inconvenience in her daily routine. She expressed no emotions, no love, and no affection. This wasn't all the time, but 85 percent of it. Nothing I did was ever good enough. I was never praised for work I did. In her words, anything I did was always "half-assed." This has affected me throughout my life, regardless of how many therapists I've seen. I don't want to paint her as a bad person. Maybe it was the way she was brought up—cold, unemotional. I'll never know. I lost her as well. Maybe some people aren't meant to be mothers or fathers, but she was the only mother I had for twenty-nine years. I had no one else to compare her to.

What was I *missing*?

I've felt throughout life, since the age of three months, that I was the only one I could trust and rely on. No one came when I was scared, when I cried, when I needed a hug or reassurance that everything would be OK. Maybe the reason I felt this way is because I spent my first few months in foster care. I got robbed of the touch of a warm, human hand, a warm body holding me close. A beating heart to listen to. I still sometimes feel like a two-year-old who never got the security he needed. How is that possible, as I am now a grown man? All I crave is to trust, love, and believe people. I don't want to think that everyone is unfaithful, that everyone lies for gain or whatever.

By the time I was ten, it was obvious that everyone in my family was different. Didn't look like each other, nor did we share the same interests or talents. I have a God-given talent for creating art. I love it and thought at one time that anyone could create art. Eventually I came to realize that my talent must have come from my other family, my "real" family. I had many, many questions about who I was. Who *am* I? My eyes are kind of Asian, almond-shaped, kind of different. Many people have complimented me on them. Where did I get my eyes? My nose? My hair? My skinny physique? My love for danger, motorcycles, daredevils, and fast cars yet my lack of interest in sports? I was street smart but not book smart. I hated school and did poorly.

I had questions but no answers. My adoptive parents had no information about my biological parents. It was all hush-hush. People assume that when you're adopted, you just naturally fit in with this strange new mom and dad. They are so wrong. You have to try *harder* at it. It's not natural, nor does it come naturally to magically blend in. Why was I given up? Was I a mistake? Was I one too many?

One day in my early twenties I had a conversation with a close buddy, Tommy. I pretty much grew up in his home, as he lived two doors down. He asked if I ever thought about my birth mom or dad and what did I think was the reason I was given up. I always gave the same answer to anyone who asked that question: "I don't know." I'd been asked it hundreds of times. This day, though, I really thought about it.

I assumed that whatever woman out there had given me up, she must have had a good reason. I accepted this as fate and never questioned my history. It didn't really matter. I was adopted into as nice, comfortable home. I had a good life, a good education, a cool, fun job teaching art at a college in Boston. I had many good friends, good health, hobbies, and money. I had a great relationship with my dad and an OK one with my mom. I had attractive girlfriends. They came and went. Some lasted a few years. I always walked away. It was on my terms. When things were getting serious, I walked. I got scared. I broke hearts, but I didn't care, or I didn't feel it. I started to realize that I kept repeating a pattern. I figured I was still too young to settle down. It was not the time or not the right one. Or they would leave me. I didn't want to feel that again.

I also felt something deep down was *missing*.

Then, in the summer of 1998, I received a letter that changed my life forever. My biological mother had left it at Catholic Charities, addressed to "Mark." A social worker, Lisa, called to let me know and invited me to come pick it up. Driving to the Catholic Charities office, I was curious, anxious, excited, even a bit scared of what that letter might say.

As I walked up the stairs to meet Lisa I was sweating. She mentioned that it was rare that a letter would be left, possibly never to be seen by the intended person. She was excited for me. She said I could open it there or take it with me. I played it cool and said I would take it and read it when I got home, but as I drove out of the parking lot my curiosity killed me and I opened it about three minutes later on the side of the road. The letter basically said that I was given up for a better life. Cool, I could live with that. My mom was sixteen when she had me. Eleven kids and two adults living in a two-bedroom apartment weren't the best conditions for a newborn. My hand-me-downs would have hand-me-downs. Money was tight. My mom and dad weren't married. I was conceived one night, the only time they were together.

I met Marie, my biological mom, five days after opening that letter. We met on a Friday, down at Revere Beach, a small coastal city just a few miles north of Boston. I was an hour early because I was so excited. I was thirty years old, she was forty-six. I sat on the beach wall and waited. She pulled into the parking area. She was beautiful. I could see the resemblance in her slight, soulful eyes. She also looked a bit sad and a bit excited. I later found out she had been carrying quite a lot of guilt since giving me up. (Please don't feel guilty, Mom. You did great!) It was such a surreal moment. I couldn't believe we were face-to-face. I wanted to show her pictures of my childhood, but she didn't want to see them, my past. That was OK; I understood.

Most stories I've heard of adoptive kids seeking out their biological parents don't end well. Mine was a storybook with nothing but positive chapters. I found out so much about my family. For instance, I have two half brothers and four half sisters. My grandfather and great-grandfather were gifted artists. My uncles are artists as well.

Now I know where it came from. It was so cool! I was invited to a big cookout, where I met what seemed like a hundred family members. I was the focal point. As I sat on a table people came over and introduced themselves one by one. Family members, neighbors, and friends. They wanted to see me, and the reaction I heard all day was how much I looked like my grandfather. A great man, I was told.

They are all exceptional people. Each one with a different personality, but all share a love for each other, a deep family sort of pride and mutual respect. There are no inner wars, inner turmoil. I envy what they have. I sensed they were all close, something I didn't experience growing up. I was accepted into my new family 100 percent. I love them all. I still feel like the new kid and probably always will.

Finally I had answers to lifelong questions. Bob, my biological father, is a nice guy, but in the past few years we really haven't stayed in touch. We really don't have much in common (though that's where I got my skinny physique). A call here and there but no real connection. The two half sisters are on his side. Two great women, and we stay in touch. Meeting all these new people in my life was incredible and a bit overwhelming as well.

Still, something was *missing*.

As I said, throughout my young adult life I lacked two major factors: trust and love. I tried to love, I tried to trust, but deep down I couldn't. I have never fallen in love. I so deeply desire to love. What is "being in love"? Is it that awesome emotion that great songs are written about, poems are written about? I know what lust is but not true love. I have distrusted anyone who has gotten close to me or me to them. I have destroyed good relationships before they could hurt me. Sabotage is what I do best. It is my way of keeping people at bay, so they can't hurt me and can't leave me or abandon me. I hate this pattern that I keep repeating. It has me. I don't need anyone, but deep down inside I do want someone. From the outside I may seem like I have it all: looks, personality, success. My married friends are envious of my free-spirit lifestyle—come and go as I please, not answering to anyone. But I am a bit envious of *their* settled-down life, with kids and a loving wife. I guess the grass is not always greener.

This lack of love and trust caused many conflicts into my thirties. I kept hurting people, and that wasn't my intention. I just couldn't get past the deep-down feeling of pain and distrust. I didn't want to hurt the ones who loved me, but I couldn't fake it either. I wore my heart on my sleeve. People could read me and my emotions like an open book.

I'm so sorry if I hurt you.

The *missing* is still there and I'm afraid it will be forever. You would think by age forty-nine I would have figured it out. Therapists have tried to help, and one made some progress. He showed me how to be aware and pick the right people in my life, instead of ones who resembled my adoptive mother—the one I could never please, no matter what I did. The unemotional one who had issues that were never dealt with and who passed her somberness to me.

I have come a long way. I see the good in people and try to trust better. I stay away from bad, broken people whom I thought I could fix. They only bring you down. I surround myself with positive friends who add to my life. The roller-coaster life I lived is past me now. Yet I still crave the normalness that I see, read about, and feel others have and share. I want *that*! I'll get it one day....

I hate you, *missing*.

THE GOODBYE

Marie Conway

I stood at the nursery window and craned my neck to get one last look at him, but even after five days, it wasn't enough. I don't remember who was beside me, but I heard "Let's go."

It was October 1965, and I was an unmarried seventeen-year-old with a year of high school to complete. I have difficulty recalling much about that day I left the hospital without my newborn. Memories fade after many years of keeping a secret. Some things are tangible, like the little prayer book given to me in the hospital by one of the nuns from the home for unwed mothers across the street. Neatly folded in that book was a copied, typewritten letter from a priest to a girl who was planning on placing her baby for adoption. This is some of the text: "While it will be a difficult final move to sever the psychological cord the quicker the better, the sooner the better. The baby needs a stable situation: mother, father, and home. He will soon need legitimacy. He will need normal emotional development the way we received it— from a normal family situation." Why I kept that book I can't answer, but at times I would retrieve it from its well-hidden spot for consolation.

During my pregnancy I didn't stay in my hometown. A plan was made by the agency affiliated with our church and my mother. I can't remember, but I must have agreed, because shortly after, I went to live with my uncle and his family. I stayed with relatives because my parents couldn't afford the cost of a few months' stay at the home. I attended academic classes at the home and received prenatal care at the clinic there. Since I would travel back and forth by public transportation, a wedding band was purchased at a local five-and-dime store. So, the deception started and so did my shame.

My first clinic visit was another step in crafting the smoke and mirrors show. Someone assigned me a different first name (I didn't get a choice) and instructed me never to use my last name, especially when talking to the other girls—another reminder that secrets were to be kept, and it felt isolating. Some of my happiest and saddest times were spent with the girls at the home. Happy to talk to someone like me and sad that one by one we would leave, alone. After the birth of my son I returned to the home to say goodbye, and the girls asked the usual questions: what name had I given him, weight, and how was the delivery? Mostly, they commented on the flatness of my stomach.

I met with my caseworker a few times while away and when I returned home. She assured me that the decision of adoption would be mine. My options were few. I wasn't getting married to the father, I didn't have a job or high school diploma, and I lived with ten younger siblings. I never questioned whether I could keep my baby. I signed the surrender papers six weeks after my son's birth, with my mother as witness and cosigner because I was not of legal age. Returning home that day I was upset and angry and I wanted to blame someone for forcing me to sign those papers. My father reminded me that I had no one to blame but myself, which stung as if he had slapped my face. This was so out of character for the man I had always known to be kind, patient, and loving.

I returned to high school believing no one knew the truth, other than my best friends, but paranoia crept in once the rumors started to swirl. My self-esteem plummeted. On the surface I seemed to be OK, but inside I was filled with anxiety and self-doubt. These feelings never left me.

I married a few years later, had four children, and life went on as "they" promised it would, but you never forget. You always wonder if the decision was the right one. Was he safe? Was he loved? On the other hand, you don't want to know, because what if he hadn't been loved or wasn't safe? Never allowing yourself to put these thoughts to words, always mindful in the loneliness of the secret, is a huge task. My children never knew they had an older brother, and for that I have regrets. I regret that I couldn't allow myself to talk to my father, mother, or close family members about my child. The secret became a burden I wished I hadn't carried so long.

The Letter

The thought of searching for my son never entered my mind until I was made aware that a paternal half sister was searching for him. It was August of 1996, and I still believed that I didn't have the right. But if I didn't have the right, who did? Honestly, I didn't want him to think that he was not important enough for his mother to search for him, but I had unconsciously listened to the voice of long ago that said I could not. Only after reading the Agreement for Adoption paper provided to me in 2000 did I understand. There it was, in black and white: "I do hereby surrender, fully and unreservedly, said child and give him to the Agency. Agreeing that I will neither seek to discover his home, attempt his removal therefrom nor in any way molest the family in which he may be placed or other parties interested."

Believing my secret might be revealed, I contacted the adoption agency by telephone and inquired if information regarding my son could be given to other interested parties. I was told that the agency would not give out that information to anyone, including me, but I could put a letter in the file. First time in thirty years I was told that I could do such a thing. The caseworker also mentioned that, according to her records, my son had not started a search. She must have heard my disappointment, because she went on to explain that many adult males seek out their biological parents when they are making life changes, such as getting married, having children, etc. A few months later, with much apprehension, I wrote and mailed that letter, realizing how many lives could change. I addressed the letter with the name I had given him at birth and told him why I had made the decision of adoption and basic information about my life. I finished the letter, letting him know if he wanted or needed more information I would provide it.

About a year later I received a call from the agency and was surprised to learn that my son had received my letter during a visit in which he had requested nonidentifying information. While I was grateful to learn that he was alive, I was numb. A feeling of loss and sadness enveloped me, and my first question to the caseworker was, "Did he have a good life?" She told me that when she had previously spoken to my son, he wanted me to know that he had had a great life. I received the phone call in a few days, and after three hours of conversation we decided to meet at the ocean a few days later. I needed time to tell my children about their older brother, and emotionally I was drained.

The Hello

My first glimpse of him was before I turned my car into the parking space next to his truck. Sitting on that seawall like a little kid with a familiarity that I can't describe was surreal. I remember just sitting in my car unable to move as I viewed him through the windshield. Finally, after a minute or two, I opened my door and was thankful that he spoke first, because I had no words. I thought tears would come, but they didn't. Guess that old guard of mine wouldn't allow them. I felt awkward, amazed, and welcomed his hug. The hug was great but sad for all the years lost. I couldn't take my eyes off of him, I remembered a baby, but I felt the bond. As the afternoon went on, he shared family photos and his life experiences. I kept my feelings distant, because I felt that I had no part in his nurturing or accomplishments.

It was shocking to me that the following day was one of agony. The uncontrollable crying and unresolved pain were almost too much to bear. I have since learned, with much help from some remarkable ladies at the Adoption Connection, that I had locked away the feelings of joy of first motherhood and replaced them with shame, guilt, and grief.

Reunion

Before the reunion I had been in great denial and had shoved the pain of surrendering my son down so deep I questioned whether it had really happened. I can understand why some birth mothers forget their child's birth date. I never imagined that one day I would have the opportunity to know my son. I bought everything they told me hook, line, and sinker. I believed that if a baby was placed with a loving adoptive family, he would never have questions regarding his origins. A first-time mother would resume her prior life, as if the birth never happened, and forget. I now know that neither is true.

At the beginning of our reunion I was an emotional wreck. I doubted my actions, reactions, thoughts, and I felt so alone. In desperation, I turned to a newly acquired home computer, seeking answers. I somehow navigated to an adoption website and connected to another birth mother. Her story was so similar to mine that we poured our hearts out to each other over a period of months. I know if I had not found her, I would have lost my mind. Thank you, Abby.

Some days were filled with such sadness that I knew I needed help to continue with the reunion. The agency recommended that I contact the Adoption Connection. I learned of their monthly meetings for anyone in the adoption triad, which consists of birth parents, adoptees, and adoptive parents. I attended many meetings, not speaking, but listened to other birth mothers and, more importantly (to me), adult adoptees. I continue to attend meetings to this day, allowing my voice freedom from the silence of shame. It has been a lifeline. Thank you, Deb.

Shortly after the reunion, I traveled to city hall, seeking the original birth certificate. I was told that it was impossible to obtain, but I could get a copy of the amended one. I went to the hospital where the records of my son's birth were kept and again received news that those were destroyed after thirty years. Frustrated, in the summer of 2000 I contacted the agency again. The caseworker sent me the young parent record—basically their case file of me during and after my son's birth, along with the surrender document. I petitioned the court for the original birth certificate. I sat in front of the judge while he examined legal document that contained my name and that of my son and was told that the record would remain sealed. I called the church where he was baptized while in foster care, and the priest denied my request for his baptismal record. On both occasions, I was told that if my son requested these documents, he could receive them. Again, sealed records reinforced that I had surrendered my rights.

I have learned that keeping secrets obscures truth. Once I gave up my secret, I felt liberated. I am hopeful that today's social climate allows young women to make their own choice regarding what serves them and their children best.

My reunion with my son has led to many life changes. My four children have welcomed and adjusted to having an older brother. My siblings have been happy for me and continue to tell him how much he resembles my father. My son was the only grandchild he saw before his death. My mother died a year before our reunion, and we never spoke about the grandson lost to adoption. I think it was too painful for her. What I wouldn't give to have a conversation with her today.

By all accounts, it has been a very good reunion of seventeen years. In the past I have struggled with our relationship of mother and son. It's so different from raising your child from infancy with no secrets or regrets attached. I continue to educate myself on adoption issues and let go of "what might have been." Lately it has been easier for me to reach out to him without fear of rejection, and I can't imagine not having him in my life.

My journey continues in reunion with hope, love, and forgiveness of self. I am mother to five, not four.

EXTENDING A FAMILY

Marvin Drake

Anniversaries have a way of creeping up on you. For me, in the first few years after my son was given up for adoption, each anniversary brought pain, shame, guilt, and sadness. But, as the adoption agency had advised, I got on with my life. And as the years went by, the anniversary began to fade into the background and only the major ones—ten, twenty, thirty, forty years—brought back the melancholy. Each one of these caught me thinking of what he might be like, where he might be, who was raising him, whether he was having the better life that had been promised by the agency.

In all those years, I heard nothing from his birth mother, whom I had dated in college, or him. I made no attempt to contact him, because we were warned never to look for him or to return to the agency for information. After I lost contact with his birth mother, I also made no attempt to contact her. I just hoped they were both doing well.

As the fiftieth anniversary approached, however, I felt in my heart of hearts that something was going to happen—either a knock on the door or a phone call or a letter from him asking to make contact. I dismissed it as wishful thinking. But the thoughts kept coming back, so I began to listen to them and consider what they might mean. I still thought of my son as a child or young man. I had no concept of him as a fifty-year-old, fully grown man who had a long life behind him. When I thought of the birth mother,

I just remembered the pretty girl she had been when we were together five decades earlier.

The history of the birth mother—I will call her Karen here—and me was typical of that time. We had a whirlwind romance that started when we sang in the college choir during a two-week tour. We continued to see each other, and it felt like the relationship was going somewhere. But in the excitement of new love, we rushed into a physical relationship without thinking of the consequences. The cold light of reality hit us when she discovered she was pregnant.

We hadn't taken precautions, since birth control wasn't available for unmarried couples back then. We talked over and over about what to do, but the only options were marriage or giving up the coming child for adoption. Abortion wasn't an option, since it was illegal and very risky. A single mother raising a child was also unheard of in those days.

Marriage was something neither of us felt prepared for. Both of us were scholarship students working part-time jobs to pay for our education. If we started a family, all of this would be gone and the education and the careers we wanted would never happen. For many reasons our families either couldn't or wouldn't help us out. That left only one option, giving up the child for adoption.

Through her doctor, Karen was put in touch with a facility for unwed mothers in a distant city, one of the Florence Crittenton Homes. We drove there without telling family or friends. Karen, we decided, would return to the campus after the baby was born as if nothing had happened. Her ploy would be to say she had taken a job for a few months to save money for school. I was to continue with my classes. We remained in contact through letters and phone calls during the months she was at the home. When I went to visit, she was in good spirits, but I felt like the scum of the earth with the eyes of the FCH staff on me. I was able to work extra hours and sent her what money I could to help with the costs.

When the baby was born, we discussed what to call him and settled on the name of my maternal grandfather and great-grandfather as his first name.

(Here I will call him David.) Karen added the name of her favorite brother for the middle name. I asked that my name be on the birth certificate, but fifty years later I discovered that that had not happened. He had been given Karen's family name, and since I was the "alleged father," my name was not legally allowed on the birth certificate. So Karen alone signed the papers to give David up for adoption. He was put in foster care shortly after the birth and was placed for adoption after the two-month waiting period dictated by the laws of that state. The agency assured us we were doing the best thing for the child, and we believed it was true.

Karen returned to campus midyear, as we had planned, to start her sophomore year. We met secretly to avoid her family's condemnation of me and to not arouse suspicion among our friends. Most of the talk between us was about the last few months and little was about the future. When we did discuss the future, it became apparent that we wanted different things in life. I thought she would head east with me when I started graduate school in the fall. But she wasn't at all sure if a future with me was what she wanted, and she still had several years of college ahead of her. After graduation I left for a summer research job in another part of the country. When I returned I couldn't find her and no one knew where she had gone. I felt I had ruined her life and should never intrude into it again. So I headed east, resolving to never cause anyone such harm again and to keep the secret of Karen and David the rest of my life.

Graduate school led to a research position, which ultimately yielded a PhD. Within two years I met Elizabeth, who became the love of my life and my wife and who has stuck with me through the ups and downs of more than five decades. After years of marriage, we had a son on whom we focused our lives. I tried to be the best father I could be, but never felt I was a good enough husband or father. This eroded my self-confidence both personally and professionally. I suffered through bouts of depression, which I attributed to stress at work and at home. I was diagnosed with fibromyalgia, along with other ailments that sapped my mental and physical strength. Finally, I sought counseling. Even there I did not at first reveal the secret of Karen and David, since I thought I had put all of that behind me. Then six years ago, I received an email through my college's alumni registry. It was from Karen. She asked if I remembered her and our days in the college choir. She was suffering from cancer, she said, and had a limited number of years to live. She wanted to bring closure to the part of her life that had been hidden.

Another surprise was that we had lived within twenty miles of each other for thirty years. She had finished her schooling and moved east to start her career. She also went on to marry and have a family and much success. Nonetheless, I felt I had ruined her life, and the feelings of shame, guilt, and sorrow that had lain dormant all those years now came back full force. I knew I had to work through these painful memories and sought counseling. I began to realize how hiding the secret from my family had impacted my marriage and my ability to be a good father. For a month I tried to work through my turmoil while continuing my contact with Karen.

Eventually, keeping the secret became unbearable, and one Sunday morning I found the courage to tell Elizabeth what had happened and pray that she would accept me as I really was, which she did. Her acceptance, love, and support has been what has gotten me through all that has followed.

Through all the years we had been together, she said, she knew there was something I was hiding, but didn't want to confront me about it. She knew that something was hurting our marriage, but didn't know what to do about it. From that day on, we have worked to make our marriage strong again and to find the happiness that we seemed to have lost.

I still had the hard task of telling our son and granddaughter about David and Karen. Our son was very upset at first and has had a hard time forgiving me for keeping the secret all those years and causing his mother such pain. On the other hand, our granddaughter said that a child out of wedlock was no big deal to her generation.

Of course, there was still one matter left unresolved. After a few months, Karen told me she wanted to search for our son. I reminded her that we had been warned, "Never try to search for him, and never come back." I felt we had no right to intrude into his life. But she wanted to know what had happened to him while she still could, and finally I relented.

Karen contacted an adoption organization and was assured it was both legal and desirable now for birth parents to search for the child they had surrendered. I learned about the support and advocacy organization Adoption Community of New England (ACONE) and joined a support group for birth parents and another that also included adoptees and adoptive parents. Elizabeth came with me to be supportive and to learn about adoption and its consequences.

I believed I would be treated like the scum of the earth. Such was not the case. We were both welcomed warmly from the very first meeting. Adoptees told me it was my duty to search for David and give him the choice whether or not to make contact. That advice was the start of a journey that was to bring great happiness into my life.

Over the following months, Karen and I traded information back and forth as we found out, bit by bit, what we could about David. The agency was located, and it still had the records on microfiche. Several weeks later we were sent redacted records of David's birth, when the adoption had taken place, and a few facts about his adoptive parents. Using cryptographic methods, I was able to establish where his adoptive parents had lived and a partial spelling of his first and last names. Karen came up with a list of all the babies born that day at that hospital in that city. By comparing the list with what we had, we came up with a complete first and last name. With this much, we were able to trace his adoptive father, through his work, to the city where David now lived. A search agency produced a possible address, and Karen immediately sent him a letter explaining who we were. David replied within days in a long letter about himself and his life. Karen then called him, and his response was warm and welcoming. A few days later I called him and also received a warm response. We talked for several hours, filling in the basic facts of our lives. He said that Karen and I had nothing to feel guilty or ashamed about since he had had a good life and thanked God every day for it. An enormous weight thus fell from my shoulders.

In the next few weeks David and I talked on the phone and exchanged emails and many photos of both of our families. The physical similarities were striking, as were the similar interests in music, religion, and other areas. David had been raised in the same faith as I. We even played some of the same instruments.

During the search, I had asked for help from our minister, who was glad to be of assistance. With his acceptance of my story, I began to tell a few close friends about David. I was a bit fearful, but their reactions were uniformly that of acceptance and gladness that I had started to heal this wound in my life. I then told my brother and his family, and they too supported me. Little by little I told my story to other friends and then to acquaintances in our church community. All the while I was drawing on support from ACONE members, who cheered me on. Gradually, I felt the burden of guilt lifting from my life and began to discover the personality I had lost. With this came a new joy in life, a new freedom, and a self-confidence that I hadn't felt in years.

Finally, David and I began planning when we would meet for the first time. It would be when he came to visit his adoptive mother, who now lived just two hours away from Elizabeth and me. The meeting took place the day after Thanksgiving, a few days after David's fiftieth birthday. Elizabeth and I met him and his girlfriend in a restaurant, and we couldn't stop talking. When they closed the first restaurant, we found another and continued the conversation. Two days later we were invited to meet his adoptive mother, Phyllis, at her home and were warmly welcomed there. I took my instrument along and David, Phyllis, and I played some jazz together.

Since then, Elizabeth and I have visited David and his girlfriend. We were introduced at his church and met many of his friends at a barbecue given in our honor. His sister (also adopted) and Phyllis were visiting at the time. My cousin and her husband, who have two adopted children, traveled from their home and had dinner with all of us. My other son and David met and are now friends on Facebook. They call each other on the phone from time to time, and David and I talk by phone on a regular basis. Phyllis has come with us on vacation the last three summers, and we play and sing music together.

On that first visit, David shared with me his feelings about his adoptive father, who had passed away more than ten years earlier. His dad wanted David to be a scientist or an engineer, but David had wanted to be a professional musician. He got a degree in computer science and was never allowed to go to music school; this conflict with his dad was never resolved. Instead, David developed his musical talent on his own and has performed professionally in bands and as a soloist. He also owns a recording studio.

David and I found that we shared a love of reading, of ballet, of canoeing, and camping. We have discussed religion, politics, and culture, as well as music and family and his hopes for a better life, a better job, and more education. I also learned more about his family's activities—mostly choirs and concerts that his mom and dad organized and led but also their travels and church participation.

I am still learning about David's struggles to be his own person and am convinced that he is a good man with a good heart and is heading in the right direction in his life. I still feel sorrow for not having been there when he could have used my help or my approval. I have grown to love David and find in him all I could have wished for in a son.

His mom, now a part of our extended family, gave David wonderful gifts of creativity and music and a love of people. Where we will go as an extended family is still not determined, but my wife and I are finding this a wonderful new part of our life. My hope is that David and his family feel the same.

A SECRET REVEALED

Elizabeth Drake

One lovely, sunny Sunday morning I was sitting at the dining room table reading the newspaper when my husband, Marvin, came in. I noticed he was tense and nervous. He said he wanted to tell me something important. It was then that he told me he had had a son born before we met and that the child had been given up for adoption. Several weeks earlier, the birth mother had made contact after many years.

On hearing the news, I was so relieved and blurted out, "Is *that* all?" At last, I knew what had been bothering him these last several weeks. He had seemed so preoccupied, agitated, and withdrawn. His behavior had scared me. Whatever was bothering him was serious, was bad news. I knew it in my bones. So now the secret of the existence of this child was out in the open. He obviously was so relieved, and with the burden off his shoulders, suddenly he looked like the person I had fallen in love with so many years ago. I told him that he and Karen, the mother, should sort out the details of their reunion after so many years. At that point, they had not met in person, only communicated by phone and email. They had a lot of catching up to do.

At some point in this process, they decided to look for their son.

Slowly, the enormity of this revelation sank in. At first, I was scared, very angry, and then afraid of the possibility that they would want to rekindle that love of so long ago. As time went on, my husband and I kept talking about the new reality that had entered our lives. (We talked a lot throughout the process.) I began to see him as the young twenty-one-year-old college student having a good time with his girlfriend.

When the pregnancy presented itself, he'd had absolutely no idea what to do and felt lost, with no emotional support or advice from anybody. My heart went out to him, and I tried to support him as well as I could.

I did not give much thought to my needs or feelings. Instead, I concentrated on being there for my husband, who appeared to be living on an emotional roller coaster.

At this point, let me explain that I grew up in another country, on the other side of the world, in a culture with clear-cut rules of behavior for girls and boys. We did not have the freedom my American counterparts had, probably because none of us had access to a car, let alone own one. Voilà! No fooling around in the back seat! I am sure pregnancies occurred then too. However, given the culture we lived in, these events were absorbed into the fabric of the family clans. I cannot remember anyone being stoned or thrown out of his or her home. My friends and I went to the same school, hung out together, and kind of moved about in a pack. When I came to the United States to go to college, I found the dating habits of my fellow (male) college mates rather strange to say the least. I had landed in another culture and was faced with different customs. By the time I was about to leave for graduate school at another university in another city, I met this graduate student. We hit it off and, yes, this fellow and I married fifty-one years ago.

I do remember I never asked him about his love life before we met, because I believed then that this was none of my business. That was his life before our relationship became more serious. Regrettably, it was my mistake for not asking about his earlier life. It could have prevented much heartache many years later.

In time, my husband started attending a support group for birth parents, and I went along, again to learn and to support him. Before that, I could find the word *adoption* in a dictionary, but I had absolutely no idea of what the true story was like. Now I would find out.

We have been going to the support groups for a few years now. I have learned much about adoption, reunion, and all the pain they can cause. Nevertheless, I want to say here that very little is said in them, nor is there much interest, in the role of spouses like me. For a birth parent to search for a child lost to adoption so many years ago is most important, and yet I feel that the support of a spouse is also important. In the meetings of birth parents and triad meetings, I have not seen many spouses in attendance. It is as if they do not exist, but perhaps more likely they do not attend because it does not involve them directly. As a spouse attending these monthly meetings, I have been asked on more than one occasion why I was there. After all, I did not have direct involvement in adoption or relinquishment. However, I continued to go to meetings with my husband because I, too, needed support and understanding. However, I have not found it often at these meetings. The support I have found has come from the friendships that were formed over the years, and those have been so important to me.

My husband and Karen started the process of finding their son and, amazingly, made connection with him in about seven months, which is considered a short time as far as searches go. After all the excitement began to fade, I became aware of my own feelings, and these were scary. The best way to describe them was that I was red-hot angry with my husband. How could he have kept this secret from me all these years and live like everything was normal? Having an old flame out there, sure, I could understand that. However, having a son somewhere out there was too much to comprehend. For a long time anger became my safe place, where I could feel and hide my ugly, vengeful thoughts.

I believed him when he told me his reason for not telling me this part of his past, but for me it was not enough. I became increasingly distraught. I remembered the many times that I felt he was hiding something or not telling me what was bothering him. When I asked and did not get a clear answer, just a "Nothing," I dropped the subject. For his entire career, my husband worked in a field that required the highest security clearances. Within the family, I called them the "spook projects" and knew he could not share anything about his work, and I thought he could not answer my questions for those reasons. Looking back now I realize this was the perfect setup for keeping "the secret," and unknowingly I helped him in this deceit. I felt betrayed, and I was furious with him.

The reunion created such intense feelings of anger, fear, sadness, and powerlessness in me that I sought help from a therapist. After I had worked with her for a while, she assured me my anger was not going to kill anybody even though I felt like it. Slowly my therapist and I worked through the emotions and sadness. I learned that I had good reason to be angry, to feel sadness and grief for the lost times of intimacy and physical connection with my love over the years.

The process of healing is slow, but I have been at it for a few years now, and I know I have become a much stronger, more compassionate person. I also know I am not so quick to trust and still very cautious in how I deal with emotional issues. My husband and I continue working on rebuilding our marriage, especially the trust we lost. No more secrets! Now whenever something comes up that does not feel right somehow, we try to bring it out in the open right away.

While I worked on this article, the tsunami of memories returned, and I thought about it almost full-time. It is not upsetting or scary anymore, but more like a reexamining of what is now part of my life in open form. It is no longer an unknown undercurrent in my marriage.

Soon Marvin will be reliving that period in his life again when he is interviewed by an author who is writing a book about birth fathers. I think the conversations will stir up those buried emotions once more, but I also think this reliving process will write finis to this chapter of his life.

MY NEW MEANING OF "FAMILY"

Diana Dunphy

When I was a college freshman, I became pregnant and wasn't married. At that time, in 1965, there were only two choices in a situation like that: get married in a hurry or disappear and place your child for adoption. I chose the latter.

A few years ago a variety of events led me to seek counseling. The counselor's specialty was adoption, and she directed me to an organization that offered support services to the adoption community. I joined the organization's birth-family group, went to the support meetings, and did lots of reading. I began poking around for information. I had no records related to my daughter's adoption. I was now living in a different state and couldn't remember the name of the agency I had used.

I shared my frustration with the members of the birth-family group. A month or two later, the facilitator of the group called and gave me a name and number to try. It took me a few days to get up the courage to make the call. I immediately reached the social worker, who was able to check the records and confirm I had used their agency to place my daughter. I told her I was interested in placing a letter in her file saying I was open to contact should she ever want that. The social worker encouraged me to search for her instead.

I wasn't ready for that. I was too scared. I felt I had no right to search. There were so many questions: Could they find her? Was she alive? Was she happy? Would she forgive me? Would I be intruding? Would she even want contact with me?

I spent time thinking about what I should do and talking with my family. They assured me they would support whatever I chose. They wanted me to be happy and healed.

I finally screwed up my courage and initiated a search. It was like jumping off a cliff into the unknown, one of the scariest things I had ever done. I chose to search through the adoption agency, because if my daughter was found, I wanted her to feel protected and be able to choose what would happen next. An agonizing six weeks of waiting followed. Finally, the social worker called. She had found my daughter. Her name was Kara, and she was excited and interested in contact with me. Holy guacamole! This was really happening. Kara and I began our correspondence cautiously, via email. We wrote to each other almost every day. I still have most of the emails archived. There was so much to learn about one another. I couldn't wait for each new message to arrive. After a couple of weeks, we were ready for a phone call. It lasted almost two hours. What pure joy! When I got off the phone, I sat down and had the cry of a lifetime. There had been decades of accumulated emotions following the adoption. It had come to a head, and the dam had finally broken.

Fast-forward: We've been reunited for years now. Kara lives an easy two-hour drive away. We see each other often and are a part of each other's lives once again.

When she accepted my offer to reunite, she had the support of her family, including her mother and father, who will always be her mom and dad. She had a wonderful upbringing, far beyond what I could have provided at the time. I wasn't in a position emotionally or financially to parent a child.

I now have three additional grandchildren, who call me Nana, and a wonderful son-in-law. I've met her family and friends, and she's met mine.

We are among the fortunate ones who have families who are open and embracing. My husband quickly viewed Kara as a daughter. My two sons were onboard from the start, and the three of them are forming their own relationships. It took Kara's sister, Beth, a while longer to adjust to our reunion. She couldn't understand how Kara could embrace me and my family so quickly. She was worried she was losing her sister to us. It took many conversations for them to get to a place of acceptance and understanding.

I remember being terrified of meeting Beth for the first time. Much to my relief, it went well. We've had many occasions since then to be together at family events. Oh, the meaning of that word just keeps expanding!

Being reunited with my daughter has changed me. I am a far more complete person: able to accept myself and be happy with who I am. There is no longer a secret to protect or grief over her loss to deal with. She's in my life again. For that, I am truly thankful.

Diana Dunphy is the birth mother of Kara Ammon.

IS EVERYBODY ONBOARD?

Kara Ammon

I'm not sure that I would have ever looked for my birth parents. I grew up in the best family anybody could hope to have, and while I was curious about my birth parents, I did not feel compelled to find them.

My parents told me that I was adopted. In fact, I do not remember ever thinking otherwise. They also said that being adopted made me very special because "they got to choose me"; that was not entirely accurate, but it conveyed to me how deeply I was loved. Mom and Dad had struggled to have a child of their own before adopting me, then became pregnant with my sister, Beth, shortly afterward. Beth and I are ten months apart and very close. If they had not adopted me, I was told, Beth would likely not exist, a fact that I delighted in pointing out to her when we were younger.

I'm pretty sure that if I had expressed an interest in searching for my biological parents, Mom and Dad would have been supportive, but at some level I always felt like it would have been a betrayal. So I never did. I had one additional concern: that I might one day look in my adoption file only to find that no one had ever tried to find me or leave a letter or note for me. This was another tiny deterrent to searching.

When I was forty-four years old a letter arrived from an adoption agency in my birth state, New Jersey. I was shocked. The letter, from a social worker, indicated that my birth mother had placed a letter in my adoption file.

She asked if I would like to have the letter. (One tiny deterrent overcome.) As a point of pride, I loathe crying. I broke my arm in kindergarten and never cried, not once, until the doctor was actually setting it. The communiqué from New Jersey did what a broken arm could not and I found myself in tears.

It was Saturday. Few government agencies would be open, so I had two days to decide what my response would be. It did not take me that long. I talked with my husband. I called my sister and my parents. Reactions varied: My parents were cautious, but affirming. My husband was onboard. My sister was unenthused and a little apprehensive. By my tally that was two in favor and one opposed. I decided to call the social worker on Monday and ask her to send me the letter. This was exciting.

A little over a week passed before a small package arrived. It contained information from my adoption record, a family medical history update, and the letter from my birth mother, Diana. I learned about the circumstances of my birth. I already knew that I had been born in Atlantic City. Over the years I'd conjured up several theories to explain my start. Chief among these was one involving a hooker and a country music singer—Johnny Cash, to be specific. I learned instead that Diana had been a scared, nineteen-year-old college student. I learned that my biological father was definitely not Johnny Cash.

I discovered that I had half siblings and a host of stepsiblings, and I found out that I had spent a small amount of time with Diana before my adoption and that she had called me Raquel. Anyone who knows me will tell you how absurdly wrong that name is for me. It has been the source of numerous jokes since. Including one night when my friends met me out for drinks. By the time I arrived at the bar, they had handed out name tags to everyone, including the waiter, that read, "Hi, My Name is Raquel!"

The best part of the package was the letter from Diana, who as it turned out lives just two hours from my home in New Hampshire. Her letter explained, briefly, the decision to place me for adoption as well as her motivation for now reaching out to me. It also contained an open invitation to contact her when I was comfortable doing so and by whatever means I chose. She included her email address; I emailed her about a week later.

This package was something I would pore over many times, trying to absorb all the contents and what they might mean for me and my family. Was I different now that I knew some of my biological family's background? Had anything really changed?

My sister will tell you that I jump right into the deep end and worry about my ability to swim much later. I was on an emotional high and hit midair before realizing that the cliff was no longer under me. If there had been a manual to accompany reunion situations this would have been a great time to consult it. In my enthusiasm I sent waves crashing down upon my family. My husband and children seemed to bounce along just fine, but my sister and parents were beginning to spin as I announced my intentions to contact Diana and possibly explore a relationship with her.

Diana and I corresponded by email for a little over a week, and then we spoke on the phone. We talked for over an hour. We had an instant connection. The emails continued until Diana and her husband, Art, returned from a trip they were on in Florida. We set up a time to meet. I drove to their house on the South Shore of Massachusetts bright and early. I was both nervous and excited as I rang the doorbell. Art answered and I'll never forget what he said to me: "You are the answer to prayers." We were off to a good start.

We spent the morning drinking coffee, looking both at pictures (hers and mine) as well as each other, trying to decide if we saw a resemblance. Art took photographs, one of which is now framed and on the cabinet in my front hall. It was an amazing day.

Over the next few months, Diana and Art would come to visit my home and my husband and the kids. We would email and chat on the phone, meet for lunch, and go shopping. I introduced Diana to a number of my close friends. Things seemed to be going right along.

As my relationship with Diana progressed, I reported it enthusiastically to my sister and parents. I told them how great it was and that they just had to meet Diana and Art. Beth wanted nothing to do with meeting anyone and cautioned me about moving too fast. It might have had something to do with the fact that I insisted on extending the scope of my "family" to include Diana. From Beth's perspective "family" was earned, not granted. Instead of backing off, I doubled down. Beth and I went round and around. We had heated discussions that led to hurt feelings. At one point Beth even sent Diana a letter telling her that she did not appreciate her inserting herself into our family. Beth and I would spend the next couple years working through, bit by bit, all that the reunion with Diana had stirred up between us.

Diana offered Beth understanding and space. Beth worked to come to terms with her feelings, while I tried to moderate my expectations. Little by little Beth's resistance melted into acceptance. She began to invite Diana to family gatherings. Beth's children, Emi and Mason, accepted Diana. Emi even lived with Diana for several months while completing an internship nearby.

The relationship between Diana and I continues to grow and deepen. I have also had the good fortune to connect with my two half brothers and their families, along with Art's extensive family and a host of relatives in New Jersey. Every one of them has been a blessing.

Kara Ammon is the birth child of Diana Dunphy and the adoptive sister of Beth Soeder.

LEFT BEHIND

Beth Soeder

The story has been told countless times. Mom and Dad could not have a baby. They tried for ten years. Finally they turned to adoption. They *chose* Kara. They could have had any baby, but they chose Kara. They wanted her with all their hearts. And then, without even trying, Mom got pregnant with me. My sister was the reason I was born, they said. It happens all the time. You adopt a child and the next thing you know, you are pregnant.

There were only the four of us: Dad, Mom, Kara, and me. Our grandparents died when Kara and I were young, and when they were alive, they lived a good distance away. Then a letter from a social worker came out of the blue, asking Kara her if she would be interested in contact with her birth mother. I was shocked.

During our teen years, Kara never talked about finding her birth parents. I asked her on several occasions growing up if she wanted to find them, and she said no. Once, just once, I think, she said "maybe": after Mom and Dad passed away she would "think about it." It was never an issue, never a topic, never a concern. I believed her. Then the letter arrived.

We are in our forties now with families of our own, and our parents are in their mid-eighties. I was sure she would reply "maybe, after my parents pass away" or even "no thank you." But contact and reunion ensued, and Kara and Diana were instantly enamored with each other.

Kara said she was interested in medical history. She probably told me that because she realized I was upset. She talked about how great Diana was and how I just *had* to meet her. I figured Diana was probably not hearing about how great Kara's sister was and that Diana had to meet *me*. I grew more concerned when Kara introduced her children so quickly to their new "Nana."

It turned out Diana lived just two hours away from Kara, whereas our parents and I were six to seven hours away and visited only twice a year, because of the distance and also busy schedules. Kara and Diana, meanwhile, visited a lot, traveled to meet other relatives, and seemingly talked daily, even more than Kara and I communicated.

It was hard for me to swallow "instant family." Kara now had two interesting and successful brothers. She bragged about their careers and sent me videos of television commercials that they had acted in. I wondered if she told them that I was a published author, that I was interesting. I doubted it. I was not a part of this "thing," just a bystander.

To be fair, I gave my sister the impression I did not want to be a part of it. I felt jealous, betrayed, replaced, excluded, and protective. I told Kara I would wait and see how the relationship worked out, after the honeymoon period, before I met Diana. My concerns fell on deaf ears.

Kara and Diana texted constantly. They made inside jokes on Facebook. Diana commented on everything the kids were doing, like a doting grandmother. I was ashamed of how jealous I was. I began to feel it was not my right to be upset about my sister's new family. I stopped telling her how I felt. I stopped fighting about meeting them and agreed to meet Diana. I wanted Kara to be happy.

When I talk to my sister now, we both agree that she and I did not handle things very well. She admits to going overboard, texting Diana over and over while I was visiting her. I admit that I did not respond very maturely.

I met Diana. And you know, I *liked* her. Time has passed, and I still like her. My sister is happy. Diana is happy. I'm happy for them.

This story is about the ripple effect that a reunion creates between a birth mother and her child in a family. Kara and I were not equipped to handle that as well as we could have. I am taking the opportunity now, as the one who was "rippled," to express what I have learned during this process. Since I was asked…

Diana,

You selflessly and bravely planted your seed in my family's flowerpot. Your seed grew and bloomed into a healthy, beautiful flower. As she grew, her roots became entangled with ours.

At first I thought of you coming to pick your flower from our pot. I was upset. I was immature, overprotective, and jealous, and for that I am sorry. I wanted nothing to do with your reunion. Time has afforded me a clear head and has calmed the emotionality of the situation.

Our family roots are so entangled that by finding Kara, you have found us. She is not just that seed or single flower anymore. She is part of our pot. Being "family" with my sister requires that you adopt us, the whole pot. We will join your garden, if you'll have us. I know this is a shock, as my rosebush has been so thorny.

Beth

Kara,

A family is forged out of time, shared experience, shared growth, an understanding of someone beyond the moment, unconditional love, and trust earned by the fact that they were there every time you looked over your shoulder.

When you instantly became family with Diana, I felt betrayed. It was different from bringing a fiancé home. At least you knew him very well before you agreed to marry him. We can trust your judgment in that type of situation. You were just getting to know Diana when you were trying to convince me to meet her. I was protective of you and our family because they mean *everything* to me.

I realize that, based on my anger, you have tried to have a separate relationship with Diana. I realize that I forced you into that because you were trying to spare my feelings, but in the end, I just needed more time to adjust to the situation. I know you feel very much like Diana is family already, and I know I will get there too, given the opportunity.

I think maybe that was what you were trying to force on me, but I wasn't ready. I'm ready now.

Love,
Beth

Beth Soeder is the adoptive sister of Kara Ammon.

THE PAST RETURNS

George Fonteno

Each adoptee has a story to tell, and mine is not exceptional, for there is nothing exceptional about loss and pain. Yet, how they affect one's life is another matter.

When my natural mother reentered my life after twenty-one years, I was in the United States Navy. I do not remember anything more about my enlistment, because I spent the rest of it pulling together every remaining bit of my common sense in order to survive.

Her return came in the form of a letter. Being somewhere between sanity and insanity, I was thrust back through time to a five-year-old child being introduced to his new parents, then to a ten-year-old boy being sent away to a boys' home because of his unwillingness to adapt to his new family. I saw this same boy sitting on his bed, looking out the window of the dormitory to see the other boys go on their regular weekend visits with their respective families. This boy grew up in other boys' homes and on occasion went to juvenile hall because of his unruly behavior and constant running away. At the age of nineteen, he was released into the world, complete with a job and a place all his own, expected to become a productive member of society.

I saw a twenty-one-year-old man waiting for hours at the bureau of adoptions for information he had requested on the whereabouts of his natural parents. The waiting came to an end with a small sheet of handwritten information identifying two nameless and faceless people, their vocations, heritage, and family history. When the young man asked if he could get in touch with them, he was told about the ramifications of such contact and what might result—the possibility of shame and retaliation, the opening of old wounds.

I saw this man reading the information given to him time and time again, all the while reconfirming to himself that he belonged nowhere in this world. I saw him wonder about a brother he'd been separated from when he was sent away. I saw him join the military, a new life for him and a chance to be part of something in which he could take pride despite an otherwise hollow existence.

A year later, the letter from my mother came, announcing her return without ever considering, it seemed, how it might affect me. I felt victimized, enraged, after so many years of accepting that I did not belong anywhere, of seeing the light of curiosity and hope regarding my natural parents stamped out, of trying to pull myself out of the invisibility of life in the military. I felt as though I'd been raped. I felt naked, deaf, dumb, and blind to my present reality. I felt a big joke had been played on me by a God who did not care.

Yet, that same person claiming to be my natural mother weathered my emotional outbursts. She showed determination and strength in the face of my resentment, arrogance, and long periods of silence and noise, relaying to me her own past of loss and painful experiences, urging me to see my shortcomings as challenges and not defeats. This she has done with much understanding and few words.

It has been thirty years since I looked back upon that ten-year-old boy watching the other kids leave for the weekend with their parents. Sometimes I go and visit the boy. Sometimes we just sit in silence. Sometimes we talk. I told him, "Our mother has come back."

FAMILIAR FACES

Mary E. Fournier, MSW, LCSW

In 2009 my spouse, Marilyn, and I decided to take our adopted daughters to Guatemala on a homeland journey. As a social worker in the adoption field, I had traveled with young adoptees and their parents to China and had seen the profoundly positive experience that homeland travel can give to adoptees. We wanted our girls to have that experience.

We had been talking with them about their birth families from the time they were each placed in our arms, four years apart—not because they were able to understand but because we wanted to get comfortable talking about it. On one evening walk when our older daughter, Lucia (not her real name), was three, she told me that she had been in my tummy. I corrected her, explaining, "You were in Ana's tummy, and then you came into our family after you were born." Because I do adoption work and have counseled many women and men who consider placing their children for adoption, I thought it would be natural and easy for me to talk about it with my own daughter, but even I got a lump in my throat as I said her birth mother's name.

I have learned a lot about the benefits of open adoption for all members of the triad—birth parents, adoptive parents, and adoptees—and not just permitting contact between birth parents and adoptees but practicing it freely. Visiting Guatemala, giving our girls the experience of their birth culture, and meeting other Guatemalan adoptees and their adoptive families seemed like good first steps in the process of opening their adoptions to birth families. We would be spending two weeks there with other families formed through adoption. We wanted to show our children not only that Guatemala was a beautiful country but also that there was a place on the earth where many people looked like them. And on our first day there, climbing off the bus, Lucia said, "See, Mom, now I look like everyone and you don't!" I knew she could see herself in the faces of the adults and children who looked into our faces.

Lucia hadn't been comfortable with the idea of searching before our trip. She was nine and, though she had lots of questions about her birth family, she had not asked to embark on a search. Over those two weeks she watched as several Guatemalan adoptees met their foster and birth families. She hovered around the periphery of reunions that were held in the courtyard of our hotel. She kept saying she thought she had seen her birth mother, and I looked over my shoulder many times, hoping to find a face that matched the photograph of her birth mother, Ana—to no avail. However, I met a searcher, Susi, during that trip who had reunited many adoptees with their biological families. I wanted to know if it was realistic to think we could find Ana. And at nine years old, was Lucia at the right age to make this decision?

Over the months after our return home, I thought more and more about my daughter's birth mother. I read an article about Susi, which made a deep impression on me. Many of the women who had been found said that they could now sleep at night knowing that their children were safe and loved. Did we have the responsibility to let our daughter's birth mother know this as soon as we could? How would we balance the timing of this with Lucia's readiness to find her birth mother? If I initiated the search, would I be robbing Lucia of the rite of passage that many adoptees embark on to search and find their identity? Surely this is the life work of many adoptees. I could find no definitive answers to these questions.

I asked myself, *What would we find?* It occurred to me that Ana could be destitute, addicted to drugs, living a desperate life, or, even worse, not alive at all. We knew there were four older siblings. Did they know about the baby who had not been raised in their family or would our searching disclose information to them that Ana hadn't shared? Was their birth father involved in the family? Would we be putting Ana at risk of domestic violence if Lucia's name came to light in her current living situation? After talking with friends and colleagues in the field, I came to realize that there were many questions that could never be answered. Like many adoptive parents, Marilyn and I had to make a decision about what was right for our daughter in her life situation.

Meanwhile, through arranging domestic adoptions I was learning about the many ways openness enhances adoption. For a birth mother, openness can reassure her that her child is alive and loved. She can see that the child is living the life she had hoped for. For adoptees, questions about their origins and the reasons they were placed for adoption can be answered. For adoptive parents, it is an opportunity to share their love and pride in their child with an extended family.

When Lucia was eleven we contacted Susi in Guatemala and got things rolling. There were papers to sort through, documents to find, monies to be paid, a photograph album to put together that Susi could take to Ana, and, most importantly, expectations to manage. The structure of the search was clearly laid out before us: Once the appropriate documents were reviewed, the searcher would go to the last known address and see if Ana was there or if neighbors remembered her. If that didn't reveal anything, she would go to the indigenous area from which the family came. Every step of the way Susi sent us emails and photographs of the places she went—photographs of herself in those places so we could see she was really there. This all took time. On our part, this took a lot of patience.

In September of 2011, Susi told me she was at a dead end. She said things might be different in six months and that I should connect with her at that time. It was hard. Our daughter had so many questions and we did not have answers for her. I grew more and more worried about what we would find. I often tell people that no news is just that, no news. It does not mean bad news—and I had to apply that mindset to our situation. But I also wanted to prepare Lucia for the possibility of bad news.

On March 1, 2012, I reached out again to Susi via email. She had been meaning to contact me, she replied, and could I call her? She had turned up some information on Ana's children, she told me over the phone, and thought she might be able to learn whether they knew her whereabouts. She advised us that this could lead directly to Ana. We would wait until we heard back before telling Lucia.

On March 3, I received an email from Susi. In the subject field it said, "I found Ana!" I lost my breath. She wrote that she had two addresses for Ana's children and found them at the second one, in a neighborhood in Guatemala City. Susi showed the photograph we had of Ana to her children and they confirmed it was their mother. They said Ana would be home after 3:00 p.m. and that they would have their mother call when she returned home. Meanwhile, Julia, Ana's second daughter, phoned her mother, who confirmed that she had placed a baby for adoption twelve years prior. Ana then rushed home to meet Susi and see the photographs we had sent. Susi sent us forty-two photographs of her meeting with Ana and her children, along with a transcript of their meeting. What had seemed so far away—the possibility of finding Lucia's birth family—was now right in front of us!

We called our daughter down to the kitchen when she got out of the shower. "Susi has found your birth mother," we said, and she burst into tears.

"Now I don't have to worry about her anymore," Lucia said. "This is the best day of my life!"

We sat down at the kitchen table and scrolled through the photographs slowly. Lucia was delighted to see three of her four siblings: Roberto, age twenty; Julia, eighteen; and Carlos, fifteen. The family resemblance was strong!

"Look," Lucia said. "She has my nose!" But no one had her smile, not that day.

WHAT WE HAVE NOW

Richard Erroll Fuller Jr.
and Susan Hamlet Nickerson

Susan: The week between Christmas and New Year's continues to be a busy time at our house. Work as usual, the kids are home for the holiday break, Christmas cleanup begins, and I'm pondering birthday and New Year's Eve plans. On this particular day, December 27, 2000, I shuffled through the pile of mail on the dining room table hoping that my paycheck was hiding among the stack of envelopes. Finding nothing besides credit card offers, a few bills, and an envelope with my name typewritten on it, I threw the pile back on the table. Two days later, while waiting for my husband to come home, I was looking forward to joining family and friends for dinner at a local restaurant. It was my forty-seventh birthday. I started thumbing through the growing stack of mail once again, and the typed envelope caught my attention. Tearing open the flap, preparing to rip up the contents and deposit it in the circular file with the rest of the junk mail, I skimmed over the page inside: Dear Susan … September 26...I was born a Hamlet….

What is this??

I returned to the top of the page, slowly reading every line. The words began to penetrate my mind. With a pounding heart and disbelief registering on my face, I realized that the unbelievable, the one thing I never thought would happen, was unfolding before me. My son, whom I had relinquished for adoption over 30 years before, was asking to meet me.

Rick: I'd decided in the summer of 1999 to search for my birth parents, ostensibly for medical reasons as I approached my thirtieth birthday. I was living on the West Coast, and someone put me in touch with a search agency in Massachusetts, where I had been born and raised.

I didn't do anything with this information right away, as it seemed so abstract and distant. Then of course, life got in the way. In the next year, I went through the end of two relationships, a cross-country relocation for a new job and the end of a close friendship and musical partnership. By the autumn of 2000 I was living alone in an off-season beach rental in Seabrook, New Hampshire, and working the overnight shift at a biopharmaceutical company. My sleep schedule was irregular, but I decided that, as long as I got to work at the right time, I'd sleep and wake as my body saw fit. Sometimes I'd go to sleep at 5:00 p.m. and wake up at 1:00 or 2:00 a.m., so I spent a lot of solitary time in that beach house, writing songs, waiting for my favorite coffee shop to open. My days off were spent bicycling, writing, and going to a recording studio in Boston, where I forged ahead with my music project despite the setbacks.

I had been in touch with the search agency, and I was told that I needed to go to the Essex Probate and Family Court in Salem, Massachusetts, and petition to open my birth records. One day in November, I woke up at 5:00 a.m. or so with nothing on my mind or schedule and decided, "This will be the day."

I drove down to the courthouse, arrived just after it opened, filled out the paperwork, and within a half hour I had a packet of photocopied documents containing my secret history.

I wandered around the Old Town plaza for a bit, breathing in the crisp autumn air and reflecting on my last few moments of not knowing. I sat down on a bench and opened the packet: Jeffrey Scott Hamlet ... Susan ... 16 years old ... unnamed father....

I wasn't prepared for the emotional reaction of learning this information about myself. Memories of my life up to that point flooded my mind, but with a different perspective this time. I never realized that I had always felt alienated, but this snapshot of my secret history gave a name to that feeling of alienation, and I felt the weight of a lifetime of adapting to unconscious insecurity and the fear of abandonment. It was like when you get an eye exam and you're looking through the lenses at the chart, and suddenly, *click*, everything comes into focus.

I was in shock.

Susan: Over the next few days I was numb with the shock of hearing from my birth son after all those years. The memories of the past, long suppressed, played over and over in my mind like an old, sad movie. It was difficult to envision a grown man named Rick while remembering walking out of the hospital and leaving behind my six-day-old infant named Jeffrey.

In his letter, Rick asked me to call him, hoping that we could meet within the next couple of weeks. Each day I struggled with the same thoughts: What do you say to your child whom you gave away, whom you've thought about, wondered about, worried about every day for thirty years? I feared that he would be angry with me or, worse, hate me for giving him away. I didn't know if he could possibly understand what it was like for me to be sixteen years old and pregnant, unmarried, ashamed, and scared to death of the future without my baby. All I knew was that he wanted to see me, and I was petrified to make the phone call.

Five days after reading Rick's letter of contact, I finally worked up enough courage to make the call. I felt that he had waited long enough to hear from me, and I couldn't begin to imagine what he may have been thinking while he waited. It never occurred to me to ignore his request, even though it meant that I would have much to explain to family and friends, including my three daughters and two of my siblings, who did not know that my son existed. He was my secret, a secret that was never discussed within my family after the relinquishment papers were signed, a secret that I waited to forget.

I sat on the floor in the den, huddled in a corner, the room lit only by the morning sun streaming through the windows of the adjoining rooms. Gripping the phone in one hand and my birth son's letter in the other, I could hear a voice repeating inside my head: "Dial the number. You have to dial the number." A calmness began to settle over me as I pressed the buttons on the telephone and listened to it ring. I wanted so badly to hang up, but my arm refused to move. Someone picked up. "Hello?"

"Richard?"

"Yes?"

There was a slight pause. "This is Susan Nickerson."

Then I listened to my son's voice for the first time in thirty years, and all my fears were washed away by tears.

Rick: The weeks of anticipation before I made contact were agonizing. When I provided the search agency with the information from my birth records, it advised me to not make contact until *after* the holidays, as that is often an emotionally sensitive time for birth parents. So I stewed in confusion and self-pity in that lonely beach house for a month. It was the most emotionally painful time of my life.

On Christmas, I drove to a friend's house for dinner. On the way, I stopped at a mailbox and deposited my letter to Susan. By the time she'd get it, the holidays would be over.

Susan: The year was 1970. I spent ten weeks in the Florence Crittenton Home for unwed mothers in Brighton, Massachusetts, to await the birth of my baby. This was my choice, as I knew that if I stayed home with my family in the small town where I grew up, I would be isolated and hidden away, my shame and embarrassment running deep. My parents supported me in my decision to go away.

I settled in at Crit, as we called it, and met many girls who would become my friends, some for years to come. We were each assigned a social worker from the home and one from the adoption agency, and they both told me that my son needed much more than I could give him, that I would go on with my life after relinquishment and I would forget that this had ever happened. What I wasn't told was that my life would be forever changed.

"You'll get married some day and have more babies," they said. I did get married, and I did have more babies, but I never forgot about my son. I returned to high school in October of my senior year, feeling like a lost soul, yet trying to be a normal teenager, when there is nothing normal about being separated from your baby. I was no longer the carefree, innocent teenager I was before. I had given my baby away, the most unnatural thing in the world that a mother can do.

When my baby was five weeks old, I signed adoption papers allowing him to be released from foster care to join his new family. The relinquishment was never spoken of again in my home. We all did a very good job of pretending it had never happened. I buried my feelings of grief and loss, yet continued with visits and letters to the social worker from the adoption agency. She was the only link to my baby, the only person I could speak with about him. For years, the word *adoption* triggered something painful inside of me. When I would see reunions on television, I would get up and leave the room. If anyone spoke of adoption, I would leave the room, fearing that someone would ask how a mother could give away her baby, her own flesh and blood. Although I had done it, I didn't have the answer to that question, and to this day, I don't know how I walked out of that hospital alone, my arms empty. Every time someone mentioned the birth father's name in a conversation, it felt like a kick in the stomach, not because I resented him, but *Jim* equaled pain, the pain of losing my son.

During the month between when I received Rick's letter and our first meeting, we communicated mostly by email, getting to know each other, our thoughts and feelings running crazily from highs to lows and everything in between. Although the excitement of communicating with my son was a gift like no other, it was difficult to grasp the idea of learning everything about him as if he were a complete stranger, yet feeling this very old and intimate connection.

My husband and I met Rick at the Museum of Fine Arts in Boston. Having him in my arms again after leaving the hospital alone was a dream come true. But only after standing face-to-face and looking into the eyes of my adult son did I fully realize the magnitude of what I had lost. I sank into a depression that left me incapable of living my life as I had known it. I withdrew from all that I had previously enjoyed. While I was thrilled to have my son back in my life, neither I nor anyone else could understand my sadness for all of the lost years, the years we could never get back.

I sought the help of a therapist who was experienced in adoption-related issues. I read everything I could find on the subject, attended support groups, and was amazed by the number of people I met who had stories similar to mine and understood all that I was experiencing. After meeting my son, I found that I was finally able to examine all that had happened in 1970. I was hungry for the information that I felt belonged to me.

I contacted the hospital in Boston where he had been born, asking for my records. I contacted the adoption agency and paid a fee to get my information, and I visited the home for unwed mothers, which no longer housed unmarried, pregnant women. I felt like I was chasing ghosts, but I needed to walk the halls and remember, to relive what happened there in order to start the healing process.

My husband and son were with me when I visited the home. We were escorted to different parts of the building. I kept wandering off by myself to different areas and stopping to feel, to remember, what it was like at that time. I also needed to know my son's time of birth, his weight and length. I needed to know the details of my visits and communications with the social worker at the agency, which I learned lasted for five years after my son was born. I also learned that I was more fortunate than many, who had no counseling at all after placing their children for adoption.

Rick was a very important part of my family for the next four years. He attended many of our family gatherings, weddings, holidays, graduations, and parties. He visited quite often, sometimes spending the night at our house. While I loved having him here, I dreaded his leaving when the visit was over, wondering when or if I would see him again. I was still dealing with my feelings of loss and not having an easy time. Of course, during this time, our visits and contact waned a bit, which I had expected would happen. He worked every other weekend and was spending his weekends off with me, and I knew he could not continue to do that for very long. The fact was, I needed him more than he needed me, and it felt like a personal rejection when he chose not to spend time with me. My logical side understood that what was happening was normal, but my heart wanted all that I could get. We planned a fun night out to mark our four years of reunion, but I was in a difficult place again and couldn't envision pretending to have a good time while feeling so sad, so I canceled our plans. That was the last time I would hear from him for three years. My biggest fear had come true.

Rick: For quite a while I experienced the highest of highs, and I felt invincible and complete. It was really exciting and healing to learn and experience so much, and my heart opened. Unfortunately, our individual feelings weren't completely in sync, and I could tell that Susan was elated but also terribly sad because of all of those lost years. The societal construct of closed adoption can be incredibly damaging. The pain caused by it seems so pointless, but after a certain point, so is obsessing over it.

Additionally, joining a family after thirty years is not the cure for feelings of alienation. In Susan's presence, to a small but excruciating extent, I felt like a ghost—the ghost of her baby instead of the grown man I was. (I had also felt like that when I was seventeen and my mother passed away; every time her family looked at me after her passing, I felt like they were seeing the ghost of her.) This feeling was, in hindsight, clearly the result of my feeling of alienation, but I was way too involved to recognize it or not be controlled by it.

So, gradually, our time together seemed to get darker and darker, sadder and sadder. We'd made a promise to each other early on to always communicate openly and honestly, and that stopped happening. I was hypervigilant during the whole reunion process because I foolishly thought we could avoid all of the reunion pitfalls I had read about. That was completely unrealistic and must have put a lot of pressure on Susan. So I was frustrated when open communication stopped. I was frustrated that our time together was being squandered. I was so angry about those canceled plans!

Ultimately, it was the feeling of being the bad guy that got to me. I overheard and observed some things that angered me, things that made me feel responsible and, worse, blamed for the difficulties that people were having.

A huge trigger for me is feeling misunderstood and having my motivations doubted. After my mother died, my support system collapsed, and I was forced to be self-sufficient at a relatively young age when I was very emotionally damaged by it all. I had been let down repeatedly by people that I trusted, so I grew up to be extremely skeptical of and oppositional towards authority or anyone who I felt was challenging me. This general resentment fueled my capacity to say, "Fuck this, I'm done," which is exactly what I did.

Susan: I tried to contact him by email, I called him on the phone and left messages, and I sent cards for different occasions. All of my efforts were ignored. I searched and found that he had moved to Colorado. I was hurt and angry that he would disappear from our lives without a word. I hurt for myself, my husband, and our daughters. Our family had been completely disrupted when he found me, and now he left us without saying goodbye. I asked him repeatedly if he needed some space or a break to process all that we had been through, and he denied it. I blamed myself for his taking flight, knowing that he was angry because I canceled our plans. He later told me he knew I was having a hard time and he felt as though I wanted him to fix it and he didn't know how. So he did what he would typically do in these types of situations. He bolted.

Rick: Yes, I was resentful and frustrated, but I also really needed to change my lifestyle. I was increasingly unhealthy in both body and mind, so I took a job in Colorado to get myself together and get healthy, play in the mountains, etc. As it turned out, coming to Colorado was both a blessing and a curse. The recreation was great, and my lifestyle improved, but due to the nature of my work, I again had to work overnights, and that really caught up with me. As I got older, my body and mind could not handle that schedule anymore, so it was difficult to think clearly and be honest with my emotions.

My partner reminded me fairly regularly that I needed to get in touch with Susan and that I was being unfair and hurtful. I promised her that I would, but I was afraid and guilty and resentful, and it took me a long time, far too long.

Susan: Three years went by and out of the blue, Rick responded to an email that I had sent wishing him a happy birthday. I was very surprised and happy to hear from him again, and we began to try to rebuild the relationship that we had previously had. This was easy for us, although I was sad that we had missed out on three more years.

A mother loves her children unconditionally. My husband was very forgiving and put his hurt aside, but our daughters were not. They are still hurt and angry, but I realize that they are all adults and have to work this out for themselves. I cannot do it for them. It comes down to how badly they want a relationship with each other.

While I don't like the disconnect and the separateness of my children, I am doing what is right for me. And that is to continue to communicate with my son, to visit when we can, make the most of what we have now and look to the future rather than the past. It took me a long time to forgive myself, and although I still regret my decision to let him go, I am grateful that he took the initiative to search for me, to reach out with open arms, and to accept me for who I am. We've been back in touch for seven years now and have settled into a new normal, and I look forward to a future that includes my son.

Rick: It was a difficult leap of faith to get back in touch, and I was terrified of rejection. This time, the rejection would have been personal and for real reasons, as opposed to when I initially made contact over fifteen years ago as a stranger. We were able to use the time to step back and work out our own stuff, but the manner in which I initiated that break caused other problems, for sure.

It was an act of self-preservation. We were all hurting terribly with no end in sight. I still feel bad for hurting Susan's husband and daughters and the mistakes I made; that's part of life. The measure of a person is what happens after the mistakes. After all of these years, I'm finally at a point where I feel that I can live my life for myself, accept my emotions, and own my choices. My motivations are no longer unconsciously informed by the abandoned, alienated child I once was. In the autumn of 2000, there was no way of knowing the journey or the outcome, but I am truly grateful for what we have now.

HOW WE GOT FROM THERE TO HERE

Ellen S. Glazer

Years ago I ran into a friend from social work school at the supermarket. I asked her what kind of work she was doing, and she told me she was involved in open adoption. For me this was a new and unfamiliar term. The year was 1981, and I was holding my newly adopted infant daughter. Three weeks earlier she had come to us in a closed adoption.

Although I cannot recall what I did last week, I can remember this supermarket encounter as though it happened yesterday. I remember the feeling of anxiety that came over me and interrupted my post-adoption, new-mother bliss. Open adoption made sense, and there I was with a baby whose birth parents were entirely unknown to me.

Fast-forward nineteen years. It is Thanksgiving Day. We are sitting around the holiday table. Everyone takes a turn saying what they are thankful for. When it comes to my daughter, Elizabeth, she says, "I am thankful to have my birth parents' first names." At the time, her words took my breath away. How profoundly sad it was that my daughter was thankful for something that most of us take for granted—the ability to know something as basic as our parents' names. Sitting there, I never imagined that eleven years later, a member of Elizabeth's birth family would officiate at her wedding and that five members of her birth family would be in her wedding party. Nor could

I have pictured Elizabeth's eighty-nine-year-old grandmother dancing the night away with eight-year-old Mitchell, Elizabeth's birth cousin. And, for sure, I couldn't have pictured the scene a year later following the birth of her son, Ryan. There we were in her hospital room—her birth father and me—fumbling together to try to change that first poopy diaper! This is the story of how all of us got from there to here.

First, some background: Elizabeth was adopted as a newborn. At the time, her dad and I were told only a few facts about her birth parents—their ages (twenty-one and twenty-two), their ethnicities (Spanish and Irish), their educational levels (college for her birth father, cosmetology school for her birth mother), their heights and weights. For eighteen years that was all we had and all we could offer Elizabeth. In adolescence, she began to ask for more information. Our response was that we would help her in any way we could when she turned eighteen.

When Elizabeth was a freshman in college, she called us on our offer. "I'm ready. I want to meet them." And with these words what turned out to be an incredibly simple and incredibly complex process began—simple in logistics, complex in emotions. Our adoption agency had closed during the years following Elizabeth's placement, but records had been sent to another agency that had a wonderful social worker devoted to search and reunion. She met with Elizabeth alone a few times and with her dad and me. In addition, Elizabeth and I traveled together to Washington, D.C., for the annual conference of the American Adoption Congress, where she heard a range of search-and-reunion stories. After several weeks of preparation, all agreed that Lisa, the search-and-reunion social worker, would embark upon a search. She told Don, Elizabeth's dad, and me that she had her "sources" and her "ways" and that it was unlikely to take long.

Lisa was able to identify both of Elizabeth's birth parents within a few days. She tried first to contact Elizabeth's birth mother (through a series of increasingly specific mailings) but received no response. Although she must have been deeply hurt by this, Elizabeth never let on. Instead she calmly asked Lisa to move on to her birth father. Thankfully, he responded immediately and, in what we would soon learn is always his way, with warmth, enthusiasm, humility, and unconditional love. Elizabeth and Bob "met" on April 5, 2000.

Bob and his wife, Karen, have a strong relationship and two terrific children, Ben and Hannah, both now out in the working world. Bob is a wonderful father, husband, and member of his community. He is a successful mortgage broker who works hard for his clients. Elizabeth is a skilled emergency room nurse with a kind heart and a gentle, soft-spoken way about her. She works hard to please and gives generously of her time and energy and often asks little in return. Two good and capable people. Two people thrilled to have found each other. One might think that it would all be easy, that reunion would be seamless. It was not. In the early years of their reunion, Elizabeth and Bob suffered through misunderstandings and bruised feelings that neither felt inclined to let go of. There were many times when each felt hurt and angry. Here are some of the reasons I think Elizabeth and Bob's first several years were so difficult.

First, I don't think anyone can really prepare for reunion. That said, there are instances in which both people are searching. Each seeks (and fears) connection with the other. Each has imagined—many times—what reunion will be like. In this reunion there was only one person searching: Elizabeth. Bob, although thrilled to be found, had not contemplated searching. And Elizabeth, the searcher, was barely nineteen years old, operating more on longing than on a well-thought-out search process. They were two people on an unplanned journey without a compass.

Next, there are some particulars about Bob's family and ours that must have complicated things. Although Bob responded immediately with warmth and delight to Elizabeth's contact, Karen, his wife, was initially cool and reserved. She had known since she and Bob first dated that he had placed a child for adoption, but she, too, had not anticipated reunion. Thankfully, Karen came around and has been wonderful to Elizabeth and to all of us. Sadly, Bob's two sisters and his mother never have. Elizabeth could not help but feel rejected by them, and Bob was stuck in the middle.

Then there are the complex issues in our family. Elizabeth's dad and I divorced when she was five. Each of us subsequently remarried, but Don's second marriage, to a woman whom Elizabeth adored, ended after five years. Although she has always had two parents who love and cherish her, Elizabeth grew up shuttling between two homes and, in one instance, dealing with a second loss. By contrast, Bob's family is stable and, in many ways, the family Elizabeth must have longed for. This, together with the fact that Bob made it clear he had wanted to parent her but her birth mother insisted on placement, may have fueled Elizabeth's probably unconscious anger at Bob for not fighting for her.

But before I lapse into more psychologizing, let me say that Elizabeth and Bob muddled through. They argued, each felt injured, each raised questions about whether the relationship was worth it, but they hung in there. Hanging in there meant seeing each other every few months, usually in a family context. Sometimes Elizabeth went to Bob's house or to one of Ben's or Hannah's sporting events. Other times, Bob and his family came to my house. And when Elizabeth got her own home, she invited them there.

One day about eight years ago, Bob went to a closing on a home that he was helping finance. The real estate broker seemed familiar and after several minutes, he put it together: she was Mary, the much younger sister of Elizabeth's birth mother. Mary was only seven years old when Elizabeth was born. Sitting there at the real estate closing, Bob was tempted to tell Mary about Elizabeth, but he kept silent—at least until he could get out the door and excitedly call Elizabeth to say, "Guess who I saw today!"

As real estate professionals in contiguous communities, Bob and Mary, he assumed, would bump into each other again. That did not happen, but about three years ago, a death notice in *The Boston Globe* caught Bob's eye: Mary's father had died. Upon reading it, he immediately called Elizabeth and told her that her birth mother, who lives in the South, would probably be in town for the funeral. He said she could go alone or with him and told her where to find the obituary. Elizabeth did not go the funeral, but she read the death notice carefully and held on to it. Which is where Facebook comes in.

"Mom, I'm going to friend Mary on Facebook."

"Who is Mary?" I asked.

"My birth aunt. I've written a note to her and I'm going to friend her. Now."

It was late at night. I'm not into Facebook. It didn't sound like a good idea. Still, I had Elizabeth read me what she planned to write, and it sounded OK enough, considering that no one expects to hear, on Facebook, from the niece you never knew you had.

And that is pretty much how we got from there to here. Elizabeth pushed send, Mary read the posting late at night and woke her husband to tell him about the message she had received. The following morning she called her mother, Della, and told her to come over, assuring her that she had some news that was startling, "but in a good way." Della reacted with a combination of surprise and delight, stunned that she had another grandchild, but thrilled to welcome her.

Elizabeth's reunion with Della, Mary and eight other members of her maternal family could not have gone better. Whether it was because none of the ten people played any role in placing her for adoption or because they were so unanimously thrilled to meet her or because they had sustained other losses as a family that made her arrival all the more welcome, we cannot know. All that matters is that it was great from the start, and that is surely what Elizabeth needed.

Elizabeth and Joe were married three and one-half years ago. Tara, her birth aunt, officiated. Three of Mary's four children were in the wedding party. Bob's daughter, Hannah, was a bridesmaid and his son, Ben, a groomsman. After the ceremony, I saw Bob and Della standing together. I walked over and heard Bob telling Della the story of Elizabeth's birth. He continued with me there, explaining to Della that he had not known his fiancée was pregnant until she was about seven months along and by that time, she was set on making an adoption plan. Della told him that when she thought back on it, she recalled noticing that her daughter looked like she might be pregnant. However, when Della asked her if she was, her daughter denied it and told her mother she had a fibroid. Then there was the poignant moment when I watched each of them look over at the beautiful bride. I imagined them thinking about what was and what might have been.

When we went inside and the DJ invited me to give a toast, I told the Thanksgiving story and then spoke of the awe and gratitude I felt because, eleven years later, fourteen members of Elizabeth's birth family were celebrating with us. I thanked all of them and singled out Bob and Della and Mary, grateful to each for the warmth and gracious ways in which they responded to being found. Then I turned to the newlyweds and said, "But my real toast is to you, Elizabeth, for your courage, determination, and vision, and to you, Joe, who has joined her in her abiding belief that there is no reason to have a single family tree when you can make a whole forest bloom."

KINDNESS UNREQUITED

Andrew Gordon

My adoptive parents had been married for fourteen years by the time I came along, and as they went through normal midlife difficulties, our house became less happy. They didn't pay a lot of attention to the effect this had on their children. I wish they had been more attuned, but there is no denying that they gave me more security than I could have had from my biological mother, especially given what I now know of her circumstances. Life wasn't perfect, but by most standards I was privileged, and my adoptive parents were my family, as far as I was concerned.

I did sometimes wonder about my birth parents and why they hadn't kept me. As I got older, I realized that my existence probably represented a matter of shame for these mysterious people. I came to feel that, in giving me up, they had earned the right to their lives, and it would be wrong to try to find them. Of course, I would have had no idea how to begin searching for them had I felt otherwise, and this made my attitude a convenient one. Questions about my origin were always fleeting, and for the most part I grew up blissfully unquestioning.

In 2006, when I was forty-seven, I heard a radio interview with Ann Fessler about her just-published book *The Girls Who Went Away*. I took a copy with me on vacation and devoured it—an eloquent, moving volume about women who gave up children for adoption in the years before *Roe v. Wade*.

It focused on individuals who regretted their decision later and found their children or hoped to be found by them. I wondered—incredibly, for the first time—whether my birth mother might have been such a person. The idea began to nag at me. How could I rest without ascertaining that she was not like the women in the book? For all I knew, she might even be one of them. By the time I turned the last page, the notion of searching for her had transformed from an unimaginable violation into a moral obligation.

Within fifteen months I had found and written to my birth mother (I'll call her Miriam). She telephoned me at her first opportunity, saying she had not regretted giving me up, but was not sorry I had found her. It was a long, cordial conversation, with one goose-bumps moment when she told me she had been waiting to hear from me for about a year, having sensed that I was looking for her.

I had imagined this conversation many times during my search. It was always underpinned with a thrilling, mystical resonance reminiscent of a chapter in George Eliot's *Daniel Deronda*, which had mesmerized me decades before. The actuality of our talk, as one might expect, did not live up to my dream. This woman was just a stranger whose story happened to involve me in a paradoxically intimate way. There was more sense of the surreal in the conversation than anything else. On the phone with me was the voice of a ghost, heavy with the strong regional accent I'd somehow managed to avoid picking up myself—but she wasn't a sphinx, just an average, unremarkable older lady like any I might have walked by on the street. As she told me about her children, I didn't feel resentment or envy, but neither could I escape a sense of irony: Miriam freely supplied voluminous detail about the life of her family, while her entire adult years had been dedicated to keeping mine a secret.

Disappointingly, she had forgotten many details, including even the date of my birth, but I was able to garner the basics of her—my—story, which had been smothered in secrecy: her sisters were told she was going away to a "special school" (they still do not know the truth as I write this); her father bribed someone at the hospital to leave her name off the birth certificate; he and her mother ordered her never to breathe a word about it to anyone, especially a future husband. Because she'd been burned the one time she played with fire, she obeyed them. She never went to a high school reunion because of the chance that someone might bring up her six-month disappearance. The past was buried.

It was sad, if unsurprising, to hear all this. The bright side was that she didn't regret my finding her; in fact, she said she was dying to meet me. After the call, I felt exhilaration that I had done the right thing in searching for her and relief that I'd managed it without causing trouble for her at home. Her sisters lived in my part of the country, and she occasionally drove to visit them, so it seemed that at some point we might actually be able to meet. (It was impractical for me to visit her, because of her husband, who knew where she was pretty much all the time.) I felt optimism, and gratitude for what she had endured in bringing me into the world, but otherwise there was surprisingly little emotion toward this woman. Still, I was recovering from the bizarreness of it all and didn't necessarily know what I felt yet, what I should feel, or what I might feel later. There was no playbook. Anything could happen, and now that I had spoken with her, it seemed it would be a continuing story, with possibilities I was open to.

Six weeks later, on the day I turned forty-nine, she called me again. It was a heartwarming and encouraging gesture. She called a couple more times that year. The conversations were always pleasant. The next year she left a message on my machine with an apology for having missed my birthday, although she had actually called two weeks early. She must have forgotten the date again. She called one other time that year. The following year, I didn't hear from her at all.

Given her initial enthusiasm, this drop-off was a disappointment, but it didn't seem hard to understand: she had said that her husband would divorce her if he ever learned about me. She said she wished now that she had disregarded her parents' instructions and told him the truth, because "things could be so different," but she couldn't tell him now, after fifty years of secrecy. Their marriage offered her so little autonomy that even the idea of her sending me any pictures of herself was out of the question. To this day, I have only seen one photo of her, gleaned from the internet and showing her as she looked in her sixties.

When I started my search, I knew that this might well be the situation I would find, and I had gone into the process with a determination that, if that should turn out to be the case, I would accept it and do nothing to disrupt her life. I told her that her security was the most important thing to me and that I would leave it up to her to contact me. In a later conversation, when the chance of a meeting seemed to be dwindling, I did make one request: I asked if she could leave some kind of note about me for her daughters, in case something should happen to her. She was afraid to put anything like that in writing and apologetically declined.

Over the next couple of years, I heard nothing more. I looked online for an obituary, but couldn't find one. Even if she was alive, she could be incapacitated; how else to explain the silence, after her calls in the first year or two? I began to wonder if I should try calling her. I didn't like the idea, but if I blocked caller ID, there would be no risk if her husband answered, and there was always the chance she might answer herself. I decided to do it.

She did answer—perfectly healthy and even a bit breezy. Her husband was out. I began by apologizing for calling her, but to my surprise, after all my agonizing, she was not angry. It was almost anticlimactic.

After that call, another silence ensued, and as time went by, I began to allow myself to look at the situation from a more selfish point of view. It was true that my search had been for her sake, not my own, but her early calls to me had seemed to offer the hope of regular contact, which I can't deny was a pleasant prospect. Now that seemed to have disappeared, and its absence began to feel like rejection. It would not change my determination not to harm her, but I now felt deliberately overlooked.

Four years went by with no further word. I wondered again if she might have died. Miriam was in her seventies; that day would have to come sometime. I decided to call one more time, still with the same precautions. If she were there, and had simply neglected to be in touch with me, I would not call her again—ever. As before, she answered. She could not talk because her husband was there, but she called back the next day. I took a more distant tone than I had previously and told her I had called to make sure she was still there and that I would appreciate hearing from her. Once a year would do; I just didn't want to be left wondering. She assented, and we chatted a bit. That was two years ago and the last time I have heard from her.

At this point, it's obvious things are stalled, at best, as long as Miriam's husband is alive. I have to consider the possibility that she simply doesn't want any further contact with me, perhaps because of my pushing her to stay in touch. This would be unfortunate, but if it is true, I'd rather have her tell me so. Still, I am not sure that this is what lies behind her reticence. She told me in one call that her life had been a lie—I particularly remember this because it struck me as such a sad thing for someone to say. I had wondered how she could have forgotten so many details about as far-reaching an experience as having a child. It seemed to border on the incomprehensible, until I imagined her having to face herself in the mirror each day and share a life with the conservative husband she had described to me. To maintain a covert relationship with me would simply remind her daily of the lie she felt she was living and perhaps force her to open doors she needed to keep shut. I suspect that if she is ever free to open those doors, she will find lost memories returning. (I base this on the reaction of one particular birth mother with whom I've discussed it.) Until that time comes, I can understand if she has a need to maintain denial. Meanwhile, I live by the promise I made to myself at the beginning: I will do nothing to cause any harm. There are so many people unwittingly involved in this story—spouses, half siblings, half nieces and nephews, aunts. What pleasure could there be in meeting any of them if they saw me as some malevolent person who showed up heedlessly to wreck their lives?

At the same time, I am not above feeling occasional resentment, perhaps anger, that my consideration is not being repaid in kind. Given the destruction I could have caused in the life of Miriam's family, might I not expect a little more kindness in return? Does my promise to protect her status mean I forfeit all acknowledgment? On my darker days, I sometimes wonder whether I will ever hear from her again. By the time I do, will I still care? If I don't, how will I find out about her death? Whom should I contact after she dies and when and how? Will that person believe me? It's hard to remain a font of pure benevolence while pondering these questions. Perhaps I am ridiculous in being so selfless. At what point does benevolence become sainthood? At what point does a saint become a doormat?

Miriam was forthcoming about my father when I asked her about him. An internet search yielded two photos and plenty of data. She did not have good things to say and didn't want to hear from him. I told her I would not try to reach him. As a result, I have no contact with that side of my birth family either. This man has stayed on my mind, though. Partly it stems from his erstwhile physical proximity: my adoptive mother still lived in my hometown for six years after I learned his identity, and his office is still located in a building I often passed when visiting her. For years, I filled up my gas tank across the street from it. More importantly, though, I look like him. I see him in the mirror every day. It's hard not to wonder what other similarities there might be and what kind of reception I'd have if I did speak with him. Although Miriam did not actively want to be found, he might feel differently. This seems so unlikely, though, that I rarely consider it.

Needless to say, this man has no idea that I know who he is. But I know, from searching the internet, that he has two daughters. I know who and where they are; until recently, one of them lived less than five miles from my adoptive mother's last residence. In an extraordinary coincidence, I once unwittingly took from the library a book that turned out to have been written by that same half sister's husband. More recently, I found a newspaper article with a picture of her and her family meeting a celebrity. I have found out many things about these people, who almost certainly do not know I exist (though I also sometimes wonder, what if they do?). I know the names of their children. I've driven by one of their houses. There are times when I feel like a stalker.

If I want to allow myself, a political progressive, to feel unbridled anger about my situation, I can direct it at the Grundyesque strictures of the 1950s. Secrecy was forced on Miriam by her parents (nasty people, according to her), and now it is forced on me, too, regardless of my own attitudes. I try to bear in mind, though, that this was a different country then, that these were not people who had the option to forgo acceptance in their community. They could not have afforded to keep me, had they even been so inclined. Frankly, I shudder to think what my life might have been if they had. They only did what most people in their situation did in a benighted time. The coldness and stupidity belonged to the mores of the day—but the results for Miriam and for me are still here sixty years later: for her, a life compartmentalized and partly denied; for me, a ghoulish need to check online obituaries with regularity.

It might seem odd, but in spite of the negatives, I don't regret my search. I accomplished what I set out to: I learned most of my story, managed to let Miriam know that I was here and OK, and silenced the questions that had nagged me after reading *The Girls Who Went Away*. I can't deny that my hope dwindles with each year, and my expectations lessen. I have become more guarded and skeptical about Miriam. But I dare to hope that there might ultimately be more to this story. Even if she can't acknowledge me, perhaps others will later. Meanwhile, I lurk offstage—unscripted, unseen, and listening for some kind of cue.

DISTANT RELATIONS

Laura Tipton Groff

The search for my birth mother began in earnest about two years after my adoptive mother passed away. That is not to say that I hadn't thought about searching before. I had always been curious about my birth parents, especially after my adoptive parents shared the nonidentifying information from my adoption records when I was a teenager. It helped to explain where I got my height, curly hair, and freckles. As I approached my twentieth birthday, I had a job in New York City, very near the agency that had arranged my adoption. I walked by the building several times but did not have the courage to go in and talk with anyone.

My curiosity rose again at age thirty, when I was pregnant with my first child. I had learned that my birth had been a cesarean, and I wanted to know the reasons behind it. I called the agency and a social worker explained that mine had been a breach birth without complications. She said my mother had shown an interest in me and made a layette. Although I was glad to get this information, I felt anger over someone else having access to information that should have been mine. I also felt anger toward my birth mother, thinking, *How could she have given up the child she was carrying?* Being pregnant, I could not imagine ever giving up a baby. It was the first time I ever felt resentment toward her. After the birth of my second child, I wrote to the adoption agency requesting more background and health information. I asked if my birth mother had ever contacted them. A social worker responded and suggested that we set up a personal interview. My responsibilities at home prevented me from traveling to New York City for this meeting. However, she sent me a detailed letter with information about my birth parents and grandparents.

In the early 1980s, adoption registries started appearing in the news. Some states were becoming more open about revealing information. Of course, as soon as it became possible, I registered with the state of New York. The application required that my adoptive parents acknowledge their agreement even though I was an adult. Upon receiving my application the registry would send me nonidentifying information, and if my birth mother registered independently, we would be given each other's name. My adoptive mother voiced concern that I might get hurt during this process. Around the same time, I registered with the Adoptees' Liberation Movement Association, a search organization. I also registered with Soundex, an international registry. At that point I wanted to be reunited with my birth mother only if it was a mutual decision.

In the fall of 1994 my adoptive father suggested that we go to an open house at my adoption agency that was open to all members of the adoption triad. By this time search and reunion was becoming more acceptable and was often aired on television shows. I joined my father, who had been a longtime supporter of the adoption agency, and we traveled by train from Boston to New York. We both attended morning seminars. I chose one about a search-and-reunion story told through the eyes of an adult adoptee and her birth mother. In the afternoon we attended a panel discussion led by a group of adult adoptees of various ages. The members of the panel discussed their feelings growing up adopted and their decision about whether to search. For the first time my "adoptee" feelings were truly validated and my wanting to know more was considered very normal. I also learned that the adoption agency could legally reveal my birth parents' first names. Even after that breakthrough, I still didn't want to pursue a more aggressive search. I didn't want to open up a can of worms. I was still hoping that my birth mother would find me on a registry.

In 1995 my adoptive mother was diagnosed with Alzheimer's disease, and I watched her steady decline over the next four years. She attended my fiftieth birthday party, in 1998, but soon after became seriously physically and mentally impaired. She passed away a year later, in May. Although somewhat relieved that her suffering had ended, I found myself grieving over a long period. She had been a wonderful mother, role model, confidant, and source of support in my life. About a year later I decided to talk to a therapist about my loss. She suggested that I might not only be grieving the loss of my mother but also the loss of my birth mother. My adoptive mother's death might have triggered the feelings of loss of my birth mother. The therapist empowered me to actively search. She gave me the sense that I was entitled to know more. I realized that if I was going to find my birth mother, I needed to do it soon, as she was already in her seventies if she was still alive.

In the fall of 2000 I had a student in my first-grade class who had been adopted fairly recently and was in an open adoption, maintaining some contact with her birth mother. Perhaps this was the impetus I needed to seriously begin my search. It was clear that my birth mother was not going to find me. In April of 2001, twenty years after my initial contact with the adoption agency, I made an appointment to finally meet with one of the social workers. She had read my earlier correspondence and sent me a letter containing new information. My husband and I went to New York and met with this social worker. I felt nervous, but I'd written down a series of questions I planned to ask. Much to my surprise, I found her to be warm and open, giving me the feeling I had a right to search. Of course, she could not give me actual names and addresses, but she gave me hints and responses to certain questions that I asked. She confirmed that my birth mother's maiden surname was the same as my original name, listed in my adoption records. By naming certain towns, I narrowed in on the rural farming area where her family lived. We learned more about where my birth mother stayed in New York during her pregnancy, interrupting her senior year of college, when she was studying to become a teacher. We also learned a little about my birth father and his family. Once again, the social worker verbally validated my need to search and wished me luck.

With the information we gained at that meeting and by using the internet, we were able to identify my birth grandfather's name and town within a matter of days. I sent away to the local paper for his obituary, and it contained a wealth of information. I learned my mother's married last name, her husband's first name, and that she had two daughters, my half sisters, four and seven years younger than I. It was easy to find addresses and phone numbers for all of them, but the question was, what was the best way to contact my birth mother, Mary? (The names of my birth family members have been changed to protect their privacy.)

I sought the advice of a local adoption search agency. I was sent a generic introductory letter that I could use as a model to write to Mary. Writing was considered a more sensitive introduction than telephoning. I soon wrote the first letter to my birth mother, explaining that she had last seen me fifty-two years earlier and that I wanted to meet for coffee. A few days after sending the letter, I attended one of the agency's monthly meetings where adoptees and birth mothers could discuss issues of search and reunion. I shared that I had just written to my birth mother and did not understand why I hadn't heard from her, either by phone or mail. I had assumed she would pick up the phone immediately after she got my letter. Members of the group told me that it probably would take time for her to process everything and I might have to wait a while, to be patient.

Patience, I learned, is the name of the game in search and reunion. On May 23, 2001, after almost four weeks, I received a letter in the mail from my birth mother. It was brief and polite but stated that my letter had come as a shock. She said she and her parents had felt they were affording the best possible future for everyone and were assured of confidentiality. She added that I had been fortunate to have been successful in my life and ended the letter by saying, "Let us put this away and be content with what we have ... thank you for respecting my wishes and privacy."

The day before I received that first letter, I had sent a second letter explaining my interest in contacting her and expressing the hope that she would respond. A second letter from her arrived the week after the first, giving me some medical information that I had requested. She ended it the same way: "Be thankful for our lives and please respect my privacy." Her handwriting was neat and her message clear and cool.

A week later I wrote again to thank her for both letters and to say that it was reassuring to know she was in good health. I acknowledged that my contacting must have come as a shock, but that my intentions were not meant to be hurtful. I further explained that I had always been curious about her and hoped that someday she would consider a meeting with me. There was no response after that. I wondered how I could communicate my need to know more while still respecting her need to forget an unpleasant past. I hadn't expected such a closed reaction and felt I had trod softly. I tried to understand her point of view but felt she had made little attempt to understand mine. She obviously didn't share my view that acknowledging one's past might be healing in some way. I decided to give her plenty of time before contacting her again.

Two months later, my husband and I took a trip to my birth mother's town as part of our summer vacation. We drove past her house to see what it looked like. We spent the afternoon in the local public library looking at old yearbooks and microfilm of the local newspaper. We found no pictures of Mary or her father but did find Mary's wedding announcement. She got married just two months after my birth. That announcement revealed the name of her college. There was a yearbook from the local high school that indicated she had been in the chorus. We also found high school pictures of my half sisters. They did not look much like me, although there was some resemblance with the younger one. We left the area feeling like we had learned a great deal, and I had some inkling of the small, conservative community I could have grown up in. I decided to subscribe to the local weekly paper so I could check the obits and village news sections.

That December I sent Mary a Christmas card. There was no response from her. Also, my husband ran an internet search on my birth father. Ten possible addresses surfaced. I wrote a form letter requesting family genealogy but received only one response, from a man in Florida who said he was sorry he couldn't help. In February a large envelope from a college library arrived. My husband had spoken with a librarian who agreed to send him Mary's yearbook photo. This was my first opportunity to see what she looked like and, yes, I could see the resemblance. She looked somewhat different than I expected, but many of her features were like mine. I felt some passing grief that I had never gotten to know this woman who had borne me. But I was exhilarated to know what one genetic half looked like!

Over my vacation that month I did a lot of reading and thinking about adoption and search. I decided to get in touch with adoption professionals who might shed insight into how I should proceed. I thought that if I approached Mary in a different way, she might be willing to meet me. I met with a social worker and we discussed my situation; she gave me some ideas for my next letter to Mary. We also discussed how I could help myself if my birth mother was unwilling to meet me.

In April of 2002, almost a year after I first heard from her, I wrote a letter to Mary trying to make her understand my need to know more while still respecting her privacy. Once again there was no response. I thought of writing to my half sister Linda, who lived an hour away, but I thought that might upset Mary and decided to put that off. On May 8, I wrote in my journal, "My thoughts this morning are angry! I really want to tell Mary how upset I am by her second rejection of me! By treating me like a nonperson, I am hurt. I don't understand why she can't come to terms with someone who is her own flesh and blood. She is not the person I imagined as my fantasy birth mother."

After some more thought I decided to focus on what I did have: fond memories of a loving mother; a father who stretched my mind and allowed me to travel the world; good friends I could talk to; two wonderful daughters whom I've passed things on to; an understanding, supportive husband; a comfortable life and job. As summer passed, though, I couldn't put the search out of my head. I felt driven to make contact. I thought of phoning Mary, formulating responses to what she might say. In the end I decided to write one more letter, indicating that my respect for her privacy could be sustained only by respect for me on her part. I kept revising this letter because I didn't want it to sound threatening or needy. I read it to the search support group. The birth mothers saw it as slightly threatening, and our group leader advised me to use a milder approach, focusing more on my birth mother than on my needs. She later sent me a revised letter that I could use. What I liked about it was that it led the way to setting up a meeting, which would be confirmed with a phone call. I sent it to Mary on September 21 and decided that if I didn't hear from her by early October, I would call.

On September 26 I got the phone call! At just after 7:00 p.m. my husband answered the phone and asked who was calling. It was Mary. She said she would agree to the meeting and asked if I knew the area. She said she would make a reservation at a local restaurant. I sent her a note confirming the date. I told her I appreciated her call and knew it wasn't easy for her. I was so thrilled to have heard her voice.

Our lunch meeting was scheduled for a month later. I anxiously anticipated it. I was even more nervous once I got to the restaurant, not knowing what she looked like. I had brought a bouquet of flowers to give her. The hostess led me to a booth where I first laid eyes on my birth mother. We both smiled and looked at one another. She had white hair in a style similar to mine. She was somewhat shorter than I expected, but looked healthy for 77. Her features were small, kind of like mine. We talked over lunch for two hours. I learned about her family, her experience being pregnant, my birth, and why she had given me up. I learned about her teaching career and her daughters. We talked about similarities in what we liked (coffee, apple crisp, crosswords), common traits (shyness, persistence). I talked about my life and shared a picture album showing what I looked like as a baby, young girl, teenager, teacher, and mother. She saw pictures of my family and my travels. Toward the end she started to tear up and said, "I told myself I wouldn't cry."

Later, I wrote my reactions to our meeting in my journal: "I feel an overwhelming sense of peace and fulfillment within me. That is what my meeting with Mary did for me. *I now know*. I know what she looks like, I know something about her personality, her likes and interests, her family, and that it was hard for her to give me up, although she did have the support of her mother and father. I know about her health history and that of her mother."

She could give me little information about my birth father other than a physical description and that they had been in college together. She admitted that she had not been careful, thus becoming pregnant. Abortion was not the way she wanted to deal with it. She talked about going to New York City and working with the adoption agency. She went to the hospital when her water broke. I was in a breach position, so they did a cesarean. As soon as she woke up from the operation, she held me and saw me for the next five or six days. She said I was a beautiful baby. She returned to New York City in six weeks to finalize the adoption. It was difficult, but she was not in a position, she said, to raise a child and give me what I needed. I didn't probe.

I felt comfortable with her as we shared our many similar interests. She told me a good deal about her parents. Mary mentioned that her mother had expressed concern about what had happened to me. "Maybe she's looking down from heaven at our reunion," she said, then added, "Nobody living today knows about the adoption except for my husband." She talked a little about her daughters. After I got home, I sent Mary a thank-you note expressing how appreciative I was that she had met with me. I told her I was touched by her openness and kindness. I told her I understood her need for privacy but hoped she wouldn't mind if I sent an occasional note.

Mary wrote back, "Your note of thanks for our luncheon meeting warmed my heart. I, too, was comfortable sharing with you. You now have some idea from whence you came. May it be of comfort to you. I am, indeed, very proud of you. I will let you know of any change in my circumstances." I hoped after that she might keep in touch.

The following April, I sent Mary a postcard when we were in London visiting our daughter Casey during her semester abroad. The summer passed without my hearing anything. In October I drafted a short note indicating that I would be passing through her area in mid-November to see Casey, now in her senior year at Ithaca College, and again in May for her graduation. I got no response by mail. However, on November 3, Mary phoned to say she had had hip replacement surgery in April and was still recuperating. She said she preferred to meet in May rather than November. I responded by saying I would contact her in May to see if we could make a time to meet.

When we finally met again, Mary let me give her a light hug, and we talked for just over an hour. At first we discussed her health and recovery from her hip operation. She seemed to have made a full recovery in the year that followed. She asked me what questions I had. I asked if my birth father had known that she was pregnant. "I don't know if he did or didn't," she said. She left college right away when she found out. The two of them had met in the drama club. I asked if he was from the college town. She said he was and that his parents were separated, and he had a sister. She also talked about her uncles, cousins, daughters, and grandchildren. She went into much greater detail about her daughters Cathy and Linda than she had during our first visit. I said I'd like to meet them someday, but she replied, "My husband is the only one that knows; I like the way you've handled this." After we were through, she let my husband take a picture of the two of us outside the restaurant.

I probably should have been satisfied with these two meetings. But on some level, I wanted to be accepted by her, not kept as a big secret. In the best of circumstances I would have liked to have had occasional contact, sharing news of our families and relatives. I would have liked to introduce her to my two daughters and be introduced to hers. I had believed that once she met me, she would see that I was a good and caring person, was not a threat to her, and would not be intrusive. But that was not to be. I wrote light, newsy notes to her on occasion, but she would never respond. I had to learn to not take this rejection personally but see it as her way of coping with the shame and guilt of an unwanted pregnancy long ago.

At the five-year mark of my initial contact with my birth mother, I had come to the conclusion that there would be no relationship between us. The question I was now pondering was whether I should reach out to my half siblings. I realized that in doing so, I would cross the lines of Mary's desire for privacy. At the same time I felt that the possibility of a relationship with another member of my birth family might be worth risking whatever it was I had with my birth mother. Or perhaps I simply felt that my half sisters should know of my existence. I gave it a great deal of thought. I brought up these issues at the search group meetings and concluded that I should at least make an attempt.

In September of 2006 I sent a letter to Linda, my younger half sister, a teacher who lived about sixty miles from my home in Massachusetts. I introduced myself and explained that I had searched for my birth mother and met with her. I also mentioned Mary's desire for privacy and her lack of response after our meetings. I explained that I wished to maintain some type of contact with my birth family and remain aware of Mary's health. As Mary's daughter, she would, I trusted, know best how to handle this situation and advise me. I was prepared to get a reaction from both Linda and Mary. However, I heard nothing from either one of them.

After six weeks of no response, I sent Linda a note asking her to acknowledge whether she had received my letter and what her thoughts might be. I added, "I've tried putting myself in your shoes wondering how I would have processed that information and certainly understand if you need more time." There was no response from this second attempt. I wondered if Mary had asked Linda not to communicate with me. I wrote in my journal, "I am disappointed with these people, but I have to put this matter to rest."

Three years went by. The only source of information about my birth family was the internet. I wondered if I should make one more attempt to communicate. There was the other half sister. The reason I had not previously written to her was that she'd been in poor health, according to Mary. She had never been able to work at a regular job, and I did not want to add to her burdens. I had chosen to contact Linda because of her close proximity and her job as a fellow teacher, thinking I would have more in common with her. That had not proved successful. I decided to bring this up at the June search group. The group leader said, "You'll do what you need to do as long as you understand the risks and ramifications." Other adoptees said, "You have nothing to lose."

In September I sent off a letter to Cathy introducing myself and inquiring about her mother's well-being. I did not ask for other information but included my phone number and email address. On September 11, the day after she received my letter, Cathy emailed me! She eloquently explained her mother's guilt/grief and Mary's inability to forgive herself and deal with the pain of the past. She wrote that I had given her mother the opportunity to heal, yet she was unable to do so. She wrote that she was "sorry," and that if I had questions I could contact her by email. Finally someone in my birth family showed understanding and compassion. Mary had told her about me after I wrote to Linda in 2006, because she assumed I would write to Cathy next. Mary had asked her never to communicate with me until after she was gone, and Cathy asked me not to write to Mary in the future and to keep our correspondence confidential. More secrets!

The next day I emailed her back, saying how appreciative I was of her response. She wrote again the next day with health information and asked if I was interested in family history. I wrote back giving her a little more information about me and indicating that I was interested in any family information she was willing to share. I didn't hear anything for several weeks, so I decided to write again, asking her about herself and her health history. This time she did respond. She brought up her physical ailments, especially allergies and stress, and mentioned the family's health issues. Our correspondence became intermittent after that. I emailed Cathy after the birth of my granddaughter in May of 2010. In the email Cathy sent, she seemed excited to hear my news and see a photo of my granddaughter. She also included news of her mother and daughter. After that I didn't hear anything for more than a year. I became discouraged again and expressed this in an email to her. Nine months later I received a response in which she wrote that she was sorry her silence had hurt me. In mid-March 2012 she sent several newsy emails saying how she was trying to reorganize her priorities. She asked if I was interested in getting to know her as a sister, explaining that she was not close to her sister Linda. She also inquired about talking on the phone.

I sent her my phone number and wrote that it would take time to get to know one another, but that I was hopeful we could continue to communicate and be supportive of each other. In June of 2012 I emailed and asked about taking her out for coffee when my husband and I passed through her town at the start of a three-month road trip we were planning. She phoned me shortly after and we talked for forty-five minutes. She sounded surprisingly upbeat. She also said that on the day we'd be in her town, she'd be going to Boston to help a friend move. I told her we'd cross paths eventually.

After that conversation we exchanged a few cards, but real communication subsided. Then in the summer of 2014 Cathy emailed me to say she was going to be in the Boston area and asked if we could meet for lunch. I arranged a place to meet, and we finally got to see each other face-to-face. We shared information with each other. The following summer, we again had lunch in Boston. This time she gave me a set of photographs of our maternal relatives. I was very grateful. I don't know what the future holds, but I feel we have established a mutual, long-distance friendship.

It has taken me almost fifteen years to sort through my feelings about the reunion with my birth family. My emotions during this journey have run the gamut. I've felt thrilled and excited upon meeting my birth mother and half sister. I've felt frustrated by the length of time it took to get responses, but was ever hopeful. I've felt anger, hurt, and disappointment when Mary closed the door on having a relationship with me. I was persistent in my efforts to reach out, but over time I had to temper my feelings and come to an acceptance of the reality. While things have not turned out to be as warm and comforting as I had hoped, I did find a half sister who has shown a genuine interest. I have learned something about my genetic heritage and have met two blood relatives. Mine is not your happy-ending reunion story, and, in fact, it's still a work in progress. This journey has been a valuable part of my life, and I have no regrets about searching. Most importantly, I have learned from whence I came.

A REVEREND'S REUNION

The Reverend Dr. Richard A. Hughes

When I was growing up I did all the right things. I made it into the honor society and sang in my church choir. I always, or almost always, did what I was supposed to do and did everything I could to make my parents proud. That's what a good adoptee does. In my case it even led me to seminary and the ministry.

When you're a good adoptee you become very good at figuring out what your parents and people want so you can please them. You do that because deep down you carry an emotional scar that comes from believing your birth mother didn't want you, and you don't want that to happen again.

So, I was a good adoptee, as opposed to a bad adoptee. Bad adoptees also carry that deep emotional scar, but their way of dealing with it is different. Instead of trying to please everyone so it doesn't happen again, bad adoptees live their lives on the wild side, so to speak. They break the rules and push the limits as if to say, "I'm going to reject you and everything that is important to you before you reject me."

Because I was a good adoptee, I never asked questions about my birth mother until I was in my early thirties. I remember the first time I thought about searching for her. It happened after I came back from a run and turned the television on and discovered that Jim Fixx had died of a sudden heart attack. Fixx was an avid runner who wrote *The Complete Book of Running*.

While there were people who wanted to believe that his death proved running isn't all that healthy for you, it was pointed out that his family had a history of congenital heart problems. At that moment I remember thinking, *Wow! I don't know if there's a history like that in my family. Who knows? Maybe all this running isn't good for me.*

That was the day I began to entertain the possibility of finding my birth mother. I didn't actually make the decision to search until a few years later. I became aware of the Adoption Connection in Peabody, Massachusetts. So, I contacted Susan Darke, the director, and with her help, a couple of months later my birth mother was located.

Now, I had to make another decision. Do I take the next step and contact this woman, who was a huge part of my life even in her absence? What would I do if she didn't want to see me? Would I be able to handle another rejection? Because I did my doctoral dissertation on adoption, I knew that 95 percent of all birth mothers welcome a reunion with a child they gave up for adoption. But what if my birth mother was one of the 5 percent who didn't want to know or meet me? I finally decided that it didn't matter. Deep down I had to know.

With the help of the Adoption Connection I wrote a letter to my birth mother and included my telephone number for her to contact me. Then I waited. A couple of weeks later I found a letter in my mailbox from her. I panicked. Because she sent a letter instead of picking up the phone and giving me a call, I was convinced she wanted nothing to do with me. I sat on the couch trembling as I held the letter in my hand. Finally, I mustered up the courage to open the envelope and read the letter. Much to my relief, she did want to meet me but wanted to take it slow. Because no one in her family knew that I existed, she suggested we meet at a restaurant.

I was excited and terrified at the same time. What would I do if we met and she didn't like me or I didn't like her? At this point there was no turning back. So, we met at a place close to where she lived. Now, this is where you have to forget about any adoption reunion you may have seen on television or in the movies. You know the ones I'm talking about, the reunions where you need a box of Kleenex as you cry along while the long-lost children and mothers are hugging joyously.

While television producers love those dramatic scenes, that's not what it's like for everyone. In my case it was very quiet and emotionally subdued. That doesn't mean, however, that it wasn't a powerful healing moment for both of us. One of the things I remember is how fascinated I was when my birth mother picked up a spoon to stir her tea and did it with her left hand. I am left-handed, and everyone in my adopted family is right-handed. My birth mother also showed me a picture of her father, and I was instantly mesmerized. I remember thinking, *Wow, I now know what I'm going to look like when I'm sixty-five!*

So, yes, the meeting was healing for both of us. I learned that I wasn't an unwanted child. And my birth mother? She learned that she didn't have to feel guilty for giving me up for adoption.

In the weeks that followed, we continued to get to know each other. There were ups and down as we adjusted to this new reality in our lives. I was blessed, though, that my adoptive parents supported me before and after I was reunited with my birth mother.

A couple of years after she and I were reunited I was called to a church in Massachusetts and maybe it was God's will that this church was in the town next to the one where my birth mother lived. I say that because of something that happened a few years later. When my birth mother was sixty-seven, she ended up in the hospital after suffering an aneurysm. Because there were complications, she eventually had to have a leg amputated and ended up in a nursing home.

A few weeks after she got there, I received a message that she was having a difficult day. So, I went to the nursing home, and when I got there, a few nurses were in her room. I waited in the corridor as the nurses went in and out. Finally, I approached one of them and introduced myself.

"Is it all right to go in and see her?" I asked.

"Yes," the nurse said, "but do you know what's going on here?"

I paused. "I'm not sure," I said, "but I think you're going to tell me that she's dying."

The nurse nodded her head as I stood there in shock. There was nothing that would have led us to anticipate that this was going to happen. So, I went in and stood beside her bed. She wasn't conscious, but as a minister I've learned over the years that that doesn't mean the person can't hear you. So, I brushed her hair back from her face and said, "Else, it's Rick. I just want you to know that I'm here, and the rest of the family is on the way." Five minutes later a nurse came back in and checked her heart. She then turned to me and told me that Else was gone. A few minutes later the rest of my birth family arrived.

Over the years I've told this story to many different people, and one of the things people often say is that she waited for me. Maybe, but what really gave me chills that day was something a cousin said as we walked out of my birth mother's room. Referring to the fact that my birth mother kept me a secret when I was born, he said, "You know, it's kind of ironic. She was alone with you when you came into the world, and you were alone with her when she went out of the world."

Because I'm a minister I don't believe in coincidences. It's been said that a coincidence is God simply choosing to remain anonymous. So, I thank God for that final grace-filled moment that I shared with my birth mother.

A few days later we gathered for her funeral service. During the eulogy I delivered, I shared with everyone that it was a little strange for me. Everyone else there was sad because of all the moments they had shared with Else over the years. I was sad because of all the moments I *didn't* share with her. For us there was no first day of school, no first tooth to put under the pillow, no celebration after graduating from college.

"But," I said, "I have lived without her once already and I can live without her again, but only because I know that in another time and in another place, there will be another reunion." Amen.

FORGIVENESS

Kathleen MacKinnon

When I was forty-two, a friend told me about a woman she had seen on TV whose agency did searches for birth parents and children who had been given up for adoption. I had waited years to hear about something like that. At last the time had come to find my daughter!

I was eighteen years old and had just graduated from high school when I found out I was pregnant. My mother had become suspicious and took me to a doctor, who confirmed it. I couldn't believe that I was going to have a baby. It was the furthest thing from my mind. My boyfriend, whom I had been going with since my senior year, had led me to think we would get married someday, so I wasn't worried about becoming pregnant. I was excited about the thought of getting married and starting my own family. So we began to make plans to get married.

My mother sent out invitations to my bridal shower. My boyfriend had his own apartment, and we were working on fixing it up. Then, suddenly, he changed his mind and said he didn't want to get married. Everything changed in a moment! When my parents found out, they began making plans for me to go away and to give up my child. I was pretty distraught. I didn't want to give the baby away.

You may wonder why I didn't just keep the baby. I was over 18. At that time, in 1965, 1966, single mothers gave their babies up for adoption. You were told that you had no right to keep your baby, to raise your child without a father. The child would be illegitimate, and his or her life would have a stigma and be a disgrace. My parents, society, and the church all agreed that the best solution was for the baby to be adopted. There was no support system backing up single mothers. The culture was very different then from what it is today.

At the home, which was run by Catholic Charities, all the girls had to go to chapel for prayers two to three times a day. There was an upstairs window that looked out over a long driveway coming into the property. I was always looking out that window, because I thought for sure my boyfriend was going to come down the driveway and get me out of there. I guess I was pretty naive. I met with a social worker once a week who told me that the baby needed a home with two parents who could provide all that the child would need, and if I loved my baby I would want to do what was best for her. The whole thing had become a nightmare.

I went into labor on a Saturday night and was taken to Saint Vincent's Hospital, which was near the home, and my daughter was born the next afternoon. A nun brought her to me when I woke up. She was beautiful, and I loved her so much. I spent five days in the hospital, and she was brought to me at feeding times. Another girl came in and gave birth to a baby boy. Because we already knew each other from the home, we loved spending time with our babies together. She was a few years older than me and was a nurse. Her name was Loretta, and she made the decision to keep the baby. I remember the social worker who worked with both of us telling me in an angry tone of voice how wrong it was for Loretta to keep her son.

My parents came Friday afternoon to take me home. When they entered my room, I was feeding the baby and they didn't want to wait for me to finish, because they wanted to get home before rush hour traffic. Hearing her cry when I put her down on the bed was shattering. I don't know how I got through it. That night when I was alone in bed in my parents' home, I cried so hard that I started to hemorrhage.

At this same time, one of my closest friends had a baby boy just one day before my daughter was born. She had gotten married, though. My uncle said we "must have been at the same party." My mother forbade me to remain friends with her. I'm sure she thought she was doing this to help me, but it didn't. Everything in my life seemed to be getting really hard. But the hardest thing I ever did was leave my daughter in that hospital room and then sign away the right to know anything about her. What kind of mother was I that I didn't keep my own child? I had allowed myself to be convinced by everyone that adoption was the right choice. And now I couldn't even find out whether she was healthy or happy. I was full of grief and anger toward my parents, my boyfriend, and myself. I just wanted to get out of my parents' home, so I started working two jobs. I would go to a bar when I got out of work. I started drinking, and I was smoking two to three packs of cigarettes a day. That was how I coped with everything. I was so nervous that I couldn't talk without stuttering.

Two years later I met my husband, Richard, at the same bar that I had been going to. When I told him where I was from, he said he had just sold his Harley-Davidson to a guy from my town. It was my former boyfriend. I couldn't believe his name came up, so I told Richard my story. We started dating, and we were married a year later. We had our first son three years after that, and when he was two, Richard and I experienced a conversion to Christ. As I began to know and understand the love of God, I started to think about how my daughter could have been with us and how tragic it was that I had lost her. I now knew that I could have been a good mother to her. She was eight years old at that time, and I vowed I would find her someday. I forgave my parents, but I still wasn't able to talk about her to them or anyone else. Everything continued to stay buried within me, but she was always my first thought in the morning when I woke up.

After hearing about the woman who did searches, and with my husband's encouragement, I got up the nerve to call the agency the following March. The person who took my call was very nice, but when I tried to speak I couldn't get the words out. I broke down crying. My husband calmly took the phone and gave her all the information I had concerning the birth and adoption of my daughter. Then the agency began its search.

Now I started to get anxious about finding her. Did she know she was adopted? Had she grown up thinking I didn't want her? That was my greatest fear. Would she want to know me after all that time? I was afraid to just barge into her life, but I knew I couldn't stop what I had started.

That summer I attended a church service to hear a speaker I knew, and the place was packed. I had a feeling my daughter might be there. That had never happened to me before, though I was always looking for her. If I saw a little girl with the right coloring or features, I would drive myself crazy wondering if she was my child. I found out later that she had not been there that night, but I had been practically sitting next to her pastor. I remember meeting him.

About two weeks later, a woman from the agency called and wanted to meet with me. She had the information I needed to make contact with Debbie. I had named her Deborah, and her parents, I later learned, kept the name but changed the spelling to *Debra*. I was elated because I had always thought of her as Debbie.

I wrote a letter to her, explaining who I was and that I wanted to know how she was doing. I included my address and phone number. After I put the letter in the mail I did not sleep for two nights. I was a wreck! I thought, "This is it. There's no going back." Debbie was twenty-four years old, and she lived about seventy miles west of me.

She called me as soon as she received the letter. It was overwhelming to hear her voice. She wanted to come and meet me the following weekend. Everything was happening fast. We planned for her and her husband and their four-year-old daughter, Melissa, to come on Saturday, which was Labor Day weekend.

Richard and I then told our sons, who were eighteen, fifteen, and ten, about Debbie. Thankfully, they were happy about it. They had always wanted a sister. I was so relieved.

When Debbie and her family arrived on Saturday morning, I ran outside to meet them. She got out of the car and we embraced. It was surreal. She was very pretty, and I couldn't take my eyes off her. She told me she had wanted to find me too, but she was afraid. We spent the day getting to know each other. We both could talk. She definitely inherited my gift of gab. Later on we decided that they would spend the night. After we all went to bed, it hit me that all my children were together under the same roof for the first time. That was exhilarating!

The next day there was church. My husband and I founded our church, which is nondenominational. He was the pastor at the time, but he was away on a mission trip. I had called my sister, Maureen, the night before. She lived near our mother, about sixty-five miles away. I asked Maureen to bring Mom to church the next morning but not to tell her why. "Drag her here if you have to," I said. Our father had died the year before, but I like to think that he was up there looking down on us and was involved in some way. So, my mother, sister, and three nieces were all there. After the sermon I stood in front of the congregation and told my story. When I said that I had found my daughter and she is here right now, it got a little emotional, especially for my mother. I invited her to come up front to meet her granddaughter. We all embraced, and it was wonderful. After all those years of never speaking about my daughter to anyone, the whole thing came out in front of a crowd.

After our reunion Debbie's parents invited us to their home to meet. They were very accepting of my relationship with Debbie, and we are still friends today. I am so grateful for that.

Over the last twenty-five years Debbie and I have stayed in close contact. There have been some good experiences and some that could have been better. We both had to work through issues of grief and anger. But I have learned, and I'm still learning, that forgiveness is the only way to have deep healing in my heart. Once I realized that, it helped me to forgive myself and others.

I'm thankful to God that Debbie is in my life and that we have had this opportunity for a second chance. It has been said that the last stage of grief is acceptance. It was so necessary for me to move beyond grief and regret. I had been stuck there for so long. I have come to realize that we are all very human and imperfect people. No one can turn back the clock and change the past. But I think with forgiveness and acceptance it is possible to have a happy future.

WHAT'S IN A NAME?

Susan Miller-Havens

How could I get this box to UPS before the movers come? What was it about moving? What was that feeling? Groundlessness maybe. Fear? As I stood in a corner of boxes, back to mind came the night the car flipped over when I was sixteen, the prop jet suddenly dropping, and years later the elevator with no escape. I don't remember traveling in cars with strangers when I was an infant, back and forth to foster care, or being alone with twenty other babies. Sometimes past traumas bubble up to the surface. Then, like on that moving day two years ago, I feel groundless and alone. I have learned to take a breath. Eventually all settles to the bottom again. Life goes on.

I grew up forty-five minutes outside of New York City in a beautiful town with perfect rose gardens and secrets. Like the TV series *Mad Men*, there were fathers who rode the Erie/Lackawanna train from the suburbs to NYC every day. Some had hidden apartments and affairs in the city; some didn't. Most were white, middle-class dads who worked nine to five. There were few divorces and even fewer moms who worked or had careers.

It was 1944. Life was good. If there was family trouble, there were ministers to talk to. No psychiatrists were consulted because we weren't "crazy." In a primarily Christian neighborhood, unpleasant feelings were to be kept to oneself. There were two churches—the Protestant one and the Protestant one. A Catholic church was in the next town. There were no synagogues or mosques. We were very Republican, racially segregated, and psychologically unaware.

Beginning in kindergarten, something felt off to me. I really didn't know what it was. I have seen early photos of a happy child who, in the next Kodachrome roll, reveals the face of a confused little girl. I alarmed my kindergarten teacher by drawing a tree in a forest and asking her to label it "The Little Tree That Growed All Alone in the Forest." She told me years later that she had called my parents. It was a perfect time for them to discuss my adoption, and yet it never happened. I was left wondering: did I drop from the sky? Why was I afraid of dying at night? Why did car rides make me uneasy? Why did I feel I didn't belong?

At around age four or five, my beloved nanny was the first to tell me the story of my arrival into the household. As we sat on the stoop at the garage entrance, she said how excited my mother was when the lady from the social services agency brought me in a basket wrapped in a pink blanket. Then there was the story my father loved to tell that I was too young to understand. "She can stay," he told the social worker, "as long as she is a Republican, Protestant, blond and blue-eyed." These stories were the first moments when it felt like the rug had been pulled out from under me and what seemed like a solid foundation suddenly gave way to a sense of groundlessness.

In our family, there was no talking about feelings or realities. Secrets were intended to protect everyone, and silence was better than truth. I had one adopted friend in town and some others where we vacationed in the summer, however, we hardly talked about anything except acknowledging our sameness. "Oh, she looks just like my son," said my adoptive aunt, trying hard to pretend I was part of the family. Her seemingly well-meaning effort was just another extension of the "let's pretend nothing happened" charade I lived in for many years.

I would not learn, even when I was pregnant with my daughter at age thirty-three, that my adoptive mother had tried every available fertility method to have babies or that her endometriosis was so bad she frequently hemorrhaged.

Not until I was in my forties did I find these facts and then only from blurry adoption records. I had told a social worker that I would speak at her conference only if I saw the records. This was not the usual mode of sealed-record access, for sure, although some social workers did bend the rules to help with searches.

The social worker brought a microfiche reel barely thirty minutes before my speech. These reels stored files on reversed-image film that could be read only through a machine and then printed out on special paper. It seemed like forever loading the machine and finding my record. I tried absorbing what I read, then suddenly I became torn apart because I had so wanted to print out hundreds of other records for those who were searching for their birth families.

Suddenly, the thirty minutes were over. All I remember about that lecture is the room, the audience I spoke to, and the ironic title of my paper—"Mommies, Babies, and Bodies."

Margaret Mary Earle "Peg" gave birth to me on June 20, 1944, in Newark, New Jersey. She named me Barbara Elaine Michael. A succession of names would follow: Barbara Elaine Earle, Susan Elizabeth Miller, Susan Elizabeth Miller-Havens, and Barbara Elaine Owens.

Your name is an essential constant that remains with you all through life. It is your passport to the world. Without your birth certificate, schooling, professional and marriage licenses, you would not be legally recognized. By 1945, the court had finalized my adoptive name. Why did my different past names matter to me?

Actors and spies take on dual identities, moving between whatever roles they are assigned. With the exception of people with split-personality disorders, most people live with one identity. Many of those who didn't know their identity or genealogy at birth have reported that a faint or looming confusion follows them around. I was one of those people. Understanding and making meaning of these dualities for all who have been disconnected from their families of origin is dear to my heart. My story isn't unusual. It is one of thousands we now see inserted into movie story lines.

My adoptive parents were told very little about where I came from. I understood that the case management plan that social workers carried out in the 1940s did not give them any helpful information. After all, the goal of sealed records was to protect the birth mother from having to wear a scarlet letter and the adoptive parents from the embarrassment of being known as infertile. The elephant in the room is always loss—loss of a child, loss of childbearing, and loss of knowledge and connection to one's roots.

To this day, even though I found my birth mother Peg and met with her twice, I have no idea why I was named Barbara. I could only assume that my middle name was a cousin's daughter's name. For five months, I was Barbara Elaine Michael. I lived in Peg's uterus for nine months, first in Tulsa, Oklahoma, and then in Orange, New Jersey. I came from a union with her and a veterinarian, Lloyd, who was a lieutenant in the Army. I was a product of their genetic pool and, I hoped, their love. Obviously, I didn't know. For a while I was hers, named by her. When she couldn't produce my father or a marriage certificate, the state changed my name to hers. Was I then partly the state's? I became Barbara Elaine Earle. Historically, I knew documents included a line denoting the legitimacy of a child to protect families from bastards who might inherit the family gold, and yet I was sad to see my birth father's name removed from the second certificate, as if my birth was a bizarre immaculate conception.

I realize now that many of the accomplishments I had achieved in my two twenty-year-long careers were partly because of the paths I had taken in order to be seen and to be acknowledged. It wasn't all about being a woman in a man's world, trying to work her way up. At times, I felt almost invisible in both worlds.

One day in the 1980s, I came home to find a note from my husband with the names of my birth parents written on it. The message was from a person in vital records who was sympathetic to searches. He said it would be easy to find my birth father, but not my birth mother. He was right. I found information on my birth father quickly, as he was a licensed veterinarian and had an Army record. Via the underground search angels, as they are called, my birth father was the first relative I found. When he was forty-five, his car had skidded into a train track in Kansas. He did not emerge from the mangled steel. Nonetheless, there was my half sister and her immense genealogical files with pictures of my aunts and uncles on a farm in Kansas. Over the next thirty years, these physical resemblances found their way into my sense of self.

My half sister and I had a DNA test done, before heritage websites Ancestry.com and 23 and Me came into being. The results revealed a relationship, just not a strong one. We ignored the weak connection because my birth mother's notes in my adoption record were so precise about who my father was and what he did. There was always a question about the red hair in the family. We let that pass—just as I let go of the feeling that my half sister and I were not compatible.

I had felt so out of place, growing so much taller than my adoptive parents. Now I saw tall aunts. At last, I felt somewhat connected. My birth father was a big-animal vet in the Midwest. He was physically strong and well educated. I, too, was strong physically, more intelligent than I knew, and loved animals. Somehow, this new knowledge, along with the photos, made me feel like I had come from somewhere, somewhere where people were tall, smart, and strong.

Whenever I drove over a train track, I imagined what it must have been like for my birth father to not have been able to get out of that car. I wrote an alumnus from his school to ask what it was like to play football with him. Sitting on our back stairs reading his response describing my birth father's sportsmanship and loyalty, tears seemingly came from nowhere. I watched the centers in football games with new interest imagining my birth father in that role.

When my half sister responded to my letter to her, she was accepting and supportive. Her sister was not receptive. She was horrified that their father would have had a child out of wedlock. The years rolled by. I framed many of the birth father family pictures and hung them in our house. Sixteen years ago, my half sister came with her daughter to my sixtieth birthday celebration, where I introduced her to all my friends. When her daughter was here in school, we saw a fair amount of her. Comparisons between my half sister and me with our daughters abounded. Pages of ancestry arrived in the mail, carefully assembled by my half sister. I was also able to talk to my birth father's elderly sister, who said she remembered him coming to her during the war and mentioning a child. I came to know that I had all the information I was going to get to assimilate my birth father into my life. I could rest assured that that search was completed.

It took seven years to find my birth mother. I became obsessed with ridding myself of being constantly taken down rabbit holes. Folders of search documents piled up on my desk, all with dead ends. I found my birth mother's mother first. Both encounters and stories are too long to write here. Suffice it to say that without social media, DNA, or open records, it was a monumental task to find either relative. Undeterred, I was drawn to the search as if I was a stick used in dowsing for groundwater.

My half brothers and I continue to look for our missing sister, so we frequently sign into Ancestry.com and 23 and Me. I have built all kinds of trees. I love helping others do their detective work. I thought I was so skilled! Actually, I am—how could I not see what was out of my sight on my own tree?

One day a year ago, I had a message from a young man who said he was my fifth cousin. Usually, that ancestral distance is a bit too far to bother following up on. Frankly, I didn't really even want to answer his inquiry. However, this time was different. He wrote that he was adopted and wondered if I could help. We went through the usual search 101 and happily found both of his birth parents pretty quickly.

When I realized that this young man's grandmother was actually my cousin, I could not make the connection. I contacted his aunt, and when she asked her mother, she said that obviously my birth father must have been her uncle. This was not the same birth father as mine. What could these people be talking about?

Curt, the man they were talking about, had passed away, so our only recourse was to get DNA from his living daughter. Who was going to bring this news to her, and why would she welcome a random, out-of-wedlock half sister? I have bucked up on many occasions in my life, receiving both good and bad news. I noticed that I really was not breathing, not taking those meditative breaths that I had learned to help my anxiety. To be honest, in that moment I was experiencing some kind of weird disconnection or lack of continuity between my thoughts.

As I rushed to get to my expired parking meter weeks later, I got a text from the family genealogist: "You may want to check your DNA matches." There it was—50:50 DNA between me and my new half sister. You would think that I could describe the feeling I had. I could not. With the exception of my missing half sister, I thought my searches were over. Had the story of my birth father that I had embraced for 30 years just vanished? To say that this turn of events was stunning is totally underreporting the size and breadth of the wrench that slowly turned my gut.

Very quickly, the calls started coming in from my new half sister and her three children.

They didn't have an aunt on either side of the family and were apparently very happy about this turn of events. Their responses were not what I was used to when I previously encountered a variety of biological family members. Then came the call from my half sister, saying, "Well, I have been waiting for this call for years. I am only disappointed that you aren't a boy." *OK*, I thought, *and what does one say now, "Sorry about that"?* I took a breath and continued to listen to a new story about my unknown family.

By the way, what happened to that box I said had to get to UPS? It contained ten pounds of certificates, Army records, maps, photographs of aunts and uncles at the Kansas farm of my named birth father. Pictures from his college days, the program from his funeral, pictures of my former half sister and her daughter at our home here. Packed away was the thirty-year-old story of my paternal heritage.

Just like that, the box went into the car and to the hands of the UPS clerk. Right down the rolling conveyer belt it went. Done, over. How appalling that all those years of trying to relate to the person I thought was my half sister were for naught and the connections that I made were false. She wondered if we would remain in contact. We wrote for a while, but in the end, we really didn't have anything in common. And so, in gaining a new birth family, I lost her and the story I had lived with for all those years.

Visiting my birth father Curt's grave in the 90-degree, dry Albuquerque, New Mexico, sun, I was overcome with sadness. I wanted to weep. I spoke to him. My hand automatically cleaned off the brush from his flat gravestone. Now I knew that he had been laid to rest there, and I had to say both hello and goodbye. My friend who had traveled with me and my half sister's husband patiently waited. They took a video. I raised my hand to stop it because I was falling apart with grief. It felt the same way as when I lost others whom I had loved. It was awful and surreal. The letting go that comes with grieving is helped, to this day, by my watching that video over and over.

No one escapes loss. I certainly have not. The only way I can explain the need to know what I and others have experienced is to equate our drive with the remarkable wherewithal families of MIAs maintain while searching for missing servicemen and -women. They will wait years until even just one tooth or bone of their dead loved one is returned to them. Then, once their loved one is buried in the ground, they can begin the task of grieving. On that day last year, seventy-five years after my birth, I let the grief for my real birth father begin.

After our visit to my birth father's grave, we drove the route through the spectacular country that he used to take from Albuquerque to Durango, Colorado. He owned Trimble Springs, a natural hot spa and a dude ranch. He was a real cowboy. He joined the rodeo at age twelve, soon after his mother left the family. He rode the range, became a rodeo star, even riding broncos in Madison Square Garden. By the time he was twenty-three, trophies and ribbons added up—as did money. Like so many athletes, and maybe especially trick riders, he was injured enough to retire. He owned a night spot in Tulsa, where I figured he met my birth mother in 1943. Then came his dude ranch and eventually selling quarter horses, all resulting in his near bankruptcy.

Inside the spa was a picture of him sitting on his favorite horse next to a picture of Marilyn Monroe and other actors who had filmed there. I felt like I was in a movie.

I don't know why I rode horses as a kid or loved country and western music. The 1950s were a great time for Western movies. We all loved Roy Rogers, Gene Autry, the Lone Ranger, and their theme music. Imagine that— my birth father was an extra in Westerns. My godfather taught me how to ride, so this is where nature and nurture cross lines.

Did my birth mother knowingly put another man's name on my birth certificate as my father? As I said earlier, there was no doubt in my former half sister's mind that my birth mother knew a great deal about her father. Did my birth mother know that one man was my father and not the other? Did she not include him in the record because she knew her own father would not approve of a former rodeo star and bar owner? A veterinarian and lieutenant certainly could be acceptable into the family.

Did I wish there had been open adoptions and that I could have gone to the ranch every year? Of course. Was I heartsick that my birth father died at fifty-five because he ignored his cancer while embracing Native American medicine men instead? Of course.

Not only do I look like my birth father, there is artistic talent through generations of family members, including my grandmother and my cousins. Yes, seemingly fearless men like my birth father rode the range, however there is an art to handling horses. The never-ending beauty in the great outdoors feeds one's visual mind. To be fair, my adoptive mother introduced me to crafts, art, and museums very early on. She herself was an accomplished craftsperson. Perhaps she fed what was lying dormant. Who knows?

Tired and elated by the breathtaking drive to Colorado, we stopped at my cousin's art show on the border of New Mexico and Colorado. When he saw me, his eyes welled up with tears. Here we were, both artists and strangers, hugging each other atop a hill in New Mexico. Our embrace carried me to a place I'd never been. The music and lyrics to the song "Purple Haze," sung by Jimi Hendrix, come to mind as I recall that moment.

Then I realized that our immediate connection and not having the opportunity to spend time together when we were younger nor in the future became painfully evident.

My friend and I arrived in Durango, the timeless Western movie set just below the Colorado Rockies. My nephews and niece were waiting for us in a bar down the street from our hotel. I felt something I had not with my mother's side of the family. Were these people part of a tribe, my tribe?

The absence of routine life experiences with these important relatives and their present enthusiastic entrance into my life is confusing. Barbara Elaine Owens one day, Susan Elizabeth Miller-Havens the next.

So, what is in a name? What's in the wrong name or two names? Maybe nothing, because what I inherited were strands of DNA that predisposed me to certain traits and a temperament. All of this genetic pool was nurtured by loving adoptive parents, who did the best they could, given what they knew.

Many years later, I am more accepting of the individual I have become. I know that I am finely tuned, sensitive to abandonment, loss, and being left out or not belonging. I tear up at ceremonies and when people win a game or a prize. Nonetheless, I have had a fascinating multilayered life, with a heightened creative sense and intuition that was born out of all my families. I have had two long careers, one as a psychotherapist, one as a portrait artist. I have good friends, spiritual fellowship, family, both adopted and extended. I am blessed and grateful.

Am I still afraid of dying at night? Yes, sometimes. Can moving vehicles and closed-in spaces get the better of me? Yes. Am I grounded? No, probably not. However, I am no longer floating. Is there more to my story? Yes.

Am I more Susan than Barbara? Yes.

Will I give up looking for my sister, even if we have been given the wrong name?

Of course not. After all, she is so much more than just her name.

THE REUNION

Denise Osterberg

It was at that moment that I knew I loved you.
Who can understand a mother's love for a child?
Your wonder was known only to God
Yet, I knew I loved you before I met you.

Songs of joy burst from my heart
As the life that I carried began to quicken.
How softly I played my guitar close to you
Enjoying this special time of my life and yours.

Oh, if only these days could last forever just you and I
But the day came and you were awesome.
You looked into my eyes with such wonder and awe
And suddenly I wanted everyone to know you.

Too soon I watched you go—how it hurt not to follow

As I placed you in the care of another who loved you.

You were always a child in my eyes

Growing strong in your mother's arms.

Who could not love this beautiful child?

Your mother held you close, and dad was so proud.

But as your birthdays drew near

I longed to share the pride that was theirs.

The day came when I learned I could meet you

Rediscover the child I held so dear.

What would you think, would you even know about me?

I know I loved you before I met you.

I counted the days as I had counted the years.

Oh, how long those days were.

While I waited to see the face I remembered

The child I had loved would soon become a young man.

The day came and I picked up the phone.

The voice I heard was like music to my ears

To hear your voice after all these years

I knew I loved you before I met you.

I said hello and how are you?

He replied I can't believe I'm talking to you.

You know, I think I look like you, and

I hear I have two sisters, whereas before I knew none.

Yes, you have two sisters most anxious to meet you

And yes, another family waiting to welcome you.

You know, I have missed you so

So glad you are well, can't wait to see you again.

The knock came at my door

I was strangely very calm and peaceful this day.

As if in a dream, I said come in, not knowing what to say.

Yes, come in, so wonderful to see you!

As I study his face, does he know how long I have waited?

As he comes into the room I wonder what is he thinking.

I only know that he is wonderful in my eyes

Does he know I loved him before I met him?

January 15, 2000

GOODBYE AGAIN

Marilynn Raben

September 6, 2014, was a pristine day. Purple, blue, and green hydrangeas adorned the entrance to the Wellesley College Club. The grounds were meticulously manicured. I walked to my car and unloaded mason jars filled with fresh cut flowers from my garden, then carried the jars to the large function room on the second floor. The windows there overlooked a lake. I paused for a moment and stared at the water.

I then tied bows neatly at the beginning of each row of chairs. From the podium I looked around at the chairs that had been set up for the event, 150 of them. It was the perfect setting for a gathering of family and friends. I would have said "Well done" to myself had it not been the memorial service for my son. And this was not the first time I had to say goodbye to him.

The first time was in 1968. I had just finished my freshman year of college. I hated college. I couldn't wait to get home for the summer and be with my friends, especially my high school boyfriend. I was as madly in love with him as any eighteen-year-old could be in love. We spent many hours together that summer. We were happy. Until I learned I was pregnant.

My boyfriend and I wanted to get married. I remember one evening snuggling up next to him in his car, looking out at the harbor and talking about setting up house, having our baby, loving that baby and each other, and living happily ever after. I savored that evening. However, the fantasy was short-lived. Marriage was out of the question. My boyfriend's father forbade it. I am sure there were many reasons for this, but the apparent one was that he did not want to complicate his son's college education.

By August I knew I had to tell my parents the news. They were pillars in the church, staunch Irish Catholics. I knew what devastation and disgrace I was about to inflict on the family. I was terrified, couldn't eat or sleep, and was gripped every day by nausea. How was I going to do it?

One morning after my father left for work, while my mother was outside hanging clothes, I snuck into the kitchen and left a note on top of the washing machine. This was the only way I dared. The note said, "I just learned that I am pregnant. We want to get married. I am sorry. I will be back in 3 hours and we can talk." I then walked four miles to Harvard Square, panicked about what would happen to me now. The slower I walked, the faster my heart beat. I couldn't get enough air.

Three hours later I arrived home and saw my father's Ford Falcon parked in front of the house. I knew the situation was bad. My father never came home from work in the middle of the day, never.

I slipped in the front door. The house was quiet. I found my parents sitting on the back porch. My mother raised a martini glass to her lips, while my father's glass sat half empty on the side table. The spotlight was on me, but filtered through Gordon's gin. I wanted to disappear.

My mother spoke for both of them. I felt tears well up behind my eyes as the words "disgrace" and "home for unwed mothers" reverberated through me. Arrangements would be made for me to go to the Florence Crittenton Home. I was dismissed and left the house to walk around in oblivion for hours.

To add to my heartbreak, my boyfriend became less and less available in the coming weeks. The end of summer brought relief to both of us. He escaped back to college out of state, and I avoided the Crittenton Home by making a plea to Catholic Charities to find me what was known as a "wage home." In exchange for room and board, I lived with a family and helped out with their four children. These wonderful people helped me in more ways than I could ever help them. The mom and dad were extraordinary human beings, supporting me every step of the way through this dark stretch of my life. To say I was lucky to have them will forever be an understatement. While I loved the family with whom I lived, I was sad and lonely during the holidays because I was separated from my own friends and family. I missed my grandmother most of all. She went to her grave never knowing that I did not spend Christmas with my college roommate that year. Just thinking about it still brings tears to my eyes.

As my baby grew and my belly got larger, I took long rests in the afternoon, working rosary beads between my fingers, praying that I would survive, and asking God to find a family with whom my baby would be safe, happy, and loved. At 4:00 a.m., March 8, 1968, my water broke. I remember the terror. I remember the pain of labor. But more vividly, I remember the emotional anguish.

Upon arrival at the hospital I was whisked away to the labor and delivery room, where I was placed in the care of a nurse who upheld society's belief that unwed mothers were to be shamed and punished. At the height of my helplessness, she leaned in close to my face and said, "Not as much fun as it was nine months ago, is it, honey?" My head fell to the side. Defeat owned me at that moment and would become part of the fabric of my life for years to come.

On my nineteenth birthday I left the hospital and said goodbye to my baby. I had been in a room by myself for four days, as it was believed to be better to isolate unwed mothers from wed mothers. Maybe it was. Earlier that morning I had been denied the right to see my son. Upon discharge, I defiantly walked to the nursery to take one last look at him. He was big and beautiful, and my heart was tiny and broken. He lay bundled in a blanket. I stared at him. Feeling empty, I turned around, put one heavy foot in front of the other and marched toward the exit door. As I left the hospital, I sent off a prayer for his safety and happiness. I then placed a huge, imaginary scarlet letter on my arm, which became my invisible tattoo for many years of my life.

* * *

In thinking back to the surrender, I realize I gave up a chunk of myself that day. I handed over dreams of being loved or deserving happiness. I fought to turn the clock back and be the same person I was before the pregnancy. Nothing worked. I didn't fit in anywhere anymore. The splintering grew and so did my loneliness. I was owned by grief and shame.

Life moved on, and an emptiness lived just under my skin. I buried myself in work and school, married, and had three daughters, all the while keeping the secret. Even though I was grateful for my husband and children, there was not a day that went by when I did not wonder about my son, imagining him riding his first bike, learning to read, playing with other children. I kept wondering if he was wondering about me. On holidays there was always an imaginary empty seat at the table that only I could see.

When my daughters were fourteen, twelve, and six years old, in spite of my best efforts my marriage was falling apart. It was time to own my lost parts. I was tired of the duplicitous life. I had a son somewhere on this earth and I wanted to know him. I called Catholic Charities to inquire about opening birth records. I made the call from my kitchen, feeling a humiliation similar to that of being in a confessional. The social worker instructed me to write an inquiry letter, and during the conversation I learned that my son had grown up in California, his current whereabouts unknown. *California?* I thought. All those years in Massachusetts I had looked for his face in every crowd, and all those years, he was three thousand miles away.

My son's name, the social worker told me, was Rob. I couldn't believe he had a name. It meant he existed. When I surrendered him, I didn't feel entitled to name him, so his birth certificate read, "Baby Boy O'Brien." My boy now had a name, a beautiful name, but any name would have been beautiful to me.

One week later I received a phone call from the same social worker. Her voice buzzed with excitement. "Your son has been looking for you for eight years," she told me. She had spoken to him that morning. I felt dizzy. After the call my body folded over itself, protecting my little broken, happy heart. Twenty minutes later I felt ready to dial my son's number. My hands were shaking. He answered the phone.

"This is your mother," I heard myself say.

There was a deep "Ahhhhhhhhh" on the other end of the line. "Happy belated Mother's Day, Mom," he said.

That day, May 20, 1994, marked the beginning of a new life for me. Rob and I spent many hours on the phone learning about each other's lives, completing each other's sentences, comparing physical traits like the odd little indentation in his left ear that I remembered feeling and seeing after he was born. I have the same odd little indentation. Talking about this small sameness filled me with happiness. No language can do justice to the joy I felt. It was like losing a limb and having it grow back after twenty-six years.

I told Rob, "I have always yearned to be a fly on the wall watching you do something you love." One thing he loved was playing basketball on the courts of Laguna Beach. Soon I began planning a trip to California, and Rob and I agreed on a day and window of time when I would secretly blend into the crowd at the beach and watch him play. When I got there, it was a beautiful beach day. I spotted him immediately. I studied every muscle, every line, every movement, every feature of his face. When I could no longer stand the excitement, I stepped out of the crowd and onto the boardwalk. Rob spun his head around, spotted me, and ran towards me. Our eyes locked. He scooped me up and we became one long embrace. I had just inhaled the freshest air on the planet.

The next ten days together were delicious. I spent an afternoon at Rob's apartment. "Would you like to see my journals?" he asked. *Do I dare?* I wondered. He took out a box filled with notebooks, page after page of his longing to know me and to know himself through me. I sat on his bed with a roll of toilet paper, weeping for hours as I read them along with his poetry. I learned that when he was eighteen his parents had accompanied him to Boston, where he stood before a judge and made a case for opening his birth record so that he could find me. Birth records were sealed at the time. The judge, however, granted this request and Rob was put in a small room by himself and handed the piece of paper I had signed when I surrendered him. He ran his fingers over my signature and wondered if it would be the closest he would ever come to touching me. He also showed me photocopied phone book pages from the surrounding towns, with all the *O'Briens* circled. There were check marks by those he had called. My family's name and address were circled, but he never got that far.

Finally, after years of angst over having been unsuccessful in his search, Rob felt he had to let me go in order to move forward with his life. With a heavy heart he went on a solitary retreat in the mountains. That was where he released me to the universe, he told me. It was shortly after his descent that we were reunited.

Our reunion was both magical and complicated. I ached with every story he told me, saddened by the years that I had lost with him and the pain he suffered from my absence. At the same time, here we were, beyond grateful to be together again.

During my visit, his parents threw a huge reunion party for us. As I entered his parents' house, my legs were weak, but his father and mother and grandmother met us at the door and the love was apparent. "Not a day has gone by in twenty-six years," his mother said, "that we have not gotten down on our knees and thanked you for giving us such a wonderful son."

"You deserve all the credit," I said. "You loved him and raised him to be a fine human being."

She took my hands in hers and said, "You birthed him, and we love you and him for that." I will forever be grateful for that evening. My cloak of shame slipped a little from my shoulders that night.

At the party there were dozens of people, from all walks of Rob's life, including a favorite elementary-school teacher. There were flowers, gifts, cards, and handwritten notes about the kind of man Rob was and what it was like to watch him grow up and grow up with him. Two moments especially stand out for me. A friend of his mother told me how Rob had always wanted to find me and that this was the happiest event she had ever attended. I barely heard a word she said, though, because all I could see was the cross that hung around her neck. For so long I had felt that I was unworthy in God's eyes. I wanted to get away from her, from the judgment I was convinced she had about me. I excused myself and headed for the bathroom, hoping to regain my composure. I would have been happy to go home at that moment, but ironically, with Rob present, I felt the most at home that I ever had.

The second moment was when the music stopped and a woman holding a sheet cake stepped forward. The cake was decorated with a stork holding a blue loin cloth. Written on the cake were the words "SPECIAL DELIVERY 26 YEARS LATER." I was numb. When the party ended, I felt relieved and tired. Did I deserve this love and attention? If I did, I had lost twenty-six years to self-disdain. Either way, I was uncomfortable.

When it was time for me to return to Massachusetts, neither one of us wanted to leave the other. Rob refused to say the word "goodbye." Rather, he said, "See you soon." That worked for me as well, and as I walked toward the plane, it seemed impossible to have such a full heart and have it hurt so much at the same time.

A few months after our reunion, Rob traveled from California to Massachusetts to meet his sisters and other members of his birth family. My youngest daughter, Elena, was in first grade. She was so proud to bring him to school one day as her show-and-tell. Her teacher called to tell me Elena had beamed sitting next to Rob as he read *Green Eggs and Ham* to the class.

He made the rounds during that trip and there were lots of memories made. But the ones I cherish most involved watching my daughters with their brother. My two oldest daughters, Kristy and Courtney, were avid soccer players, and Rob attended their separate games. You can imagine how both of the girls became star of the day as they introduced their older brother to their friends. At halftime, from the bleachers, I watched Rob kick around the soccer ball with the two of them and their friends, allowing the girls to outplay him every time. Often I had to pinch my arm to see if this was real.

In the years that followed, Rob came for holidays and vacations. He considered it a treat to have his three sisters laying all over him while watching *Ferris Bueller's Day Off*—over and over again. With a full heart, I watched the four of them on the couch.

* * *

ROB HAD TWO life dreams: to find his birth family and to become a doctor. He achieved both. At age thirty-seven, eleven years after our reunion, Rob graduated from medical school. It was both rewarding and arduous. He loved his patients, loved learning, loved his colleagues, yet I could see that he was exhausted. He studied feverishly, and medical school never seemed to end. Following medical school there was residency and then finally a fellowship in infectious disease, which was especially demanding. We only saw him twice a year, around the holidays. He and I continued to talk several times a week. Our conversations were like eating a yummy meal together. We were both fed and our relationship deepened with time. We became confidants, colleagues, Words with Friends buddies, and mother and son in a way that is hard to describe.

While navigating the tough terrain of medicine, Rob also tried to navigate his way to love. He was not as successful at this as he was at practicing medicine. My chest ached when he talked about his loneliness. While he had many relationships with women, his inability to sustain intimacy was his primal wound. He was burdened by it and openly shared this burden with me. In spite of this, he tirelessly searched for love until the day he died. Very late at night, in my most private moments, I have wondered if that unsuccessful, endless effort was a result of my surrendering him at birth. Would he have been able to find and keep love if I had found a way to raise him?

Despite all of Rob's academic, intellectual achievements, his true passion was sitting at a patient's bedside getting to know the human being he was caring for. His deepest desire was to do this in a rural setting where he could help the underserved. This dream became a reality upon completion of this fellowship, when he accepted a position at a small hospital in Montana. There he practiced medicine for nine months. Many of his patients were from the local Indian reservation. He loved learning the native tongue, Salish, and took time to appreciate the culture of both the Salish and Kootenai tribes. He was both disheartened by and determined to find a solution to the rampant alcoholism and meth addiction that afflicted the local community. He had one young patient who was especially dear to him. She had had multiple hospitalizations, but the one she had at Christmastime 2013 would be her last. She arrived at the hospital critically ill with end-stage liver disease. She and Rob had a quiet, gentle conversation in which she said she wanted to go home for Christmas. Rob helped to stabilize her, and she did go home for Christmas. She died on January 3. He and I debriefed for a long time on the phone afterward. He then attended her burial.

At dusk, the evening of July 19, 2014, I was beginning to pack up at my beach condo in Plymouth, Massachusetts, planning to return home to Framingham the next morning. The sky was painted with a beautiful sunset. I took a picture and texted it to Rob. We texted nearly daily and often shared our photos. He usually texted me back right away even when he was at the hospital. I didn't hear back from him that day and assumed he was busy. At noon the next day I returned home to four messages on my phone from Rob's mother: "Marilynn, can you give me a call when you have a minute?..." "Hi Marilynn, I'd like to speak with you. Give me a call...." "Marilynn, I've been trying to reach you. It's important that I speak with you...." The last message was "Rob has gone missing on the lake."

A lump filled my throat. My insides shook as I called her back. It hurt to breathe. I reached her on her cell phone right away and learned that Rob had taken out his kayak around 11:30 a.m. the day before. He texted a friend a picture of the shore around noon, the surf just kicking up. That was his final communication. A squall came up on the lake and took him. His body surfaced five days later.

* * *

THE TRIP TO Montana seemed endless. His parents, my daughters, and I shared a house for the next several days. The hospital had a memorial service for him. His parents and I sat in the front of the room. I was flanked by my girls and felt like I was watching a movie that had nothing to do with me. Our last day in Montana, the sheriff took us out on the lake and showed us the spot from which my son had sent his final text. He also took us to the spot where Rob's body had been found. There, his mother and father, my daughters, and I joined hands and recited the Lord's Prayer. We floated in silence for a few minutes. All I could hear was my barely beating broken heart.

In the months and years since, I have asked myself the same questions over and over again: Did the surf tip him over? Did he drop his phone after texting and then reach for it? For how long did he struggle in the water? The final questions that bring tears to my eyes are: Was he afraid? And did it hurt to drown? I will never have the answers.

Although there had been one service in Montana, I wanted a memorial service for Rob here at home. His adoptive parents were unable to make the trip and they encouraged me to do whatever I wanted. While alone in my bedroom, writing the eulogy, I felt lost. This was not your typical memorial service. I didn't raise my son. I found him as an adult. I didn't usher him through the conflicts of his adolescence. I didn't send him to college. Was my loss legitimate enough for me to have this ceremony?

* * *

AFTER I FINISHED the final detail of folding Rob's favorite shirt for display on the table, I walked over to the banister at the top of the stairs that overlooked the foyer. I watched people as they entered through the main door below, and I saw car after car pull into the parking lot.

I felt detached, dazed, not in my body. After a moment to regain my composure, I greeted people as they came up the stairs. A calm slowly came over me. I took a moment to look each person in the eye. What I saw was love. For so long I had thought that people were ashamed of me and I longed for their forgiveness. As everyone took their seats I watched their faces and suddenly sensed that I was the only one who thought I needed it. I then began to forgive myself.

* * *

I STOOD BEHIND the podium. It was time for the service to begin. I was the first person to speak: "I am overwhelmed by the number of people in this room. And I am struck by the contrast between forty-six years ago, when I gave birth to Rob in the shadows of shame, and now, how in this very public way we are all birthing him to a new dimension, ushering him on with full acknowledgement. It is exactly as it should be. He would be very happy."

With each word I felt a little more relaxed, a little more whole. I stood up straighter, my shoulders relaxed, dropping to where they were supposed to hang, and I felt my feet firmly touch the floor. I looked out at the lake again and welcomed a deep exhale.

Even though there are still days that I see the world through a lens of black grief, I remember one moment that September day at the Wellesley College Club, after the service, as I carried the last mason jar to my car. I looked out over the sprawling lawn toward the water and caught a glimpse of Rob in the sunlight. He smiled as if to say, "Well done."

SISTERS

Mary Salem

I always knew that I had been adopted as a baby. In fact, when my parents were trying to adopt their second and third children, I went with them to the same orphanage in Manchester, New Hampshire, where I had been born and placed for adoption.

I loved visiting the nuns and seeing the babies in their cribs. I was perhaps four or five years old at that time and didn't mind hearing about the adoption process. As I grew, however, I became uncomfortable if talk turned to my adoption in front of others. Looking back, I can see that I felt set apart from children raised by their natural parents, and I didn't want to be set apart.

However, I did ask questions of my parents about my birth family and heritage. The questions were met with hesitation by my parents, and I soon learned that I shouldn't go there.

During my early teens I would fantasize about who my mother might have been, but as the years went on, my questions (not spoken aloud) became more definitive: What was she like? Who did I resemble? Why did she give me up? Was it painful for her, and did she think of me over the years? The fact that I had a birth father as well didn't seem to matter at that point. My thoughts revolved around that special woman who had given birth to me.

When my dad passed away, I began my search in earnest. In 1972 I learned about an adoption service in a nearby town. After calling to make an appointment, and armed with only my altered birth certificate, date and place of birth, and baptismal certificate, I met with two extremely helpful and caring women in their office. With their support and suggestions, I stepped out onto an unknown and sometimes frightening path in my life.

Over a period of about two years, I was able to learn my original last name when paperwork in old adoption files was found. It was only a notation written up by a social worker who had done a one-year follow-up after my placement, but with that vital last name, I drove to the probate courthouse in Nashua, New Hampshire, where, I was told, my adoption records would have been filed. When I nervously approached a woman behind the counter and asked for my birth certificate, she obligingly went to look it up. After pulling out my file and consulting with another person in the office for several minutes, she told me that, because it had been an adoption, I couldn't see it. I remember feeling quite upset that perhaps another door had been closed to me, as well as a feeling of anger that these strangers could read all of my information and had the power to keep it from me. Never having been an aggressive person, I was surprised to find myself briefly wondering if I could leap over the counter, grab my information from their hands, and charge out of the building. What I did instead was to simply thank them for their time and drive back home in frustration.

After a few weeks' recuperation, my spirits seemed to recharge themselves, and I again spoke with my friends at the adoption agency and got back to work on my search. It was suggested that I take a trip to the Bureau of Vital Statistics (now called the Division of Vital Records Administration) in Concord, New Hampshire, to see if my birth mother's last name appeared anywhere. She had either lived in New Hampshire or had gone there, to Manchester, to give birth to me, and it was possible, therefore, that there would be some information on her in Concord. That trip, however, provided me with no further facts.

The next step the agency suggested was that I write to a particular probate judge and ask for access to my original records. After I obtained the name of this judge, and after a year of writing letters back and forth, with my answering his questions and assuring him of my intentions to not impose upon my birth mother's life if she did not wish it, he granted my request. Seeing her full name was something I will never forget. The only address given, however, was for the orphanage in Manchester.

This particular orphanage had long been closed. However, there were still nuns who resided in the old building, so a trip to Manchester ensued, and I had a lovely visit with one of the nuns in charge. She was very sympathetic but told me that most of the old records had been burned.

I began writing to the bureaus of vital statistics in all six New England states, asking for birth certificates in my mother's name, as well as making many phone calls to families with the same surname, explaining that I was interested in my genealogy. Everyone was very helpful, and I did get a few leads, but none of them worked out. This was back when we had to pay AT&T for every long-distance phone call, so I tried to spread this out over a period of several months.

The next suggestion given to me was to visit libraries, pore through their telephone books of different states, and see in which areas that particular surname seemed to show up the most. I was open to any and all ideas. It was amazing to find so much information in old telephone directories. As it turned out, my birth mother's last name seemed to show up more in the midwestern states, and that's where I focused my search.

Again, requests for birth certificates as well as marriage certificates ensued in several states in order to cross-reference maiden names with name changes because of marriage. This gave me good leads, and it was in April of 1984 that I finally found my birth mother, in a small town in Iowa. It took me hours and many prayers to compose a letter to her in which I simply gave my date of birth and asked for any information that might help in my search for information about my family. In this way, if any of her family were to see the letter, she could easily explain that it was just someone doing a genealogical search. I also enclosed a picture.

The weeks that went by were nerve-racking, but she finally answered, included a picture of herself, and stated that she had always hoped her past would remain covered. She seemed anxious over my sudden emergence. I remember feeling disappointed that she preferred not to meet at that particular time in her life, but she didn't object to occasional phone calls, which I then made to her over a period of a year and a half. I believe she realized I meant her no harm. So, it was that later, in the summer of 1986, I sat in a chair in my living room, with a telephone in my hand, praying that I would use the right words in the call I was about to make to my birth mother. I told her my husband and I were willing to drive to Iowa so that we could meet if she was willing to do so, and she agreed. I was elated. She wanted our meeting to be a distance from her home, so we chose a small town about an hour's drive for her.

My husband and I drove to Iowa, registered at a small hotel across the street from a shopping center where my birth mother told me she would meet me, and on August 26, 1986, I sat in my car in the parking lot of that shopping center and watched as she drove in at 1:10 p.m. and looked around. When I stepped out of my car, I dropped my purse and keys and it was all I could do to walk over to her with some semblance of control. We talked for a while in her car and then drove over to the hotel to spend a few precious hours together.

About an hour into our visit she became visibly nervous, rubbing her hands, apparently upset or bothered greatly by something, and she said: "I have prayed for guidance in what I am going to say to you today. You have often said that you wonder who you might look like, who might be like you. Would it help you to know that you have a close relative who may be interested in your existence?" I replied that of course I would be, and she then told me that there had been another child—a girl—born seven years before me, and she, too, had been given up for adoption. This was a completely unexpected turn of events that just about left me speechless. I remember asking, almost in a whisper, if it was the same father, and she said that, yes, it was. I had a full sister.

My sister had contacted her ten years earlier, she said, but she had told her that she could not meet with her and that there could be no further contact. She said my sister had abided by her wishes, but that I was more persistent. I remember saying, "Aren't you glad about that now?" She simply smiled and that was good enough for me. She then withdrew a piece of paper from her purse and handed it to me. On it was my sister's name and phone number. She said she had written it down at the time of their conversation ten years before and hadn't known where it was in all the intervening years. It had just "shown up" in the past few days, she said, and she took that as a sign that she was to give the information to me.

My sister's name is Connie. She was born in Iowa and was still living there. I called her that very evening and we talked for over an hour. We liked each other immediately and made plans to meet the next morning. Needless to say, I didn't get much sleep that night, and I later learned that Connie spent most of the night cleaning and preparing for our visit.

When we arrived in Cedar Rapids in the morning, I called her from a designated stop with access to a public telephone. Connie and her husband drove there to meet us and take us back to their home. When their car pulled into the parking lot, our eyes locked together and we couldn't seem to get out of our cars fast enough in order to wrap our arms around each other. I was holding my sister, a link to a past that I had never known.

It wasn't until the following year, when I traveled out to Iowa by train to spend a week with Connie, that she met our birth mother for the first time. We called and asked if she would be willing to meet with us and she agreed. We had a good visit with her, and Connie and I told her about our lives together as sisters. This pleased her very much. She had told me earlier that she had fears it might not turn out well for us. Connie and I gave her a gift we had created—a necklace made with antique buttons, which she immediately put around her neck. It was a good thing to be reunited, even for a short time that one day.

After that I phoned our birth mother from time to time and she enjoyed hearing about the times that Connie and I had gotten together. Connie refrained from further contact with our birth mother, however, because, she said, meeting her in person on that special day answered all of her questions, and she was more than satisfied with the outcome of having been given a sister.

Our birth mother passed away at the age of ninety-one in 2005. Connie and I have visited her grave site to say a silent prayer and to leave flowers.

From the beginning, I never wanted to hurt anyone and have always prayed that God would be with me in this search for my roots. Well, He apparently agreed, because every time a door seemed to be closed to me, another would open.

The past years have been a wonderful and growth-filled time in my life with my sister. Connie and her family still live in the Midwest, while I live with my family on the East Coast, but we visit each other and have met with and been happily accepted by each other's families and friends. While together during the summer, we enjoy our mutual love for painting (she with acrylics and I with oils), while our husbands go out fishing. I am grateful for the entire search and reunion experience and especially to God for the gift of my sister, Connie.

NOW I KNOW

Ginny Smith

I gave up my baby for adoption in 1975, when there were no agency-sanctioned open adoptions. Adoption meant relinquishing all rights to your child. Even basic knowledge about his or her whereabouts and health, progress, and problems were all forbidden. I knew I wanted an open adoption even then, although I did not have the words to describe it. I sought information throughout my pregnancy in regular visits to the adoption agency, finally requesting concessions such as "Can I be notified if something bad happens to him?" In the end, my social worker said, yes, they would notify me "if he were to become very ill or if he were to die." However, when I called the agency fourteen or fifteen years later, they did not even know his whereabouts. And I have since found out that he *was* very ill at one time, having had an accident. I, of course, never knew this until much later, when my "baby" and I finally met again, in 2002.

Unlike many birth mothers with unplanned pregnancies, I did quite a bit of research—starting with the choice of an adoption agency. My doctor had hoped to arrange an adoption with a couple not able to conceive, but I chose a public agency because the social worker seemed to answer my questions honestly and promised good record keeping.

I was twenty-three years old, and a few of my peers were already starting families. It was very important to me for my child to have a good and stable home with both a mother and father. In my meetings with the agency's social worker, I learned that my son's parents had already been chosen and that they were "a very special couple." I asked what qualities were sought in adoptive parents and succeeded in finding out how parents were chosen in general, but nothing specific about my child's parents. Still, I made my preferences clear: a similar background, a high value on education, a stable couple with a strong relationship. While I received only the barest of acknowledgment in this, I was glad that I had the opportunity to share this preference, though I was not really sure how much my wishes influenced the agency's choice.

The strange mores of the times dictated that the agency had all the information and rights; birth mothers had none. In fact, this notion was so successfully communicated to me that I did not give my son a name, nor did I dare to take a picture of him in the hospital, as much as I wanted one. I did not believe I had any rights at all, reinforced at numerous times in many ways, most memorably by my hospital roommate, who said as I was holding my baby, "You really should not do that. You are just teasing him. You won't be there!" I felt so mortified that I could not speak to her again after this exchange.

After giving birth, I felt an overwhelming connection and love for my baby that forced me to reevaluate my decision. I called a young woman I knew from high school, with whom I hadn't spoken in years, because I knew she was unmarried and raising a baby. She agreed to talk with me, but when I visited, I noticed her attempts to concentrate on a soap opera as her baby fussed unhappily in a playpen. I called the few day care centers in the area at the time and found just one that would take infants at six months of age, but it had a two-year waiting list. Through my health insurer, I attempted to negotiate hospital health care coverage, but they repeatedly made it clear they did not cover "unwed pregnancy" hospitalizations. Fortunately, my doctor offered to treat me gratis, and I gratefully accepted.

I visited my baby on two or three occasions while he was in foster care and once in the hospital after he had turned blue while eating. I worried about this, thinking I must keep him if he were unwell, but he recovered fully. My mother, seeing my confusion, finally said something I remember clearly: "I will not stop you from keeping your baby, but I am not going to be the mother."

After writing to a married woman I had met during my pregnancy, who was expecting a baby about the same time as me, I received a discouraging reply: "If I read between the lines I can see you have doubts about giving him up.... A relative of mine did this....All the stress shows in little Joe.... It's really hard, even when you have a caring husband," as she did.

Although most people supported my plan for adoption, one close friend said, "So what if you go on welfare? It won't be forever." She had a family and knew how sad I would feel about giving up my son. I also remember one comment about "giving up your own flesh and blood," which reinforced my sense of guilt. What feels like a lack of imagination, or courage, led me down a path to relinquishment rather than face what seemed to me the impossible task of raising a child alone.

Looking back, though, there was a way. I could have collected what was referred to then as "welfare" (quite a stigma at that time), rented a small apartment, and somehow cobbled together a life for us, difficult though it might have been. Support from my baby's father did not seem like an option. He and I had parted ways contentiously fairly early in my pregnancy after I expressed my firm commitment to having my baby. We had been dating for several months by then, and I had already begun to feel we were not suited for a future together. Our needs, tastes, and lifestyles were different, and he was recovering from a bitter divorce, which was causing me to feel that, in his eyes, I was merely a replacement for his wife. When I told him about the pregnancy, he initially suggested we could be together ("What about us?"), but this did not feel right to me. After that discussion, he became unsupportive, saying, "You have no idea what you're getting into." True.

Somehow, amidst all my doubts and fears, I felt a sense of pride and a feeling that something magical had happened. But I still ended up feeling that keeping my baby was not the right thing to do, a view reinforced by society in general and most individuals with whom I discussed the decision—key in these being my social worker at the adoption agency.

During my period of reevaluation, my son's foster mother confided that their family loved "Teddy" and would love to adopt him. I conveyed this to my social worker, excited at the prospect that I might be able to know his whereabouts, visit him, and be part of his life. She shook her head, very seriously, unwilling to negotiate, and explained that his parents had been selected and were waiting for him. I came to terms with my decision over the ensuing months (and years). I finally signed relinquishment papers almost four months after my baby's birth, with some pressure from the adoption agency, after a final visit with my baby in his foster home.

I found a new job, returned to work feeling as though I were leading a double life, always thinking about my baby. While I was pregnant, I had met a man who admired me in spite of my situation, or perhaps because of it, and we fell in together as romantic partners. He had chosen me and I was a bit unsure, but I certainly enjoyed his attention. He was a fun type of person, loved little adventures, and I sorely needed some lightheartedness. I had given birth early in January 1975. My new friend and I moved in together in June, and, whether because of internal or external pressures, we began planning a wedding. We were married in September. Looking back, I was naive. Someone, or I, should have said, "No, wait—too soon!" We developed problems soon after I became pregnant the following year, in 1976. Issues surfaced of which I had been unaware and that led to serious misgivings on my part. I had not even known him well! As much as I loved my new baby, his infancy was a trying time. Finances were a serious challenge, and I felt isolated and unable to share this information with anyone. I recall some weeks wondering if we would have enough for basic needs. I also recall a lot of sadness—whether about my floundering marriage or my other baby, I couldn't tell. I simply felt confused and alone.

As time passed, our marriage deteriorated irrevocably. Having returned to college, a long-standing plan, I was suddenly alone with a young child and a lot of responsibility. Two weeks after he left, my mother, who had agreed to watch my son part-time while I was a student, suffered a heart attack. It was a terrible time. I had frequent and recurrent thoughts and regrets about my first baby. I wished to have him back, but you cannot change your mind in adoption; this I always knew.

A few months after we separated, I met someone new and fell in love almost immediately. He was responsible, financially secure, and really liked my son! We married and seemed to thrive as a family, but I felt skittish about having more children. My new husband was a very good father, humorous in a way that enlivened us all, and he seemed right for both me and my son (and us for him). My ex-husband ended contact with our son, and a few years later my new husband adopted my son. For several years, I was plagued by doubts about having another child, and since my husband left it up to me, we kept our little family as it was, a decision that I realized only years later was at least partly related to my feelings of inadequacy as a parent for having given up a child. At some point, I regretted the decision, but now I am at peace with my choice.

I still thought of my adopted baby all the time, and when I had a bout of unexplained but severe illness in 1989, I contacted the agency, fearing I might die, and placed a letter in his file with family contact information. I also attempted to initiate a search but was told by a search agency that adolescence would not be a good time to disrupt his life, and I accepted this. Eleven years later, in 2000, I contacted the agency again and, two years after that, seemingly out of the blue, the agency contacted me with the news that my son would be in Boston, where I live, and wanted to meet me—the next week! I was euphoric but also a nervous wreck: one week's time to prepare—get pictures together and try to process the reality of this momentous event.

We met at the hotel where he was staying in Boston with his then wife and discussed our lives, including my family medical history. He brought a laptop and showed me pictures of his friends and adventures. Absent were photos of his childhood, although he told me about camping expeditions with his father, about his mother's love of horses and, much to my relief, about his parents' being "very special people." I laughed as he told me about his younger sisters' adolescent competitions. He also told me about a serious accident he'd had while hiking a few years prior. I was reminded of the agency's promise so long ago and felt sad that I had not been there for him then and throughout his growing years. Before we parted, he asked about his birth father, saying he understood that his birth father was not a very good person. I tried to correct this assumption and conjured up old memories about his birth father's positive attributes: his sense of humor, love of sports, and coaching youth basketball locally.

When we parted I melted into tears and a terrible sadness; I was reminded of how I had felt when I left my little baby at the hospital. In the next days and weeks, totally preoccupied, I would get lost driving on familiar roads and startle at the slightest noise. I fell into a state of grief, just barely functioning. I did manage to work but would cry when I got home. This went on for months, maybe more.

In my tears and actual wailing, I began to hate myself for being so self-absorbed. Why wasn't I happy that my son had had a good upbringing with loving parents and was entering a promising adulthood? After our reunion, I had emailed him, sent him cards, at least one or two letters, and got no reply. I focused on why he did not want contact. I became obsessed with what had gone wrong.

Although he had seemed pleased to meet me, had in fact given me a college paper he had written about being an adoptee and the courage shown by birth mothers who give up their children, he also said it was painful at times to be adopted. He reported that "I don't tell just anyone." When he did not respond to my attempts to stay connected, I became fearful that he disliked me and would not want any further contact. I just did not understand it all—my strong feelings, the silence of my birth son. Compounding my anxious state, my birth son's birth father contacted me a month or two after the reunion, seeking information that I did not feel at liberty to share. While I did provide the name of the adoption agency, I asked him not to call me about this again, and he has respected my request. I now know that he has suffered, too, not knowing, wondering, and I am occasionally tempted to contact him and tell him that our son is well, but more often I feel it best to leave any decisions about contact to my birth son. Suffice it to say, I was stunned and shaken by these events and my reactions to them.

Within a year or so, I began counseling, but each session left me feeling misunderstood. When I learned of an organization that held conferences for all members of the adoption triad, Adoption Conference of New England, I attended and met two other birth mothers. One described the same feelings of despair and isolation after meeting her birth son that I was experiencing. I attended more of the organization's gatherings and met more birth mothers. Everyone thought about their birth children, I learned. I was not alone.

Soon I began counseling again, this time with a birth mother, and tentatively began communicating with my birth son again. For several years we did not communicate often, but this seemed like a big step. Today he and I communicate quite regularly, and I no longer feel as insecure about his acceptance. We have a relationship—not the "I'm so glad to have you back" relationship that I craved after our reunion, but it's warm and friendly. I enjoy communicating with him and hearing about his family. I believe that, in addition to the healing powers of time, I can thank his new wife for opening up the channels of communication a bit more. Soon after meeting her a few years ago, he wrote to tell me that he had finally told his parents about meeting me. I have not met them but would still very much like to do so. He lives on the opposite coast, and I believe that limits our relationship, but I rarely feel the overwhelming grief anymore over what I lost—such a familiar impulse in the first years after meeting him. I am grateful for the knowledge of his welfare and his whereabouts. Because he and his wife maintain a blog showing family photos, I am able to follow their adventures and the progress of their two children, and this is a huge gift.

I now realize my expectations for our relationship after the reunion were unrealistic. For years I had carried a fantasy that after finally meeting again we would share a close relationship, not mother-son but similar; that he would tell me all about his life growing up and I would tell him about the years without him; that he would want frequent communication, maybe even asking my opinions about things; that he and my other son would forge a strong bond; that other members of my family would welcome him and he would reciprocate. That I never considered his viewpoint now surprises me and causes me to feel very naive, humbled by my own blindness.

While I strongly believe I needed that fantasy in order to survive all the years with no information about his welfare, my birth son had a family and was not seeking another one. He certainly did not need a close relationship with a grief-stricken woman who saw herself as a mother figure. What he needed was time and space to process the reality of meeting me. He needed to find out who I was and why I chose to give him up.

I no longer view my situation with the intense sadness I felt off and on when he was growing up and, particularly, post-reunion. Rather, I see a set of unfortunate circumstances in which at least two lives (and really more) contained needless suffering created by a misguided system of closed doors and secrecy. For some birth families, the decision does indeed have tragic results, such as when adoptees do *not* have the unconditional love of caring parents or suffer with feelings that they do not "belong" to their family, a situation I have heard about too frequently in adoption circles. Some birth mothers feel they should have kept their babies and could have provided a better life. I believe them. For myself, I still do not know whether I did the best thing. I certainly could not have offered my birth son the financial opportunities he enjoyed as part of his adoptive family. Could I have provided as much caring and support? I certainly would have loved him, but in retrospect, I can see that my life lacked stability in those young adult years. I have also come to realize I was a bit smothering as a mother. Was this the result of my still-raw loss when my son was born, my shaky marriage, or my own upbringing? I do not really know for certain. Perhaps all of these were factors.

The loss and confusion caused by the shame and silence of closed adoptions did cast a dark shadow—for my birth son, feeling "different" throughout his childhood, probably carrying a sense of abandonment, wondering who gave him up and why, and for me, forever looking for my child in the faces of other children, carrying a burden of grief tinged with a sense of failure. I perceive it as a loss for my raised son, too, who could have shared love with a brother, even for my whole family, since they also would have loved him. When I learned my birth son was going through a divorce and shared this information with my husband, he said, "We should have been able to help." In spite of this, I also feel relief and gratitude that the strange system of closed adoption no longer exists. I feel very grateful to my birth son's parents, who provided a caring, stable home and who truly did want children with whom to share themselves and their hearts.

I now believe—considering the rules and customs of the times and my own circumstances in those times—that things turned out as well as could be expected for my birth son. I am grateful that he met someone with whom to share a life and children, grateful he has the love of his family, and very glad he and his wife wanted children, which I believe shows confidence and faith in the future. I wish only the very best for their future.

Giving up a baby goes so deeply against a mother's nature. It is bound to wreak grief and havoc when these ties are severed, for both mother and child. I am very relieved (and perhaps a bit envious) for the awareness in today's adoption world that these ties should be preserved in whatever way is healthy and possible. To have no knowledge of or contact with one's child (or one's parent) is unnecessarily cruel and totally unnatural. My child was lost to me for many years, but forty years later and thirteen years after meeting him as an adult, I can face this reality with peace and acceptance. Our story has not ended. It is still unfolding.

UNBREAKABLE BOND

Robin Stolarz

My boyfriend and I lived together for a month after I found out I was pregnant, when I felt there was no way I could face my family and honestly tell them the predicament I had gotten myself in. I packed up and ran off. He wanted to get married. I was just scared. I wanted my mother. I wanted to be home. I wanted this to go away.

My parents came to get me after a few tearful phone calls back and forth. They swiftly packed me up and took me back home after I promised to not contact the birth father anymore. I was allowed one last goodbye call. I never saw him again.

The months at home were peaceful, as I was hidden away from neighbors and family. I felt like the naughty girl taken back by loving parents. Spending days with my mother, crocheting and reading, led me to believe it wasn't all that bad. My parents sent me for counseling at a church organization, but no one ever explained that it was really an adoption agency and would later place my daughter with new parents.

No one ever told me how that little person would so affect my life. No one told me I was forever bonded to her, no matter how far away they took her.

I went to counseling and stopped frequently at my childhood church, praying my hardest to God and asking Mary to watch over us and guide us.

After my baby was born, I waited nine weeks to sign the relinquishment papers, hoping something or someone would come to our rescue. It was nine weeks of hell. Reality had struck. There was no one to save me.

My father's signature as a witness is glaringly obvious below mine on the papers. My parents drove me that day and they watched me sign. They drove me home as I sat sandwiched between them in the car, crying my heart out.

I told my mother I wanted to go and see my baby in foster care and she said no, stating that I could never make my mind up rationally and repeatedly telling me to think with my head and not my heart.

So, that is what I did.

But no one told me it was my heart that I would have to live with forever.

I learned my daughter was put into an incredibly dysfunctional home. She ended up anorexic and depressed and has been in therapy most of her life. She went on to an abusive marriage and is now trying to maneuver through a divorce.

The pain of the situation has left me deeply ambivalent about adoption.

When I met my daughter again at eighteen, she was very, very angry and shut me out for years until she started having children and contacted me. From there I suggested we respectfully email one another and start a dialogue about our relationship, past and present. This went on for a year. I got her some much-needed counseling and since then we have been a work in progress. Right now I am very much in her life, supporting her through this divorce, and she has finally, at forty-two, realized I am in her court, supporting her, loving her, backing her up, as I have always been.

* * *

ALL I WANTED to do after relinquishing my daughter was have a family. Get married, have children, be happy.

Or so I thought.

Only years later did I realize I could not put the past behind me. It didn't work. I couldn't replace what was lost. I secretly started the beginning of a search, afraid to share this with family. She was still young and under-age, and I knew I had a long road ahead, so I began simply—buying birthday cards, writing to her, journaling, and reading whatever I could get my hands on about adoption and birth mothers.

I joined a support group for birth mothers and scoured every news-letter, pulling them out over and over again, reading other birth mothers' stories and feeling a glimmer of hope that we would one day have our own story to tell.

I eventually married and had three more children, making the reality of what had happened even more apparent. All my children were beautiful and loved, and I always believed that God looked upon me kindly, sorrowfully.

I insisted on being an at-home mother, holding my children close and vowing to make amends, to make it right, to prove I could be a mother to be proud of and shower them with all the love I could not give the first time around. I started explaining to them early on that they had another sister and someday we would find her.

My husband was supportive, and when I finally had the courage to tell my mother, she was positive and ended up being my staunchest believer in my journey back to locate my daughter. We attended monthly birth mother meetings for years, sharing stories with other birth mothers. It gave me strength to find that there were others who agreed that adoption was not always the answer.

These meetings were my lifeline. For the first time, I could be open in telling my story, and no one judged me. There I met many birth mothers who also felt that our only crime was being young, unmarried, and naive.

I believed it was only a matter of time for me and I would then repair the damage done. My daughter would be back in my life, happy to be there, and the adoptive parents would accept me, grateful for the gift I unselfishly gave them. Of course, they would love me too.

I was counseled and walked through every step of reunion at a time when it was still believed by society that to leave it alone was best. Reunions were just starting to be public stories, and I could not have been happier. This was before the time of computers and the internet, and search progress moved at a snail's pace.

I returned to the agency throughout the years, hoping they would slip with some information with regard to my daughter. I did receive sympathy along with nonidentifying information and the opportunity to leave a letter in her file. I continued to plead for just the first name, but the answer was always no, because that was the law in Massachusetts at the time. Agencies were not allowed to give out identifying information.

Meanwhile, I was searching through other channels and fairly easily acquired all my hospital records. The sight of my daughter's little footprints left me reeling for months after. I requested my relinquishment documents, and seeing them with my name clearly written on them was a staggering jolt.

As hard as all this was, I knew it was preparing me for the obvious. It was baby steps back to her. I would never turn back now. I was hell-bent on bringing this to fruition.

Two weeks before my daughter turned eighteen, some searchers helping me came up with her name and where she lived, only half an hour from me. She was very close all along.

I will forever remember this day and hearing her name spoken for the first time. A beautiful name, Kara.

My Kara. My daughter. Had she thought of me all these years? Did she even care? Would she want to hear our story and meet her two half brothers and half sister, who had always known about her and anxiously awaited the day of her return?

I sent her parents a letter, with an unsealed letter to Kara inside. I wanted them involved, supportive, and approving, with the option to give her the letter. Or not. It took many minutes at the mailbox before I allowed that letter to fall into the dark abyss, which then left me with the feeling that I wanted to jump in the mailbox, fish it out, and go home. But it was done, and it would be two weeks before pictures and the letter came back to me, along with tears, happiness, incredibility, and family visiting me to congratulate and see pictures for the first time.

She was beautiful beyond words. My daughter was back. She was home. She was happy I had found her. All was well, and we were on our way. Or so I thought.

Against her adoptive father's wishes, Kara and I started a relationship. She met all the family and appeared happy but overwhelmed all the time. She was quiet. I tried to explain all that had happened, but I knew she was young, and I had a sense that there were walls up between us. She told me she was happy and had a great life, but it was apparent to me that Kara had never explored how being adopted might have really affected her.

Our visits were sporadic and only at my invitation. She didn't seem comfortable coming alone and would bring a friend. The distance that I sensed was not comfortable and we were both realizing you can't always get back what you have lost.

I knew when she went off to college that it would make or break the relationship, and it was a tearful conversation when she said she couldn't lie to her parents anymore about us and ended it.

It would be another fifteen years before I set eyes on her again.

Letting go the second time was torment. Knowing that I had to let her have her freedom was like giving up after I had worked so hard to get her back. But now she was an adult and she had made a conscious decision to not have me in her life, and I had to respect it.

I didn't call again. I didn't write. I did not pressure her but sent Christmas and birthday cards, never knowing if she received them.

Those were agonizing years, and back I went to the church, always talking to God, asking that he watch over her, keep her safe and loved. I only wanted her happiness, and if that meant without me in her life, then so be it. It didn't make me angry. Just sad. Profoundly sad that she felt she had to wipe me out of her life. She didn't trust me to act according to her wishes, and it was easier for her to pretend I didn't exist. My children were devastated and cried for her, not understanding her quick exit with no explanation.

Funny thing: all those years I thought I was the only one having pain and loss and never looked further than that for how our story had gone so horribly wrong.

I never once contemplated the idea that adoption had not served her well, had left her scarred. How could that be? I'd been told that giving her up was the best solution for everyone. But my daughter was in pain. She *did* feel loss. No one had acknowledged her pain. No one counseled her or saw the sadness within. My realization of this came through much reading, from meetings and talking about my journey, writing about it and speaking at conferences. I came to understand that adoption for Kara and me had brought only pain.

Kara never should have left me. I didn't have the courage, fortitude, and foresight to see it differently when I was younger, and that is what I struggle with to this day. We never should have been separated from each other.

I also had difficulty understanding all the secrecy that had once surrounded adoption. That was wrong. It is adoptees' inherent right to know who they are and who they came from. Every adopted adult deserves to have their records legally and quickly accessible. I believe a person's birth name should stay with them, and amended birth certificates should no longer exist.

Adoptees need to have their voices heard and acknowledged.

For Kara and me it has ended well. The glue for us is love. I believe in the power of love. Sometimes love stands back and takes a back seat for a bit. I believe all of us who love must couple that love with respect.

Cautiously, Kara and I approached reunion again through counseling, talking, and emailing for almost a year. I listened and I heard how her pain and loss affected her life. I don't know that I can ever find peace in knowing how she suffered.

I have beautiful grandchildren whom I love dearly. We have journeyed through and now make our own choices and decisions about what is best for us.

Kara is beautiful. Inside and out. Vulnerable and feisty. Smart and loving. I love her with all my heart, and I have learned through experience that the mother-child bond is strong and despite damage it can grow if it is nourished. It can forgive and heal.

We have argued and disagreed as we have ventured forth in finding a place in each other's life. At times it has left me with a tenuous, shaky thought that sets us back, but years have proven that with our differences come strength and a very real relationship. No phony stuff.

I try to really listen and hear the pain and acknowledge it and give it a place.

I am forever blessed to have all my children and beautiful grandchildren, and my best days are when they are all by my side. It has not been easy, but I have never given up. I never will.

Giving up my child for adoption has been the biggest event in my life, the one that has affected me the most and the longest.

I can only try to make peace with it and go on lovingly and not bitterly. Believing that all things happen for a reason has left me baffled on this one. Kara and I are forever changed with this event, and I now know that we both courageously bear battle scars, but knowing we are forever bound, physically and by the heart, gives me peace and the understanding that no one can keep us from each other ever again.

FAR FROM ME

James Sweeney

I was forty years old, with three kids, a wife, and our yellow Lab, Jake. My life centered on youth sports, school projects, and keeping the grass trimmed, just like any dad. Every day at lunch I would visit my mom, who didn't live far, to check in and chat. One spring day, however, our lunch was a little different than all the others.

It was the normal small talk and me trying to rush back to work. I was always in a hurry. "I really have to go, Ma."

"Stay a little longer, Jim," she said, urging me to sit down. "I have to tell you something." From the tone of her voice, I knew it was serious. At first I thought she was sick. I mean, at eighty years old, she *was* starting to slow down, but no, that wasn't it. "You were adopted. You and your sister, Maria."

I thought she had lost her mind. "Ma, are you OK?"

"If you don't believe me, here are your adoption papers."

She handed me a few musty documents, yellowed with age, written in German. They looked like they'd been stashed away, untouched since being signed forty years earlier. There was a notary seal and a blue and white thread that served as a page marker. They certainly looked official. I didn't need to be fluent in German to figure that out.

As I flipped through the pages, I was able to translate a few sentences and learned that my name at birth was James Francis Fischer. I then came across a page with two words that were not typed. Neatly written and perfectly legible in black ink was a signature, Maria Fischer, my birth mother. I stared and stared at it. I must have held onto that page for five minutes. I could not speak. I just looked at the documents.

If you see a punch coming, you can prepare yourself for it. This was one I hadn't foreseen. Nothing in my forty years of living as James Sweeney hinted that there was another part of my life that had not been told, but the papers proved her story was fact, not fiction.

My adoptive mother had been born in Germany, so I spoke German as a child but had little interest in our family history or in Germany itself. I had never visited it, never really thought about it. It was something I always took for granted.

My sister, however, had always suspected she was adopted. She would constantly ask as a child, but our parents steadily denied it and had an explanation: The missing pictures had been destroyed in a fire aboard the ship when we traveled from Germany to America, our mother would explain. That seemed plausible.

Me, on the other hand—the thought of being adopted never crossed my mind. I looked like my dad, had his quirks and personality. There were even baby pictures of me and the family. There was nothing suspicious. All the pieces fit.

Everything my parents had told me was true, except that they neglected one small fact: they were my adoptive parents, not my birth parents. It took my mother forty years to fill in that detail.

My father passed away while I was in college, so the secret came to rest on her shoulders alone. As time went on it became even more difficult to come clean. She told me that afternoon during my lunch break that she'd been having headaches and could not stop thinking about the adoptions. (Something like this would have consumed me, too.) I believe she wanted to find some inner peace and not carry the secret to her grave.

I had grown up knowing that I was the child of a German mother and a father who'd been a soldier with the United States Army stationed in Germany after World War II. Which was all true, just a different pair of German and American lovers. My mother told me that afternoon that she and my dad had met after the war and a year later were married. They adopted a two-year- old girl from a Würzburg orphanage, and during the adoption the social worker informed them that she knew of another woman who was pregnant and planning to place the child for adoption. My parents said they would be interested in adopting *only* if that baby was a boy. A few months later, in April 1960, I was adopted and brought home from the hospital just two days after my birth.

* * *

I HAD SO many questions for my mother: "Does my sister know? Does anyone know? Why did you wait so long to tell me? Did you know my mother?"

One question I didn't have was whether I would look for the woman who had signed those papers forty years prior. I had to put a face, a personality, to that signature. A signature that gave a baby away.

That night I stared in the mirror for a long time. *Who am I? Where did I come from?* I knew nothing about myself. That morning I woke up James Sweeney. That night I went to bed James Fischer. Everything I thought to be true was false. That morning I thought my birth mother lived one mile away from me. That night I thought she could be anywhere. That morning I knew my mother was alive. That night I couldn't answer that question. And now I had a question that had never crossed my mind. That morning I knew my mother loved me. That night I wondered if she ever even thought about me.

* * *

IMMEDIATELY AFTER LEARNING of my adoption, I became engrossed with learning about Germany—reading everything I could, taking German language classes. I was obsessed with my adoption. I spent hours at my computer after work each night searching adoption websites and trying to find out how to conduct a search for birth parents. I eventually came across a site dedicated to German-born adoptees. Later I contacted the website, provided them the name of my birth mother and other details, and they went to work. Two months later, I received an early Christmas gift: the address and phone number of my birth mother.

That was the easy part. The hard part was deciding what to do with the information, and writing my birth mother proved to be even more difficult. What does one include in a letter to someone who may or may not have ever held you or even looked at you? At first, nothing I wrote seemed to fit. Finally, after many drafts, and deciding on the perfect stationery, I finished the letter and sent it off.

* * *

ON NEW YEAR'S Day 2001, my birth mother called me. I couldn't believe it. I was ecstatic.

Over the next few months we exchanged a few letters. Our relationship, though surface level, seemed to be going well until one of my letters was returned. The envelope was stamped by the post office with various options for why a letter might be returned. One box was checked off: "Delivery Refused."

I was confused, furious; I couldn't let it go.

Is that it? I decided to call. I began dialing but quickly hung up. I didn't know what to say. Despite taking German language classes, I knew my German was not what it could be. A few days later, I prepared some questions with the help of my German teacher. Finally, I was ready to call.

I dialed all but the last number, then hung up. I did that several times. I was so nervous my hands were trembling. I dialed the wrong number, then dialed again. The number seemed longer this time, adding to my doubts: first the U.S. exit code, then the country code, then the area code, and finally her number. I pressed the last number. I could hear the phone ring. A woman answered. I said, "This is Jim," but before I could continue, she hung up. I looked at the phone in disbelief.

Before the call, I had had a feeling deep down that it wasn't going to be helpful, but I wasn't expecting *that*. My disbelief turned into anger, but at the same time, I was relieved. The thought of her telling me she wanted no contact with me or hearing her say she wished I had never been born would have been far more painful than the click of a phone. But it couldn't end like this. The next day I booked a flight to Germany.

I had no plan, only an address and a photo of my birth mother that she had sent me. A little over four weeks after my last "phone call," I stood outside my birth mother's apartment building, within arm's reach of the tenant listing and her doorbell. I ran my finger down the list, then stopped. There it was, the name I had read two years earlier, clear as could be: Fischer.

One problem: I wasn't ready to meet her. After a sleepless night followed by a long plane ride, it would be best, I decided, to return the next day.

After another sleepless night, morning finally arrived. This would be the day, and now I had a plan. I would ring her doorbell. If that did not work, I would ring other tenants' bells until somebody allowed me into the building. Once inside, I would leave a card with flowers at her apartment door.

I found a flower shop and bought a bouquet, then attached a small card that explained I would be in Munich for a couple of days. I included the name and phone number of the hotel where I was staying and wrote a short note: "I hope you can find the time in your day and a place in your heart to meet with me."

It was only a short walk from the flower shop to my birth mother's apartment. On the way I began to wonder, *What if she refuses to meet with me? What then? What if I can't get into the building? What if she does not read my note?* The confidence I had while booking my flight was nowhere to be found. I felt alone, very alone.

As I got closer to her building, my doubts only increased. I turned the corner onto her street and walked to the door, then looked down the tenant listing, but before I had a chance to ring her bell, my plan took a turn. She was standing there, at the door of her apartment building just about to leave.

A sudden sense of calm came over me. I knew it was her from the photograph she had sent, but am not sure even now whether she recognized me. I called her name and said I was Jim.

Her jaw dropped and she stared at me like I had stared at her signature months earlier, paralyzed. Before she could say anything, I handed her the card and flowers and told her I was in Munich for a couple of days and hoped she would call. She said she was on her way to a doctor's appointment but would call later and that she wanted to go back to her apartment to put the flowers in water. She then turned around without saying a word, opened the door to her apartment building, and went inside, leaving me outside, alone.

Of all the possibilities and scenarios I had envisioned, I never considered this. It felt as though I was her neighbor, someone she sees every day, a momentary interruption in her schedule. I waited on the sidewalk until she returned, then reminded her I would be in town for only a short while. She nodded and walked down the street. I watched her until she turned the corner and was out of sight.

Was that it? Did I just meet my birth mother for the first and last time— no tears, no hug? Perhaps the sheer surprise had been too much for her, but I had dreamed it would be different. Very different.

Afterward, I half-heartedly toured the city on my own, trying to enjoy myself as best I could, wondering if my birth mother would call. To my surprise, later that evening she did. We agreed that her boyfriend would meet me at my hotel and accompany me to her apartment. That night I met him in the lobby and we talked for a few minutes. He spoke no English, and with my German being less than perfect, I asked the clerk at the front desk to act as an interpreter. The boyfriend and I were approximately the same age, some 30 years younger than my birth mother. The clerk, understanding that I had a strong desire to see this woman before I returned to the United States, assumed we were talking about an ex-girlfriend and seemed uneasy at first aiding my efforts to meet her.

Finally, my birth mother's boyfriend or companion—I'm not sure what to call him—walked me to the apartment. It was a small studio with a Murphy bed. We talked, though it was rather strange conversation, with my birth mother being so much older than her boyfriend.

I didn't stay long, and the discussion did not go very deep into my birth or her avoidance of me. There were so many questions I was afraid to ask: Who was my father? What were the circumstances of my birth? Did I have any brothers or sisters? I was talking to my birth mother, but at the same time a complete stranger in a plain, one-room apartment with no photos or keepsakes—nothing that would reveal any of her past. I wondered if she had removed them before I arrived or if they even existed. I assured her I had been adopted by a good family and told her how I had learned of the adoption. As far as what drove me to cross an ocean to see her or why she hung up on me, those details were left at the door.

The next day, she and I traveled by train to her hometown to meet her sister. The sister had married an American and spent many years in the United States before returning to Germany. Unlike my birth mother, she spoke English, which made the meeting less stressful than the one the night before.

My birth mother and I spoke in English, with the sister acting as translator. The sister talked about her years in the United States, and I learned that my birth mother had often visited her there, but not long enough to learn English. There was an uneasy calm in the air.

I explained that I had hoped to learn about the circumstances surrounding my birth. My birth mother claimed she couldn't remember my father's name. I didn't believe her. How could she forget something like that? Later, after I discovered on my own that she had five other children, each with different men, it became more believable.

In the years that followed, there were letters and Christmas cards. As time passed, the letters and cards became fewer and fewer. Like our correspondence, the enthusiasm and joy I felt while searching for my birth mother faded. I came to see I would never get the answers I wanted from her. I also knew I would never be able to ask some of the questions I wanted to ask without pushing her further away.

I realize now that maybe we were too much alike—no opening up on either side, unable or unwilling to talk or write about our emotions. Now they seem like such easy questions that I wish I had asked. I think I was more afraid of hearing the truth than of asking the questions. *Did you ever think of me? Did you look at me in the moments after my birth? Did you ever hold me? Did you ever kiss me? Did you regret giving me up?*

Fifteen years after I learned of my adoption, in July of 2015, my birth mother died alone in her apartment. To this day I find those questions difficult to contemplate. I know I can only imagine the answers.

MY ROOTS AND MY WINGS

Dana Ann Whidden

I remember being told at age three that I was adopted and special. I loved hearing the story of how I came to be adopted. When my adoptive mother first saw me, she said, it was love at first sight. When she and my adoptive father would come to visit me in my foster home I would run to her every time.

My adoptive parents had lost a child years before at the tender of age of fifteen months. My adoptive mother had such an emptiness in her heart after that and badly wanted another child. My adoptive father wasn't on board because of the lost child. The loss and pain felt too much for him, but my adoptive mother's pain was even greater, and he would do anything to ease her pain. He knew this was her medicine. We both needed each other, because I, too, was starved for love and affection.

Once the decision was made to adopt me, it took a few years to be finalized. During that time they would tell me they were worried the system might take me away. It is still unclear why it took so long. Fortunately, my adoptive parents' fears were unwarranted.

They already had three children. I became their last child, the baby of the family. To this day, I am very close to my siblings and relatives, and it still brings tears to my eyes that I was so loved and wanted. I am convinced that my baby brother in heaven had a hand in my adoption.

My adoptive parents took very serious risks in adopting me. They were in their forties, and I had severe emotional problems, but my adoptive family never gave up on me. With infinite patience and love and painstaking work on my speech and eating, we all got through it. I never heard anyone say, "This is my adopted daughter." I was their daughter, sister, niece, cousin, grandchild, aunt, and now great-great-aunt.

In 1980, when I was thirty-three years old, there was a thyroid scare. I heard on the news that anyone who had had radiation on their thyroid or neck in the '40s or '50s should contact their physician. I wasn't sure if I had had a treatment, but I was told I had had experimental surgeries when I was quite young. Not long after this, I had a dream that I was in my birth mother's womb. It startled me, and I knew I had to find out my medical history. So I wrote to the hospital and received extensive medical information. That triggered a desire to find my birth parents, particularly my birth mother, to find out what had happened and why I was adopted. I knew part of the answer: My birth parents were young, and shortly after I was born, they filed for divorce. But I needed to hear it from her and to get my complete medical history.

Before I started to search for my birth parents, I wanted my adoptive parents' blessings. My mother was supportive, but my father was not happy. He felt I was his child. I tried to explain to him that I needed to find out why I was adopted and get medical information. I told him, "If you think I'm going to run away, you are crazy. I will always be your daughter." He then seemed to understand my need to do a search, and he gave me my amended birth certificate and adoption papers.

I found my birth father in Texas. I had learned from a former neighbor here in Massachusetts that he and his family had moved there in the '70s. I already had his name and age, and the neighbor suggested that I write to the Texas Department of Motor Vehicles. I took his suggestion and within a week or so, I received a copy of his license with all the information. I wrote to him and, a few days later, the phone call came. I will never forget the day. It was March 2, 1982.

I was relieved to find out that he was healthy and happy. We met a few months later at my home in Massachusetts and hugged for what seemed like forever. We then talked for a very long time.

I discovered during our conversation that my birth father was French, and that I have some Micmac Canadian Indian in my background. I also learned I have five half siblings—three sisters and two brothers—who are alive and well. I am the oldest in my birth family.

For a while the reunion went very well. But my birth father's wife was uncomfortable with the relationship and twenty years lapsed without communication, partly because he became ill. My husband and I did get to see my birth father a few more times before he passed away in 2006. I have a photo of him, his wife and me, with my birth father and I holding hands.

I found my birth mother on February 8, 1983. It was a challenge because she was married three times. She never had any more children. I found her in Florida and first spoke with her husband. "Wait till Babe hears this!" he said. That evening, my birth mother called. However, she was not the easiest person to get along with. Early on I told her I thought she was a nice woman. I was taken aback when she replied, "I am not a nice woman." I should have picked up on that comment. We had a tumultuous relationship, strained at best. I remember her telling me she didn't like children.

"What about me?" I asked.

"You're my daughter. Of course I love you."

It warmed my heart to hear that. I wish we could have had a better relationship, but knowing what I know, about the three marriages and all, I understand why it was so very difficult for her.

In 2006 she called from a rehabilitation center. She was recovering from hip surgery and was told she was not rallying like she should. She said she couldn't gain weight. At the time it didn't occur to me that she might be seriously ill. Boy, was I wrong.

Not long after, I got a call saying she had passed away. She had died on the anniversary of the day we met. I was deeply shocked, saddened, and angry all at once. I wished we had had more time.

Later, to my surprise, I received a call from a crematory in Florida saying I was listed as next of kin and they needed my permission to bury her with her husband. Of course I gave it to them.

It took a few years to come to terms with my grief, from her death and my birth father's. But I think it's important to answer the questions you have about your past, no matter what the answers may be, to find out where you come from and how you were formed. I definitely resemble both of my birth parents. I have my birth mother's fingers, her physique. I have my birth father's skin tone, his eyes, his widow's peak. I am a voracious reader like he was.

I have no regrets. The reunion with my birth parents was not perfect, but I wouldn't have changed a thing. I now have my roots and my wings, my birth family and my adoptive family.

Acknowledgements

LOVE NEVER LEAVES never would have been completed without the love, support, and encouragement of my family, friends, the adoption community, and so many others along the way.

Heartfelt thanks to the following people, who made the second part of this book, In Their Own Words, possible: Kara Ammon, Jimmy Birmingham, Marie Conway, Elizabeth Drake, Marvin Drake, Diana Dunphy, George Fonteno, Mary E. Fournier, Richard Erroll Fuller Jr., Ellen S. Glazer, Andrew Gordon, Laura Tipton Groff, Susan Miller-Havens, the Reverend Dr. Richard A. Hughes, Kathleen MacKinnon, Susan Hamlet Nickerson, Denise Osterberg, Marilynn Raben, Mary Salem, Ginny Smith, Beth Soeder, Robin Stolarz, James Sweeney, Dana Ann Whidden. Thanks also to Lori White.

To my daughter, Denise, for how she kept me sane when I thought my laptop had swallowed twenty chapters of my manuscript and informed me how to protect everything with something called a backup drive. Thanks, Denise, for your loving patience and all of your computer expertise. Without it I would have drowned in an area I knew nothing about.

To Emily Rosen, who was always there for me, guiding me through the labyrinth and pitfalls of the publishing world and whom I always could rely on for complete honesty.